"Kathy is a force—a pioneer, an entrepreneur, and the unofficial princess of San Francisco's Chinatown. Walking beside her is an education in Chinese American cuisine, from hidden market stalls to the kitchen of her family's legendary restaurant, where she and her father effortlessly craft dishes rooted in tradition yet alive with innovation. For any great cook, it all starts with the broth, and when a jar of the Fangs' golden, fragrant stock arrived at my door, I knew they were people to learn from. This book is a love letter—to history, to family, to the ever-evolving flavors of a culture—and a gift to anyone who believes that food is more than just a meal; it's a story."

ZAC POSEN, FASHION DESIGNER

"Peter and Kathy Fang have graciously opened the doors to their (many!)-decades-old and iconic San Francisco restaurant House of Nanking in this beautiful book. What began humbly as a small restaurant where Peter Fang cooked all the food in a single wok has grown into something larger and immeasurable in stature. This book shares a large array of Chinese recipes that have graced the tables of the restaurant and tells the story of the family that is legendary in the San Francisco food community. From the congees to the pickles to the noodles, the recipes are accessible and unique at the same time. I have earmarked many pages, and I encourage you to do the same."

ALEX GUARNASCHELLI, CHEF, COOKBOOK AUTHOR, AND TV HOST

"Just reading the list of dishes from House of Nanking makes me crave these elegant Chinese flavors. I've been an admirer of this cuisine since my childhood, and now the secrets are available to all of us. I can't wait to start cooking these recipes."

BOBBY FLAY, JAMES BEARD AWARD–WINNING CHEF, TV HOST, RESTAURATEUR, AND COOKBOOK AUTHOR

HOUSE OF NANKING

南 京 小 館

HOUSE OF NANKING

南 京 小 館

Family Recipes from San Francisco's Favorite Chinese Restaurant

KATHY AND PETER FANG
with Emily Timberlake

Photographs by Quentin Bacon

ABRAMS, NEW YORK

Trade Mark
Grant
SAN FRANCISCO MUNICIPAL RAILWAY

CONTENTS

Chapter 4: SOUPS & CONGEES

Chapter 5: VEGETABLES & TOFU

Chapter 6:
EGGS, POULTRY & MEAT

Chapter 7:
SEAFOOD

Chapter 8:
PICKLES, PRESERVES, CONDIMENTS & SAUCES

TO CHINATOWN,

KATHY: As I stroll down Jackson, Kearny, Stockton, and Columbus, I'm not just walking along streets; I'm traversing the pages of my childhood album. Every corner whispers a story, every storefront holds a memory. This is Chinatown, San Francisco: twenty-four square blocks that have shaped my life and the lives of countless immigrants, including my parents, who stepped off a plane from China and found a new world within these boundaries.

The sights, sounds, and smells transport me back: my grandmother guiding me through the red-light district to her apartment overlooking North Beach; my aunts hurrying me through bustling markets; a stern-faced vendor shaking her head as I sneak a taste of dried shrimp from one of her cardboard boxes. I can almost taste the steamed har gow I used to eat from a red and white checkered paper bowl, a favorite treat before my daily visit to House of Nanking.

This neighborhood isn't just a place; it's a living, breathing entity that has nurtured generations. It's where I grew up, where I went to the doctor and the dentist, and even where I watched my first movie (at the Great Star Theater, which is still there on Jackson Street). And, remarkably, much of it remains unchanged, a testament to the resilience of our community.

The markets on Stockton Street are the lifeblood of Chinatown, supporting local businesses and restaurants alike. When we opened Fang, our second restaurant, in San Francisco's SoMa district, we worried about sourcing ingredients from our trusted Chinatown vendors—many didn't have delivery trucks. But our business was so important to them that they found a solution: One dedicated man, pushing a handcart loaded with our daily produce order, made the trek from Chinatown to the new spot. Even now, you can spot him around 3 p.m., starting his journey from the corner of Stockton and Jackson, navigating through the Stockton tunnel, emerging into Union Square, and finally reaching us at Fang. This daily pilgrimage is more than a delivery; it's a reflection of our community's spirit. When he arrives, breathless but smiling, he chats with our kitchen staff on break. We've developed a warm ritual: He brings us seasonal fruits to enjoy, and we send him off with a couple of sodas for the road back. It's in these small exchanges—produce for refreshments, stories for smiles—that the true heart of our Chinatown community shines through.

SAN FRANCISCO

Chinatown, like House of Nanking, may appear different to different people—exotic, exciting, touristic, authentic, or, at times, dirty and rundown. But beneath the surface lies the true essence: the soul of immigrant families who have poured their dreams into every nook and cranny. It's a tapestry woven with threads of determination, sacrifice, and hope.

As I reflect on our thirty-five-plus years at House of Nanking, I'm filled with deep respect for immigrants like my parents who have fought tirelessly to succeed. And I'm overwhelmed with gratitude for every customer who has walked through our doors—from San Francisco locals to travelers from across the globe. Your support has been OUR lifeblood.

This cookbook is more than a collection of recipes; it's a love letter to Chinatown, to the immigrant experience, and to the beautiful synergy of our community. Each dish tells a story of resilience, creativity, and the power of food to bring people together. As you cook these recipes, know that you're not just preparing a meal—you're becoming part of our story, our family, our Chinatown.

WELCOME TO THE HEART OF HOUSE OF NANKING. WELCOME HOME.

Kathy shopping on Stockton Street in San Francisco's Chinatown

献给旧金

Kathy on Jackson Street in Chinatown

凯茜: 凯茜: 当我漫步在杰克逊街、凯尼街、 斯托克顿街和哥伦布大道时，我不仅仅是在走过街道巷口，我是在翻阅我童年的相册。每个街角都低语着故事；每个店面都承载着回忆。这就是旧金山的中国城-24个街区塑造了我的人生和无数移民的生活，包括我的父母。他们从来自中国的飞机上下来，在这里找到了一个新世界。

那些景象、声音、和气味把我带回过去。我的祖母带我穿过红灯区，来到她俯瞰北滩的公寓；我的姑姑们催促着我穿过熙熙攘攘的市场，当我从她的纸箱里偷吃一只干虾时一个面色严肃的商贩摇了摇头。我几乎能品尝到曾经从红白格子的纸碗中吃到的蒸虾饺。那是我每天拜访南京小馆前最喜欢的点心。

这个社区不仅仅是一个地方，它是一个有生命，有呼吸的实体，哺育了一代又一代人。这里是我成长的地方 - 我在这里看医生和牙医，甚至在这里看了我的第一部电影（在大明星剧院，现在仍然在杰克逊街上）。值得注意的是，它仍然保持不变，见证了我们社区的韧性。

斯托克顿街的市场是中国城的生命线，支持着当地的商家和餐馆。当我们在旧金山的Soma区开设第二家餐厅Fang时，我们担心如何从我们信赖的中国城供应商那里采购食材因为许多人没有送货卡车。但我们的业务对他们来说是如此重要，以至于他们找到了解决方案一位敬业的男子推着装满我们每日农产品订单的手推车，从中国城跋涉到新店。即使现在，你也可以在下午3点左右看到他。从斯托克顿和杰克逊的拐角处出发，穿过斯托克顿隧道进入联合广场，最终到达我们的Fang餐厅。

山的中国城

这个每日的旅程不仅仅是一次送货，它反映了我们社区的精神。当他到达时，气喘吁吁但面带着微笑和正在休息的厨房员工聊天。我们形成了一个温暖的仪式 - 他带当季的水果给我们享用，我们送他几瓶汽水作为回程的补给。在这些小小的交流中，农产品换取饮料，故事换取微笑，我们的中国城社区的真正核心闪耀着光芒。

中国城像南京小馆一样，对不同的人可能呈现出不同的面貌 - 异国情调、刺激、旅游胜地、正宗或者有时是脏乱和破旧的。但在表面之下，真正隐藏着的本质是那些将梦想倾注到每一个角落的移民家庭的灵魂。这是一幅用决心、牺牲和希望的线编织而成的锦缎。

当我回顾南京小馆三十五年以上的历程时，我对像我父母一样不懈奋斗的移民充满了深深的敬意。我也对每一位走进我们店里的顾客，从旧金山的当地人到来自全球的游客，心存感激。你们的支持一直是我们的生命线。

这本食谱不仅仅是菜谱的合集，它是一封献给中国城、献给移民经历和我们社区美丽和谐的情书。每道菜都讲述了韧性、创造力和食物将人们聚在一起的力量。当你烹饪这些菜肴时，请知道你不仅仅是在准备一顿饭菜，你正在成为我们故事的一部分，我们家庭的一部分，还有我们中国城的一部分。

欢迎来到南京小馆的心脏。欢迎回家。

CLOCKWISE FROM LEFT:

Lily and Peter standing in front of the shelves Peter built by hand, in the first month after opening Nanking

Lily, shortly after immigrating to the United States, at one of the first restaurants where she worked as a waitress

The infamous line at 3 p.m.

INTRODUCTION

KATHY: If you visited our restaurant, House of Nanking, on any given day in the late 1980s or early 1990s, it is very likely you would have encountered the following scene:

A line of excited, reasonably patient diners waiting for a spot to open up at our tiny bar or one of the six small tables inside. The line started at our address, 919 Kearny Street, and on busy days wrapped all the way around the block and spilled onto the next street, Columbus Avenue, toward City Lights Bookstore.

My dad, Peter Fang, visible through the large, steamy window facing the street at the front of the restaurant. This was the site of our original tiny kitchen, where my dad, the only cook, manned the one wok he used to cook all the restaurant's food. If the line was too long, he'd probably have a concerned expression on his face, and would be moving even more lightning-fast than usual. He didn't like the long lines; he was always nervous that people would walk away and he'd lose customers. That didn't happen too often, though.

My mom, Lily Fang, working the front of house, where she showed guests to their tables, served them food and drinks, bussed dishes back to our dishwasher (the only other employee, who did his best to keep up with the churn), handled checks, and basically did everything else that needed doing.

Me, a tiny little kid sitting at the tall bar, either folding napkins, drying plates, filling chili oil containers, or, more likely, precociously chatting with one of the restaurant regulars sitting next to me (and not realizing he was famous film director Francis Ford Coppola).

Our customers were an amazing cross-section of San Francisco at the time. Locals from all over the city rubbed shoulders with tourists from far-flung places and, sometimes, even movie stars. One regular reminisced about a time he was waiting in line with about thirty other people when, as he approached the window, he noticed Keanu Reeves, Francis Ford Coppola, Gary Oldman, Winona Ryder, and Anthony Hopkins all squeezed around a tight table, drinking Tsingtao beers, laughing, and stuffing their faces with sesame chicken and pan-fried veggie buns dipped in peanut sauce.

Fast-forward thirty years, and you'll find that the restaurant is now about twice its original size—we actually have servers, a kitchen, and more cooks than just my dad working in a whirlwind at the wok. There are new dishes we've added, as our tastes evolve and we get excited to offer customers new preparations. But the important things remain the same. The list of celebrity fans and decades-long regulars who support us is rich and unwavering. You can still get our famous sesame chicken

CLOCKWISE FROM TOP LEFT:
Peter, baby Kathy, and Lily in 1984

Kathy and Cān guǎn Nǎi nai eating glutinous rice balls with black sesame during Chinese New Year (page 218) the way it was when my dad first invented it—the best sweet-and-sour chicken you've ever had in your life, lightly battered, with no red food coloring, tender and juicy because of its marinade. Most iconic of all, Dad's sesame chicken is paired with thinly sliced, quickly fried sweet potatoes. He tells me that little inspiration came from Americans asking him to make them something Thanksgiving-inspired. We don't do turkey at Nanking, and I think we can all agree succulent dark-meat chicken with a crispy coating and sweet potatoes is way better. This dish is so good that our competitors in Chinatown started trying to copy it. As a kid, I spent a lot of time watching people eat (what else did I have to do?), and I noticed the hardcore fans—these are people who would come and order it almost every day—perfected the Nanking chicken bite. First nibble the chicken while it's still steaming hot, then pierce the sweet potato with your fork, then add rice to the end of the fork, so your bite includes rice, sweet potato, and chicken. Pure joy on their faces. To this day it is not unusual to see four cases of sweet potatoes—that's 160 pounds, or 75 kilos!—getting delivered to HoNK (some of our regulars' clever acronym for "House of Nanking") in a day.

House of Nanking remains one of the most popular Chinese restaurants in the country; it comes up again and again in tourist guides and must-visit lists for San Francisco. In 2020, it was named an official legacy business by the city of San Francisco—an honor that means so much to me and my family. I am a first-generation Chinese American, and my parents and grandparents are immigrants to this country. To be told that we are part of the fabric that makes San Francisco, our home for the last four decades, great? Nothing could make us prouder.

Our business has always been a family affair, and I'm not just talking about the three of us, who run the actual business. House of Nanking wouldn't exist without my extended family—my aunts, grandparents, and god-grandparents, who I called Cān guǎn Yé ye ("Restaurant Grandpa") and Cān guǎn Nǎi nai ("Restaurant Grandma")—who took turns living with us and taking care of me while Mom and Dad worked long days, every day, at the restaurant.

The book you are holding in your hands is a family cookbook, in the same way House of Nanking is a family restaurant. There are recipes for all of the dishes that put us on the map, such as the sesame chicken with sweet potato (page 218), garlic eggplant (page 168), and shrimp in Tsingtao beer sauce (page 246), that inspired people to line up and wait for as long as it took to get a seat. (Or, as sometimes happened when I was in middle and high school, inspired people to try to slip me $20 to help them skip the line or get in faster. I would obviously not take the money.) But there are also home-cooked dishes from my childhood, like the elegant steamed beef seasoned with ginger-scallion water (page 239) my pó po (my mother's mother) would make, and the spicy pork, chili, and fried egg dish (page 223), which we called "Bastard Eggs" because of a childhood translation fail, that my aunt would fix me and my cousins. There are dishes that my father used to eat as a boy in Shanghai in the 1950s, dishes that I created for our second restaurant, Fang, which we co-opened in 2009, and dishes from every stage of our lives in between.

House of Nanking opened in 1988, and people have been asking my dad to reveal his culinary secrets ever since. He'd usually laugh and say, "No, I'm not going to share my recipes." I think it has to do with his upbringing; he was taught to protect and hold close the things he'd worked hardest for. There's also the fact that he was, and is, busy. My dad is now seventy-three and my mom is seventy-four, and they continue to work every single day. House of Nanking is open seven days a week, from 11 a.m. to 9 p.m., and closes one day a year, for Thanksgiving Day. We used to close on Christmas Eve, but my dad reverted after realizing he had customers who still wanted to come in—he said people would be too disappointed if we closed, which is how we ended up as the family restaurant that only closes one day a year. How many owners do you know who still work seven days a week, and, at ages seventy-three and seventy-four? I have the utmost respect for my parents. I always joke that I'll never beat them when it comes to work. I can't beat the deep love, appreciation, and respect they have from their community, either.

A couple of exciting things happened in recent years, which helped me convince my dad it's finally time to write a book. First, we had the opportunity to create a reality television show for Food Network, *Chef Dynasty: House of Fang*. It aired in 2022 and focused primarily on my life running Fang—specifically, what it means to run a legacy business with your dad. Plenty of laughter, plenty of good times, and a lot of very predictable frustration.

After the show aired, we'd get letters, or guests would come into the restaurants and say, "We're from Canada, we're celebrating a wedding anniversary, and we were trying to decide where to go. We picked San Francisco because of your show. We love your dad and your food!" Even more inspiring were the people who, often with tears in their eyes, would share how much our show and story had meant to them. A lot of the time, they were also the children of immigrants—sometimes from China and other parts of Asia, but not always—and they'd say, "Your story is my story. My parents worked so hard, and were very limited when it came to expressing emotion, but they would show their love through action. Their words were harsh, but I saw the love was there."

Hearing that, a light turned on for me. You don't have to be Chinese for the Fang family story to move you. Our story is our own, but it resonated with others because it's not that extraordinary. So many immigrants share our experience.

For my dad, the last episode of *Chef Dynasty* was particularly special, because the producers delved a bit further into our family's history and my dad's origins in Shanghai. When he saw it, he said, "Oh, this is very neat; a historical document has been created for our family." Only then did I realize how much he craved that, and how much he had truly lost. The pharmacy that his father's family had owned in Shanghai was gone, demolished, and there weren't even photos of it left. The same is true of the paper manufacturing plant his mother's family had owned. The only thing he had were his own memories, which he passed to us by word of mouth. The details are getting less and less vivid with each passing year, and my children, who are currently three and five, are getting diluted versions.

This cookbook is our family's legacy, and the legacy of a restaurant that not only became a culinary landmark in one of the world's greatest food cities, but also redefined ingredient-driven, multiregional Chinese cooking in America. It is a document of who we are and where we came from, the priorities in my family, and the food that connects us to each other and to the world.

Our hope is that by sharing our stories and favorite dishes, you will be reminded of what is special about your own family. Maybe my grandmother's recipes are reminiscent of something your grandmother used to make. Maybe the recipes from House of Nanking and Fang remind you of outings to your favorite Chinese restaurant growing up. Maybe you're one of the nearly four million people who have visited us in San Francisco over the last three decades, and you're excited to recreate those taste memories in your home kitchen.

As you cook through the book, I hope you'll take photos and share your food journey with us. Nothing will make us happier than if some of these dishes become part of your repertoire, and your family's culinary legacy. Kuài lè pēng rèn—happy cooking!

OPPOSITE:
Peter (looking particularly intense) in front of the new kitchen after the restaurant expanded into the space next door

CLOCKWISE FROM TOP:
Peter with a customer at the original restaurant counter

Peter and Lily enjoying lunch at Nanking

Lily working as a waitress at Nanking in the early days

PETER'S STORY

PETER: People have asked me to describe my earliest food memories, and it's hard for me, because growing up all food seemed so delicious and memorable. I'd walk past grocery stores or restaurants in Shanghai, my hometown, savoring the sights and smells, and it didn't matter what was hanging in the window, I wanted to try it all. Spicy, mild, starchy, greasy, fatty: all flavors and textures were attractive to me.

This is for two reasons: because I was a teenager, and growing boys are always hungry and thinking about food; and because at that time in China, there were food shortages and it wasn't always easy to put meals on the table.

It wasn't always that way. I still remember the Shanghai of my very early childhood. The Bund (Wài tān), the waterfront area of the historic old town, was beautiful, but without all the flashing lights of today. The architecture was so grand: European-style buildings, lined up along the Huangpu River. Across the way was East Bund, Pudong, which is now the tech center of Shanghai, with skyscrapers and Pearl Tower. But when I was growing up, it was just farmland.

As a child, my favorite place to visit was Chéng huáng Miào, or City God's Temple. It's a large collection of temple-like buildings, traditional Chinese architecture, filled with restaurants and street food stalls. You could buy anything there, from little trinkets and toys to amazing small eats. My favorite was Ningbo-style lard and black sesame–filled tāng yuan (sweet rice balls). For an extra-special treat, you can add osmanthus syrup to the broth. The smell was out of this world. On colder days, these piping-hot glutinous rice balls filled our stomachs with sweetness and warmth. Imagine crisp, cold weather, enjoying bamboo steamers filled with juicy soup dumplings from Nan Xiang, and then finishing the meal off with sweet rice balls. My memories from that time were as rich as the food.

My mom was an incredible cook. There's a saying in China, even today, that if a woman wants to be happy in her marriage, she should marry a Shanghainese man, because he will walk into the kitchen and know what he's doing. Often, he'll take the job of cooking away from the wife. Well, in my family, it was the opposite. My mom's whole family were foodies, loved food—I'm sure that's where my own interest came from—but my dad was clueless. He'd just sit there and eat all the delicious things my mom prepared for us.

One of my favorite family activities was when the whole family—there were five of us kids—would visit the markets together and shop for ingredients. Back then, everything in Shanghai was based entirely on seasons. Winter was the only time you could get shepherd's purse, ta gu choi (tatsoi), and winter bamboo shoots. In spring, we looked forward to celtuce and spring bamboo shoots. It was during those visits,

CLOCKWISE FROM TOP:
From left: Peter; Peter's father; Peter's oldest sister, Jean (above); Peter's younger sister and Kathy's frugal aunt (below); Peter's mother; Peter's eldest brother, A Ming (above); and Peter's youngest brother, Xiǎo Dì

Peter and Dà Yí in Hong Kong, during his two-week stay before flying to the United States

Kathy doing dishes with her grandfather, Peter's father

when I'd watch my mom carefully select the ingredients for our meals, that I learned how to buy vegetables. Then we would all go home, watch her cook, and enjoy the fruits of her labor. I crave everything from those early childhood days. It seemed like everything tasted better. The vegetables, the seafood, the meat, the noodles—everything.

One thing that set our family apart was that we were always open to Western food and influences, especially my mom. She was quick to adapt flavors and make them her own. My maternal grandpa owned a paper manufacturing plant, which produced the paper used to wrap cigarettes. He often did business with foreigners, which meant we had access to many international and Western-style ingredients: Worcestershire sauce and sardines, for example. A typical breakfast might be pork chops and congee with buttered white toast, fried eggs, and black coffee. My mom made a beautiful Russian-inspired borscht soup (we've included a recipe on page 137). On one very special occasion, my mom decided to splurge on a fancy meal and took us to Red House Western Restaurant (Hóng Fáng zi). It was French style, and I remember eating braised oxtails with carrots and potato, French onion soup (but without the bread and cheese I now see at French restaurants), escargots, and potato salad. It was such a treat to be able to try all this, and fairly uncommon for kids at the time. Soon after, my mom started making her own potato salad with homemade mayonnaise, since she couldn't buy it in stores. Soon guests were flocking to our house to try her potato salad, a specialty that they had heard about but could only try at the Fang household.

Those were happy days.

When our family's circumstances changed, as they did for so many families in China, my mom's love of food stayed the same. She just had to be resourceful—work harder and differently—to feed us the way she wanted to. In my early childhood, every meal was an elaborate banquet, with multiple courses that she would make by hand: egg omelet–wrapped pork dumplings with bean thread noodles, napa cabbage, and fried belt fish soup in casserole (dàn jiāo fěn sī bái cài dài yú tang); red fermented bean curd stewed with cuttlefish and red-braised pork belly (fǔ rǔ hóng shāo roù dùn wū zéi); or duck marinated in seafood oil (hǎi xiān yóu yān yā zi).

Later, the meals were simpler, but still delicious, like the curry chicken soup (gā lí jī tang, page 135) she would make with just chicken bones, which were cheaper than meat, and a thinner broth that she could stretch to feed me and my four siblings. She adapted cài fán (rice with Shanghai bok choy and salted pork, see page 113), which is traditionally meant to be a starchy side dish accompanying protein-based mains, like lion's head meatballs. But my mom turned it into a one-pot meal by fortifying it with fava beans, which made it way more filling. And the texture worked beautifully with the rice. I remember the smell of her stir-frying lard with minced salted pork (the lard was a way to cheaply enhance the flavor), then adding bok choy and beans, which she coated in that delicious fat. We didn't miss the meat. It was perfect.

Eventually, my family decided to leave Shanghai and move to the United States. In those days, the only way into and out of China was through Hong Kong, which was still under British colonial rule. My mom's sister, Aunt Dà Yí, was the first to leave; she immigrated to Hong Kong, where she opened a successful nightclub. I was next. I still remember the day I left Shanghai. I had all my belongings in a suitcase, plus a small television set my mom wanted me to bring to her sister in Hong Kong. My younger brother, Jason (Xiǎo Dì), accompanied me to the train station, which was the first step of my journey. The plan was for me to stay with Dà Yí for two weeks, until my flight to San Francisco.

I am a confident person and was even more confident at thirty-one than I am now. But I still remember the fear I felt when I looked at my brother and realized I might never see him again. In 1980, there was no easy way to telephone my family back in Shanghai. The best I could do was send a letter and hope it might get to them eventually. My brother and I looked at each other and said, "Take care, be careful, and good luck." And I boarded my train.

Those first few days in Hong Kong were . . . memorable. Life with my aunt at her nightclub was very different from the life we were living in Shanghai. My first reaction upon seeing Hong Kong was that I couldn't believe how bright it was, even brighter at night than during the day. I was not accustomed to an entire city being flooded with so many neon lights. It felt like it could never get dark in Hong Kong. It was exciting at first, but in truth, it made me miss Shanghai and the dark, quiet, familiar alleys I used to walk to get home. The noise of Hong Kong was almost too much for me to handle.

That stay in Hong Kong was my first real experience of Cantonese food. I remember my first bowl of Hong Kong–style wonton noodle soup: I went to a wonton stall, sat down, and ordered. When the tiny bowl came, I thought I had made a mistake—it was possible, as Hong Kong uses the Cantonese dialect, and back in Shanghai I spoke Mandarin or Shanghainese. I was used to a huge bowl of large, soft, pillowy wontons with thick skins, filled with pork and vegetables. These Hong Kong wontons were smaller and had a bouncy texture, and the noodles were springy with a little alkaline aroma, very different from the smooth, soft noodles I was used to. Then there was the fact that the serving size was puny, half of what I was used to.

I mostly ate meals at home with my aunt, but when I did explore the city, I found the dai pa dongs (street food stalls) to be particularly exciting. Unfortunately, I couldn't try any of the food, because I had to save all my money for San Francisco—but boy, did I want to. I encountered seafood I'd never seen before. It felt like an open-air aquarium. There were colorful fruits and vegetables, amazing smells, smoke, happy people eating on the streets, low tables, low chairs. It was all a bit dirty and super casual; people wore slippers and tank tops and smoked openly while eating and cooking. Back in Shanghai during this time, there were no neighborhoods like this, nowhere where you could just hang out on the streets, eating, yelling, wearing whatever the hell you wanted. It was more proper back home, buttoned up.

Before I had time to really get used to the Hong Kong lifestyle, after a short two weeks, I was aboard a plane to San Francisco.

I can distinctly remember the moment I stepped off the plane at SFO. Specifically, I remember the air. It smelled so clean and fresh. On the ride into San Francisco, I was mesmerized by the beauty of the city: the blue water, blue skies, Bay Bridge, tall buildings. The geography and landscape of the city was so interesting to me. I had seen nothing like it before. The weather was incredibly nice. In fact, I remember San Francisco weather back then being even more perfect than it is now. There were warm days when I would wear short sleeves and shorts all day. It was a drastic change from the sweltering summers in China, where you step outside and can barely breathe. Later, fall and winter rolled around and it was a little breezy, but not so cold I needed a coat or sweater. Compare that to the cold winters in Shanghai, where we would sleep with rubber bags filled with hot boiling water and wore shoes that had fur inside because if you wore only socks and shoes, you would lose feeling in your toes. San Francisco was just perfect.

When I arrived, I lived with my dad's cousin Ya Shuo and his wife, Sung Sung, who Kathy would later call Cān guǎn Yé ye and Cān guǎn Nǎi nai. They were so kind to me, always willing to lend a hand. They even made their two kids share a room so that I could have my own room in their North Beach apartment. The first place they took me was to Chinatown, where they introduced me to their network of friends. My initial reaction was, Wow, I can't believe I can feel like I'm at home in America. Chinatown felt familiar because I saw people who were like me, markets that reminded me of home. Although the dialect was different, the energy and food was familiar. But I didn't get to do much touring or walking around—I had to make money, and there was no time to waste. I went straight to work. Like many recent émigrés, I started working in restaurants—as a bartender, dishwasher, server, or wherever I was needed.

Chinatown was very lively during those days. Many restaurants were open late-night and served food until 2 a.m. There was even a twenty-four-hour restaurant, Yuet Lee. There were jazz clubs underneath some of the Chinese restaurants, and I worked as a bartender at one of them—Da Dong Restaurant on Jackson Street, which was open only at night and served Cantonese food for Americans on the main floor and had live jazz in the basement bar.

Even though I didn't have a ton of money to spend on meals out, I was fascinated by all the bustling Chinatown restaurants: Hing Lung on Broadway, known for its congee; Lin Yuen, where my wife, Lily, worked for years and served Cantonese-style Western food like prime rib with spaghetti, corn soup, black pepper chicken steak, red wine–braised oxtails with carrots and potato, and apple pie; Ocean Seafood Restaurant, which specialized in delicious clay pot rice dishes; and Ping Yuen, a fancy dark wood restaurant with booth seating. It was the 1980s in America and business was booming.

I married Lily soon after moving to San Francisco. My sister Jean had actually met Lily's father at an immigration office back in Shanghai—he had needed some help with an English-language portion of the paperwork—and when they realized that we were all planning to move to San Francisco, they arranged a meeting. I was a young man and had plenty of girlfriends at the time, no plans to settle down. Lily had a different plan. She says that she just had a gut feeling about me. Not necessarily love at first sight; she just knew we should get married. I admired her conviction! In fact, it's something I've always liked about Lily: When she sets her mind to achieving something, she really goes for it. She's always been the risk-taker in our family. She decided to take a risk on me.

It wasn't long before we were married and had our daughter, Kathy. My younger brother, Xiǎo Dì, eventually moved to San Francisco, followed by my parents, older brother, and younger sister. They took turns living with us and helping to take care of Kathy while Lily and I worked.

There was nothing particularly special about the restaurant where I first worked as a cook. One day, the guy who ran the place asked me if I thought I could work in the kitchen. With full confidence, I said yes. I started asking him follow-up questions and quickly realized, Hey, I know way more about food than he does. I had spent years standing behind my mom, watching her cook, especially in Shanghai, when her creativity had saved us from boring food and hunger. I'd watched street-food vendors and restaurant chefs cook. I had lots of experience feeding myself and my siblings back home. What this guy was asking me to do was easy.

Lily and I worked for years in other people's restaurants. We lived in SROs in Chinatown, and made a quick detour to Sacramento, because I'd heard it was cheaper to live out there. It wasn't for us—really, it wasn't for Kathy. Even as a three-year-old, she wanted the city life. Whenever we came to visit family in San Francisco Chinatown, she would clap in her baby seat and laugh. When we left to return back to Sacramento, she'd cry the whole ride. Eventually we took the hint and moved back to San Francisco, where we saved as much as we could with the hope of someday opening our own place. I was also running a real estate business on the side.

KATHY: The best part about Dad's real estate side hustle was that I was his "assistant." Because he was busy working in restaurants all the time and never home, he was afraid of missing calls. So, he trained me to repeat these exact words if someone called: "Hi, you've reached Peter Fang's number, a real estate agent from Century 21. Can I take your number? He will call you back."

Can you imagine trying to call your real estate agent, only to get a child answering the line? I'm on the other end, sitting on a pink plastic kid's stool, doing a job that probably should have been left to an answering machine. Why didn't we just have an answering machine handle this? Not everything immigrant parents do makes sense.

PETER: I just wanted to make a living, and real estate seemed like a better path than restaurants. But I was much better at cooking than at real estate.

Luckily, by the time Kathy was seven years old we had saved up enough money to open our own place. Lily enlisted her dad to help find the location. Both of them believe in fēng shuǐ 风水; my father-in-law is always reading and studying books on the subject.

When he found the listing at 919 Kearny Street, I visited it and did not like the location at all. It was on the edge of Chinatown, far away from the main action. But Lily and her dad didn't care about that. They said, according to fēng shuǐ, this was it. In Chinese culture, you respect your elders—and give them the final say. When your father-in-law tells you, "This is the site of your new restaurant," you don't argue.

KATHY: When it came to naming the place, the logic made even less sense than the location. My gōng gong (grandpa) told my parents to name it House of Nanking because my grandpa had spent quite a bit of time in Nanking during his formative years as a student. Nanking (often Anglicized as Nanjing) was the former imperial capital of China—but apart from Gōng Gong loving it there when he was a teenager, we had no connection to the place whatsoever. So as a business decision, the name makes no sense. We don't serve any food from Nanking; our cuisine is not even inspired by the food of Nanking. It's the equivalent of naming your pizza joint "Pizzeria di NYC" . . . except your pizza is Chicago-style and you don't serve any New York–style pizza at all. Even to this day, Chinese tourists come to our restaurant, sit down, and ask for Nanking dishes. They look so confused when we tell them we don't serve any Nanking food—"But the sign . . ."

Our sign has of course become a very famous and beloved San Francisco landmark, but it has a funny and fortuitous origin story. The rainbow-colored marquee has become somewhat legendary in restaurant and graphic design circles. We are constantly selling out of merch with the rainbow logo on it, and many people assume that some hot, expensive graphic-design firm created it for us.

But no, the rainbow-colored branding was just something my dad thought might catch drivers' eyes as they whizzed down Kearny Street. That was it! All the other signage in North Beach was brightly lit neon, and in Chinatown, it was all the predictable red and gold. Dad wanted something different.

Right now you're probably thinking, *Wow, what vision and foresight!* Except that rainbow sign wasn't ever supposed to be the restaurant's actual logo. If you could track down one of our very first business cards, you'd see an image of a duck holding a sign that read "House of Nanking," with no colors. That was our logo. Dad got the idea by looking at one of my Scholastic book-ordering catalogs—the ones kids got from school every month. He was sifting through it one day while taking a break from remodeling the restaurant—and yes, he did all the remodeling himself. He built the chairs, cabinets, and moldings, because he had to be as frugal as possible. Anyway, he saw a picture of a duck on one of the books in the catalog, and then started doodling a really short duck standing on two webbed feet, holding a sign.

PETER: Americans love duck, and duck is a very Chinese dish!

KATHY: First of all, why is the logo on the business card different from our street sign? Shouldn't they be the same thing? At the very least, the duck should show up on the signage. Oh, and we don't specialize in duck at House of Nanking. Yet another confusing business move. It's a good thing we had fēng shuǐ on our side!

PETER: Originally, I wanted House of Nanking to be a traditional Shanghainese restaurant. That was what I knew how to cook. So the initial menu had dishes like fried gluten wheat with black fungus and ginkgo nut (hóng shāo kǎo fū) and cold drunken squab (lěng zuì rǔ gē). What I discovered was that there wasn't really a market for this type of food. San Franciscans at the time were used to moo goo gai pan and egg foo yung, and the majority of people who lived in San Francisco's Chinatown were Cantonese and Toisan, from Southern China. My only customers were my relatives' friends from the Mahjong Benevolent Associations. There were maybe ten people in all of San Francisco at the time who could appreciate authentic Shanghainese food, and we knew all of them.

KATHY: Those early days were rough. The restaurant was empty most days and nights. One of our first customers came in and didn't enjoy the dish my dad had made for him. I remember how disappointing it felt to all of us watching on the sideline—me, my mom, gōng gong, and dad. Dad knew that something had to change, or we'd risk going under.

PETER: I believe that most people are given a few chances in life. The people who can grasp those chances and capitalize on them are the ones who become successful. But if you don't grasp them—if you let them go—you may never get another chance again. And you may miss the window to change your life.

My chance came when a Shanghainese gal walked by House of Nanking with her American friend. Turns out, that gal was Jiang Xiaozhen, a filmmaker and the daughter of Bai Yang, one of China's most popular actresses. Her friend was Peter Kaufman, the son of director, screenwriter, and producer Phil Kaufman. Of course, I didn't know any of that at the time. All I knew is that a lady smelled what I was cooking and it stopped her in her tracks.

She popped her head in the door and told me the food smelled like home. Turns out, she was from Shanghai, too! We instantly connected, and struck up a conversation as I served her Shanghainese specialties like garlic eggplant and mock goose meat filled with dried shiitake mushrooms (shù jī).

Then her friend Peter mentioned she was the daughter of Bai Yang. Every Chinese person knows who Bai Yang is! No pressure, right? Just me in an empty restaurant, cooking for the daughter of one of the most famous people in China. For Jiang Xiaozhen, my food offered the flavors of a hometown she missed very much. For Peter, this was simply the best eggplant he'd ever had—so flavorful, juicy, buttery, and soft. They were both so impressed that Peter decided to bring his father, Phil, and food critic Patricia Unterman to try out this hidden gem.

CLOCKWISE FROM TOP LEFT:

Peter on the flight from Hong Kong to San Francisco, immigrating to his new home in the United States

Peter landing in San Francisco and seeing the city for the first time

Lily, Kathy, and Peter celebrating Kathy's birthday at a restaurant in Chinatown

Lily with newborn Kathy inside their SRO in Chinatown

Lily's parents, Kathy's pó po and gōng gong

I remember the day Patricia came to the restaurant. I didn't know she was a food critic at the time, but I could tell she was a food lover. I was so surprised by how much she knew about Chinese food—I don't know if she'd studied it, or what. But her order and her comments made me think, I didn't know a Caucasian person could know this much!

Lucky for me, she really liked the food. And shortly after her visit, she published her review in the *San Francisco Chronicle*: three stars, the highest possible, literally on the same page as a three-star review of the French Laundry. Nice company!

> This nondescript little restaurant on Kearny turns out some of the most delicious, homestyle Shanghai cooking I've ever tasted. It's all prepared by Peter Fang, a recent emigre, who discovered that he is a natural chef. He and his wife run this tiny place from morning 'til night with a dedication rarely seen. They shop twice daily in Chinatown for the freshest seasonal produce. The kitchen prep work is meticulous, and the resulting dishes are colorful and luscious. The delicate, yeasted Shanghai buns, chicken in beer sauce, fish soup, crispy pan fried noodle pancake topped with tiny Chinese eggplant, green beans and chicken, cold spicy noodles, deep fried squid, and hard bean curd with Chinese chives are just a few of the remarkably clean dishes turned out, one by one, by Fang. House of Nanking is a treasure, worth a wait to get into.

In the days before Yelp or Instagram, a review like this could change your life. The next day, people were lined up outside the door to get in.

I had never seen that many people wanting to eat at my restaurant, so I was excited and a little bit nervous. But I was also confident. I knew that if I cooked good food, with good flavor, people would enjoy it. It's as simple as that. It doesn't matter where in the world you come from—if the meat is cooked properly, customers will be happy.

KATHY: My dad is one of the most observant people I know. He's always watching, analyzing, and thinking. When he was cooking at his wok, pressed up against the big front window, he was observing everyone: the people who were seated and people who were waiting in line. He saw their wide-eyed expressions when the wok flames shot up, so he'd do it more. They started calling him "the One-Wok Man" because he steamed, pan-fried, deep-fried, sauteed, and braised all in one wok. We literally had one burner to feed the whole restaurant. He did everything himself, and he cooked ten times faster than any human should be able to cook.

PETER: House of Nanking was my chance, my opportunity. There's an expression in Cantonese used to describe a restaurant on slow nights: "paak wū yīng," swatting flies. I didn't want to go back to swatting flies all night, waiting for customers. I didn't want to underwhelm or disappoint people.

KATHY: Dad watched and learned what people liked and didn't like. He worked twelve-plus-hour days, then lay in bed at night thinking about the next day's menu and service.

PETER: The people in San Francisco wanted something different! I wanted them to try food that tasted and was presented in a different way than they'd ever had before. I didn't want to cook the same thing as the guy next door. The interesting thing about San Francisco at that time was, you had 150 different Chinese restaurants, but they all had one menu. The name would change—Wong's Café, Dragon Restaurant—but the food was the same. And I told myself, These people deserve to have something different. All that delicious food that I remember from China—I should give them the chance to have that.

At the same time, I knew how risky it was. The cooking was never hard for me, but writing a menu—that was the hardest part. So there was some trial and error, and watching to see what people liked. Turns out, everyone likes tender, well-cooked meat. So that part was easy. But some people like their sauce spicy, some like a milder flavor, some like it strong. But at the end of the day, I couldn't think too much about that. I had to cook what I knew was good food. I don't like food that is overly spicy because I think it kills the palate. Even if a guest thinks they want chicken fried rice, I'm not making that. He can go next door and get that.

KATHY: You loved ordering for people, and it sort of became part of your schtick—Kathy Griffin even joked in a stand-up set that she loved to come to San Francisco and have Peter Fang tell her what to eat. But what some people didn't realize was, it was an efficiency thing. You only had one burner and one wok, and if all of a sudden you had fifty tickets with fifty different dishes, service would grind to a halt. So rather than give people the opportunity to order all over the place, you'd just make the same thing for twenty people. Once those twenty people tasted it and realized how good it was, suddenly they were coming back and saying, "Nope, no menu . . . Peter will order for us."

PETER: Business was good—really good.

KATHY: We were one of the busiest restaurants in San Francisco. People loved the food, even if the service was known for being a bit . . . brusque. Things moved so fast, you'd get plates tossed at you like Frisbees, and water glasses showed up still wet because we could barely finish washing and drying them before we needed them for the next batch of customers. On crowded nights, guests sat on beer boxes and soy sauce buckets because chairs would break on us. Sometimes we'd get multiple produce deliveries in a day to avoid selling out of dishes too soon.

PETER: In 1994, we had the opportunity to expand into the building next door. We knocked down a wall and more than doubled our capacity. We hired more cooks, more servers, but I continued to work the line every single day. And House of Nanking took on a life of its own.

TOP: The Fang family at a Chinese New Year feast at home

BOTTOM: Peter receiving an award for "Best Chinese Restaurant" from Chef Focus

KATHY'S STORY

KATHY: If you had asked me when I was younger whether I was going to end up in the restaurant industry, I would have very forcefully said no, never. During my angsty teenage years, I worked at House of Nanking during summer breaks. When I was younger, I spent most weekends helping out at Restaurant Grandma's place, Star Lunch, which was a tiny thirteen-seater with only barstools and an open kitchen that served food from Ningbo. But I resented my "abnormal" upbringing. I hated the long hours and the time I was forced to spend away from my parents. I would watch my friends get picked up from school on time, while I sat on the stairs with my buddy the security guard, waiting for my dad—who sometimes completely forgot to pick me up. I longed for the stereotypical weeknight family dinners at home, which I never got. Three or four days a week, Dad would take me out after school to some new spot in Chinatown, where he'd have a late lunch and I'd have an afternoon snack and we'd talk about the dishes we were eating and how we could improve them. On weekends after Nanking's dinner service ended, Mom and Dad would pick me up from Restaurant Grandma's house and we'd go to Italian red-sauce joints in North Beach for an 11 p.m. dinner. (This is why I witnessed my first bar fight when I was ten years old—two guys decided to duke it out in the middle of our dinner. When my dad told me to leave the table, I ran in the wrong direction, toward the bar—but he caught me and pulled me toward the second exit. See what I mean about him always being observant?) I could count the hours we spent together during any given week on two hands, and it wasn't enough. It felt like my parents were choosing work over me.

It took me a long time to appreciate my parents' dedication to their craft, how hard it must have been to raise a kid amid all that uncertainty, and how beautiful it was to be raised in the proverbial village of my extended family. My parents' siblings and my grandparents on both sides alternated taking care of me: They would live at our house for anywhere between one to three years to help watch me.

So, I got to have dinner with my relatives every day—and I was exposed to all of their interesting and eclectic cooking styles.

Of course, it was my dad's cooking at Nanking that ignited the spark of my culinary passion. From a very young age, I was his sounding board and taste-tester. If it sounds hard to believe that my dad would trust the opinions of an eight-year-old, just know that many Chinese immigrants at the time worked in a sort of bubble—we'd never ask people outside of the family for help, advice, or guidance. So my dad could only trust me and my mom to give him the blunt, direct feedback he needed.

That's how I ended up accompanying him on produce shopping trips to Chinatown markets, or to Costco to learn about Western fish. I was never a kid who ate for sustenance—I was always analyzing dishes, dissecting them, brainstorming with Dad how to make them better. It was an incredible education.

My dad's cooking style is only one piece of the puzzle of my culinary influences. My taste was also shaped by the aunts, uncles, and grandparents who cooked for me every single day when I was growing up. As a kid, I loved noticing the cultural differences evident in our seemingly unified family. My dad's older sister, for example, was very traditional. She took after their mom when it came to cooking meals: six to eight different dishes for dinner, including two or three cold dishes, one soup, at least two hot protein-based dishes, and one or two simple vegetable dishes. My aunt's dinner table had a lazy Susan to accommodate all the different components of her meals. My dad's younger sister, by contrast, was the most frugal of the bunch. When she cooked for me, she would make only one dish and boast how far she'd stretched a dollar in order to feed us. Her dishes always had a tiny portion of protein and lots of vegetables, fortified with either noodles or rice. The beef and jalapeño stir-fry on page 237 is a great example. My dad's dad (Aya) only knew how to make three dishes: microwaved whole tilapia (page 256), egg fried rice, and glass soup. And no matter what my grandma made and how amazing it all was (she was the best cook from the Fang family, apart from my dad), my grandpa always wanted to finish his meal with his own egg-fried rice and glass soup.

My mom's family has ties to Hunan, Shanghai, and Hong Kong, and the dishes I ate growing up reflect all those different influences. My gōng gong (mom's dad) is originally from Hunan, where the food is often stewed, pot-roasted, braised, or fried. Food from Hunan is also on the spicier side, using a lot of chilis, garlic, and green onions. They often use smoked meats to enhance dishes. All these elements show up in my mom's cooking: She likes pickled vegetables and uses them in stir-fries with chili and protein, to amp up the bold flavors that Hunan cuisine is known for. The Spicy Pickled Long Beans with Ground Turkey on page 180 is a perfect example. And now I realize how much her cooking has influenced my own.

After a busy childhood helping my folks with Nanking, I attended college at the University of Southern California and worked at Merrill Lynch and Johnson & Johnson. For years, I lived the life I thought I wanted and tried to quiet the tiny voice in my head that told me I missed restaurants.

Eventually, that voice became too loud to ignore. That hectic, erratic, unstable lifestyle that I had resented so much as a kid? Turned out, I needed it. I told my dad I wanted to move back to San Francisco and join the family business.

PETER: I was so happy. Over the years, so many people had asked me to franchise House of Nanking. But it's out of the question. There will never be a House of Nanking Las Vegas or anything like that. The restaurant business is so grueling, and every little detail matters. If you get one detail wrong, it could jeopardize all of your success. That is just too much responsibility for anyone except for someone you trust completely. And for me, franchising would just be about money. The restaurant was never about money for me; it was about making people happy.

Before Kathy came on, I feared that once I was gone, House of Nanking would have to close. It would be the end of a decades-long legacy.

KATHY: In 2009, after I'd earned my degree from Le Cordon Bleu, my dad and I opened our second restaurant, Fang, in the SoMa district of San Francisco. It was the restaurant he and I had always dreamed of: three stories, with banquet rooms large enough to host large events. Over the decades, so many people had begged us to host their weddings, anniversaries, or corporate events at House of Nanking. We always had to say no; we just didn't have the space or the logistics to make it work.

Fang was supposed to feel like an extension of our home. We wanted it to feel personal, which is why we gave the restaurant our last name. In Chinese, the restaurant is called dà tang fāng chú, a play on words, since Tang, my mom's last name, has the same pronunciation as dà táng, which refers to a dining hall. Fang is our last name, and fāng chú is "chef Fang."

We didn't hire an interior decorator or designer; my dad and I hung up the décor and picked out the paint

CLOCKWISE FROM TOP LEFT:
Chinese New Year at Restaurant Grandma's house

Little Kathy in the first house she, Lily, and Peter lived in

Kathy at Restaurant Grandma's house

Kathy on her seventh birthday, the year the restaurant was opened

PRODUCE OF USA
unless otherwise marked
PRODUCE OF CANADA
PRODUCE OF MEXICO
EGGPLANT
FANCY
CHOICE
LARGE
CUCUMBERS
PEPPERS
JUMBO
EX-LARGE
LARGE
MEDIUM
SELECT
RED
SUNTAN

colors ourselves. If it feels like you're in our living room, it's because my dad is the type of guy who will get excited about a review or a photo of Keanu Reeves and then print out twenty copies and paste them all over the place.

The food is also a reflection of who we are as a family: a little bit modern, a little bit old-school, with regional influences from Shanghai, Canton, and everywhere we've traveled to over the years. Our cooking is always guided by the produce, ingredients, and places that inspire us.

PETER: People taste our food and say it has that "Nanking flavor." But they aren't talking about the city of Nanking; they're talking about the Fangs' unique style. There are many reasons I am happy to be in business with my daughter. One is that we speak the same language. She or I can describe a dish that we have in our heads, and the other one immediately understands. We don't have to use too many words; we just know how to cook together.

KATHY: For me, working with my dad is a way to make up for lost time. My parents may not have been around as much as I wanted when I was a kid, but now I see them every day—to the point where I buy paper towels for their house and schedule all of their doctors' appointments. Some people might think that's weird, but I love it.

PETER: My hope is that when people cook from this book, they love the process of cooking and they love the food. Because if they love what they are cooking it will make the food taste better, and then everyone will be happy. These recipes have brought much happiness to me and my family over the years, and I hope they do the same for yours.

OUR COOKING STYLE AT HOUSE OF NANKING & FANG RESTAURANTS

KATHY: People always ask, "What kind of Chinese food do you cook at House of Nanking and Fang?" The answer isn't simple. It's not just Shanghainese, or Cantonese, or any one style. "It's ours," I say, pointing to my head, then my heart. "It's all here, and here."

This book? It's a collection of experiences, a journey through the vast landscape of Chinese cuisines we've encountered in our lifetimes. Yes, you'll see dishes rooted in Shanghai, where my father was born. You'll taste the Cantonese influences I encountered in restaurants in San Francisco's Chinatown, as well as at the table of my pó po, where she shared dishes she learned in Hong Kong. There's even a touch of fiery Hunan in there from my gōng gong , my mom's dad.

But more than that, you'll see our own interpretations. At House of Nanking and Fang, we cook without boundaries. Why? Because our lives have been a blend of these amazing cuisines. We take the best of what we've learned, mix it with our own ideas, and create something uniquely ours.

In these pages, you'll find dishes that might seem familiar, but with a twist that's pure Fang. You'll also see traditional recipes both my father and I grew up with. We're not about sticking to one style. Sometimes, we honor the styles we've encountered by showcasing them in their original form; others, we honor them by fusing them into something new.

Chinese cuisine is like a big family: We're all related, but each branch has its own personality. Chinese cuisine is also incredibly diverse, with some experts recognizing as many as eight to ten major regional cuisines, often referred to as the Eight Great Traditions. However, this classification only scratches the surface, as there are dozens, if not hundreds, of distinct regional styles across China. Each province, city, and sometimes even village has its own culinary specialties. On the following page I've included a short intro to the three major Chinese cuisines we cover in this book, as these are the three cuisines most clearly reflected in our life experiences.

A NOTE ON TRANSLATIONS

For most of the Chinese translations in this book, we've provided pinyin (the romanized spelling of Mandarin, with tonal marks) followed by simplified Chinese. However, for the ingredients section on page 47 and in the glossary on page 281, we are also providing the Cantonese pronunciations—since, depending on where you live and shop for ingredients, the retailers near you may speak Cantonese.

Shanghainese cuisine: Originating from the Jiangsu province in eastern China, Shanghainese cuisine is known for its sweet and rich flavors, often with a touch of alcohol from locally made Shaoxing wine. The cooking style emphasizes braising and slow-cooking techniques. It's been a running joke in our family that the key ingredients of Shanghainese cuisine are soy sauce, rice wine, sugar, and MSG. But when I traveled to Shanghai, I discovered there was far more than just what my family joked about. I learned that freshwater fish and seafood were also key ingredients, which makes sense, since Shanghai is a major port city right on the coast where the Yangtze River meets the sea.

Cantonese cuisine: Hailing from Guangdong province in southern China, Cantonese cuisine is renowned for its emphasis on freshness and natural flavors. Dishes tend to be a lot more subtle than those you might encounter elsewhere in China, often slightly sweet, savory, with natural umami flavors and a focus on the inherent tastes of ingredients. Cooking techniques such as steaming and stir-frying are designed to enhance rather than mask original flavors; the goal is achieving harmonious balance in dishes. The most iconic food from Guangdong that many Americans know is dim sum. *Dim sum*, which translates to "touch the heart" in Cantonese, refers to a style of Chinese cuisine characterized by small portions of food typically served in steamer baskets or on small plates. This culinary tradition originated in the tea houses of Guangdong province, in the city of Guangzhou (Canton), centuries ago.

Hunan cuisine: Originating from the Hunan province in south-central China, Hunan cuisine is famous for its bold, spicy flavors: hot, sour, and often smoky. Chili peppers, smoked meats, garlic, shallots, and pickled ingredients are commonly used. Hunan's hot and humid climate influenced the development of its spicy cuisine, since spicy food is believed to help with perspiration and cooling down.

ESSENTIAL EQUIPMENT, INGREDIENTS, AND TECHNIQUES

KATHY: Pó po only had an electric burner, so she didn't have a wok in her home kitchen in San Francisco. She would steam, braise, and boil a lot of her food, which actually suited her Cantonese style of cooking (Cantonese cuisine is known for steaming, braising, and poaching). You can tell from her dishes that she favors lighter flavors and healthier ways of cooking.

My a niàng (Dad's mom), on the other hand, had a gas burner. There's no way she would have accepted living in a place that didn't have one. She had to have a wok to make dishes she loved from back home.

I mention all this because I think it's important that American readers know that amazing, home-cooked Chinese food is achievable, whatever your kitchen setup. When I was a little kid, my family moved around from tiny SRO (single-room occupancy) to tiny SRO—which meant we didn't have a ton of kitchen gear to move around with and made do with a very limited number of tools. Before we annexed the space next door, House of Nanking was tiny—Dad's kitchen space was literally 81 inches wide and 55 inches deep. That's basically 6 by 4½ feet. So, naturally, we didn't have room for extraneous gear! And even to this day, the House of Nanking kitchen is still incredibly small, with two wok stations, a fryer station, and one boiler: 120 inches wide and 82 inches deep—a whopping 12 by 6 feet!

That said, there are a few tools that will make your life easier if you want to really channel the spirit of House of Nanking at home. For our recommendations on where to buy these items, turn to the Resources on page 291.

The Essentials

Wok with lid (chǎo cài guō 炒菜锅): A wok is such a beautiful, all-purpose tool. You can use it for stir-frying and deep-frying, and with its lid, for steaming and boiling. Carbon steel is preferred for its light weight, quick heating, and ability to develop a natural nonstick patina. (Do not let someone trick you into buying a stainless steel, or, even worse, a nonstick wok; it is far better to season your own carbon steel wok.)

If you have an electric or induction range, you'll need a flat-bottomed wok. If you have a gas range, opt for a traditional round-bottom wok. For tips on choosing and caring for your wok, see "More on Woks" on page 44. For tips on wok cooking, see page 54.

Wok spatula (chǎn zi 铲子): A metal wok spatula with a wooden handle is your best friend when stir-frying in your wok. It is specially designed to work with the curves of your wok, and allows you to easily toss, flip, and pick up ingredients. You can use a large, sturdy metal or wooden spatula instead.

Rice cooker (diàn fàn guō 电饭锅): We went back and forth about whether to include a rice cooker in the "essentials" or "extra credit" section. Technically, you don't need a rice cooker; you could cook your rice on the stovetop in a simple pot with a tight-fitting lid. However, for our family (and most Asian families), rice is LIFE, and life without a rice cooker is unimaginable. Many Western families are surprised when they learn about the ubiquity of rice cookers in Asian households. Maybe they think it's "cheating" to use a machine to cook such a staple food. But when you cook rice every single day (literally!), sometimes for breakfast, lunch, and dinner, a rice cooker makes cooking rice as simple as pushing a button.

A rice cooker isn't just for making perfect, fluffy rice—although that's a pretty sweet deal right there. This bad boy is a multitasking genius! It can steam proteins, keep your food warm for those crazy days when everyone is eating at different times, prepare congees, and even steam up cakes.

A rice cooker is so essential, I've seen Asian friends of mine pack theirs in their suitcases when they travel. I'm not even kidding! Passport? Check. Toothbrush? Check. Rice cooker? Double-check!

I never learned how to ride a bike, but you sure as hell know my parents made me learn to make rice in a rice cooker before I was even seven years old. When I started cooking all my own meals, I had a mini rice cooker that made single-serving rice, which is great for small spaces and doesn't waste food. Now, I have a Zojirushi (Xiàng yìn 象印) brand cooker at home. This is the Rolls-Royce of rice cookers, and the one that most families use. It's known for its advanced "fuzzy logic" technology, multiple rice settings, and a keep-warm function that lasts days.

Cleaver (cài dāo 菜刀): A Chinese cleaver is a multipurpose knife used for chopping, slicing, and mincing. Its wide, flat edge is also handy for tenderizing meat and transferring food. Look for a cleaver with a high-carbon stainless steel blade and a wood handle. Alternatively, you can use a Western chef's knife or santoku knife.

Strainer (zhào lí 笊篱): A spider strainer is ideal for removing food from hot oil or water. Look for a stainless steel mesh with a bamboo or heat-resistant plastic handle. Alternatively, you can use a large slotted spoon or mesh skimmer.

Steamer setup (zhēng guō 蒸锅): For steaming dumplings, vegetables, fish (see page 256), and other proteins (see page 210), you'll need some sort of steamer setup. One option is to buy a bamboo or metal steamer. (At Fang, we use both bamboo and stainless steel, depending on what we're steaming.) You'll also want a basic steaming rack, called a zhēng jià 蒸架 or zhēng lóng jià 蒸笼架. This is a circular stainless steel or aluminum rack with an open-wire design to allow steam to pass through and legs that elevate it above water in a wok or pot. It comes in various sizes, usually ranging from 7 to 11 inches (17 to 28 cm) in diameter and 1½ to 3 inches (4 to 7.5 cm) in height. Make sure to use heatproof plates or bowls on the rack.

At home, we prefer to use a stainless steel or aluminum steamer (jīn shǔ zhēng guō 金属蒸锅), which is durable and resists corrosion. The pot base holds water, while the steamer sits above. It is easy to clean (most are dishwasher safe and don't absorb odors) and doubles as a pot: You can boil food in the pot and steam in the top rack.

However, there are many pros to the traditional bamboo steamer. Bamboo absorbs excess moisture, which helps keep food from becoming soggy, is stackable, which allows you to steam multiple dishes simultaneously, imparts a subtle, pleasant aroma, and is generally more affordable. But it also requires more maintenance: Bamboo steamers need to be cleaned carefully and dried thoroughly after each use, or they might warp or develop mold.

Cooking chopsticks (chǎo cài kuài 炒菜筷): We like to use cooking chopsticks, which are longer than eating chopsticks, for stirring, mixing, and picking up food while cooking. Look for chopsticks made from bamboo (for its heat resistance and traditional feel) or wood. Alternatively, you can use long-handled tongs or a wooden cooking spoon.

Nonstick skillet (píng dǐ bù zhān guō 平底不沾锅): Several recipes in this book call for a 10- to 12-inch (25 to 30 cm) nonstick skillet.

Large pot or stockpot (tāng guō 汤锅): For soups and broths.

Braising pot (dùn guō 炖锅): This can be a clay pot (see opposite), a medium Dutch oven, or any heavy-bottomed pot with a lid.

STEAMER HACK

As I love to tell people who take my cooking classes, you can create a steamer setup with pretty much anything you have at home. Start with a plate or shallow bowl that has raised edges to catch any delicious juices. Then find a pot that is large enough to comfortably fit the plate or bowl. If the pot has a lid, great. If it doesn't have a lid, find a baking sheet or something else large enough to completely cover it. Now bunch up aluminum foil to form four foil balls. Arrange the balls in the pot to form a square, then the plate on top of the balls. Fill the pot with water lower than the level of the plate (you don't want it to bubble onto the plate). Cover with whatever lid you've landed on and voilà, you have a steamer setup.

Extra Credit

Clay pot (shā guō 砂锅): The most authentic way to cook the clay pot rice recipe on page 110 is in—you guessed it—a traditional Chinese clay pot. But you can use your clay pot for slow-cooking or braising meats or legumes; cooking dried and fresh seafood low and slow; making soups, stews, or saucy noodle dishes; or cooking flavorful rice dishes.

When shopping for a clay pot, look for unglazed zǐ shā clay, which is purplish brown. Avoid pots with a shiny glaze on the interior; they won't season as well. The pot should have a slightly rough interior, which is better for flavor absorption. Heavier pots retain heat better, and the lid should fit snugly but not airtight. A flat base is more stable, and a one- to two-quart pot should feed two or three people. Fun fact: Those little cracks? They're not flaws, they're flavor channels! As long as they don't leak, a cracked pot has even more character. The best clay pots look humble but cook like champions!

Did you know your clay pot is like a fine wine? It gets better with age, just like a well-seasoned wok or skillet. The more you cook, the more flavor it absorbs. Caring for your clay pot is similar to caring for your wok: Never use soap, just hot water and a soft brush. Air-dry it upside-down, then store it with the lid slightly ajar (your clay pot needs to breathe!). Avoid sudden temperature changes—for example, when you wash your clay pot, wait for it to cool slightly, rather than plunging a hot pot directly into cold water.

Deep-fry thermometer (wēn dù jì [yóu zhá] 温度计 [油炸]): For measuring the temperature of your frying oil. Also called a candy thermometer.

Fine-mesh strainer (xì shāi 细筛): For sifting dry ingredients, straining liquids, and rinsing small grains like rice. Look for stainless-steel mesh with a metal or plastic rim.

Cleaver sharpener (mó dāo shí 磨刀石): Used for maintaining the sharp edge of the Chinese cleaver and other kitchen knives. Whetstones—typically a combination of medium grit (around 1000) and fine grit (around 3000 to 6000)—are ideal. Diamond or ceramic stones can work as well.

Stainless-steel shallow steaming pans (bú xiù gāng zhēng pán 不锈钢蒸盘): If you plan to steam a lot, it is worth investing in a few shallow, stainless-steel pans you can place on a steaming rack in a wok or steamer.

Metal steaming tongs (zhēng pán jiā 蒸盘夹): And while you're at it, specially designed tongs will help you safely handle and remove hot steaming pans or dishes from steamers or woks.

Wok ring (guō jià 锅架): If you're new to wok cooking and using a round-bottomed wok, a wok stand or ring goes on top of your gas burner and helps stabilize the wok.

MORE ON WOKS

PETER: Ah, the wok. This is my favorite piece of cooking equipment. Every morning, when we open Nanking, the sound of our cooks firing up the woks is like music to my ears. The loud whoosh of the flames, the sizzle of the first drops of oil hitting the hot metal, it's all part of the symphony. Add in the rush of running water as we prep, the rumble of the boiler next to the wok, the rhythmic chopping of vegetables, the yelling over the phone for our daily produce orders from the Chinatown markets—it's the heartbeat of our kitchen.

Some people might find all that noise overwhelming. I know, because we have customers who come in for the first time and I can see it in their eyes. They first notice the sounds from the kitchen, then our servers yelling orders, then the dishwasher in the back. It's a lot to take in, I know, but it's exciting! Entering House of Nanking as a customer reminds me of entering my favorite restaurants in Shanghai. Noise means there's life, activity, and that means there's good business to be made. I don't want quiet in a restaurant. When it's loud, it's soothing to me. It settles me. It tells me that another day of creating delicious food for our customers has begun. It's a sound I've woken up to every day for nearly four decades, and I still love it. And the core piece of equipment at House of Nanking that has fed all those millions of people over the decades is the wok. To me it isn't just a tool; it's the soul of Chinese cooking.

Entire books have been written about woks and wok cookery. Two of our favorites are Grace Young's *The Breath of a Wok* and J. Kenji López-Alt's *The Wok*. We encourage you to explore both of these well-researched books. The former is beautifully written, personal, and thorough. The latter is nearly seven hundred pages long and includes all sorts of tips and hacks for approximating restaurant wok cooking on your home stove.

In the meantime, we want to offer a few wok basics to get you started, and to help you cook the recipes in this book as successfully as possible.

WOK STYLE

- **Flat or round?** If you have an electric or induction range, you'll need to go with flat-bottomed, because round will not balance on your stovetop. If you have a gas range, the traditional round-bottomed wok is the way to go.
- **Material?** Carbon steel or bust, baby. It's durable, conducts heat well, and develops a natural nonstick patina over time.
- **Thickness?** Look for 14-gauge (about 2 mm thick) for a balance of heat responsiveness and durability.
- **Finish?** Hand-hammered woks distribute heat more evenly than machine-made ones.
- **Size?** A 14-inch diameter is versatile for most home cooks. It's large enough for family meals but not too heavy and clunky.
- **Handle?** For home use, a long wooden handle stays cool and offers good control. You can buy a one-handled wok (dān bǐng chǎo cài guō 单柄炒菜锅) or two-handled wok (shuāng ěr chǎo cài guō 双耳炒菜锅), but if you'll only buy one, buy a one-handled wok, which is better for stir-frying and tossing ingredients. The single handle gives it greater maneuverability but is less stable with large volumes. Two-handled woks have two smaller handles and are better for deep-frying, braising, and soups. Most professional chefs are skilled with both types and choose based on the specific dish they're preparing rather than strictly adhering to one type.
- **Brand?** Consider reputable brands like Joyce Chen, Craft Wok, or Lodge for quality assurance.
- **Where to buy?** Flip to the Resources section on page 291.

WOK CARE

The first step when you buy a new wok is the initial seasoning (kāi guō 开锅).

1. First, thoroughly wash the wok, inside and out, with hot water and mild soap to remove any machine oil or grease (this was likely applied at the factory to reduce rusting before the first use). This will be the last time you use soap on your wok!
2. Dry the wok thoroughly with a towel, then heat on your stovetop until it smokes.
3. Rub the hot wok with a high-smoke-point oil. Use paper towels (you can hold the towels with tongs, if you want to be extra careful not to burn yourself) to thoroughly rub and coat the interior with the oil.
4. Heat until the oil smokes, then turn off the heat and wipe the wok clean.
5. Repeat the process of rubbing the wok with oil, heating until it smokes, and wiping clean two or three more times.

You're now ready to cook with your wok! When it comes to regular wok care, there are just a few rules to follow:

1. Soon after use, while the wok is still warm (but not so hot you risk burning yourself), clean and scrub the wok with hot water only—no soap, which is too abrasive and will damage that nonstick patina we're working to maintain.
2. Immediately wipe the wok dry with a towel, then heat it again on the stovetop to evaporate any remaining moisture (moisture causes rusting).
3. Apply a thin layer of oil before you store your wok.
4. If, despite your best efforts, your wok develops some rust, don't worry: Simply scrub with steel wool, rinse, dry, and repeat the initial seasoning process. If you feel your wok is losing its nonstick seasoning, repeat the initial seasoning process.

BEST SCRUBBERS FOR CLEANING A WOK

- **Bamboo wok brush (zhú shuā 竹刷)**: This is your best overall choice. Made from natural materials, it is effective at removing food residue while still being gentle on a seasoned wok. It also dries quickly, which reduces bacterial growth.
- **Chain mail scrubber (liàn jiǎ shuā 链甲刷)**: Use this if you encounter stubborn residue. It is durable and long-lasting, and safe for seasoned surfaces if used gently.
- **Soft bristle brush (ruǎn máo shuā 软毛刷)**: Good for general cleaning. Choose one with heat-resistant handle.

Avoid metal scrubbers, abrasive scouring pads, and soap-filled sponges, all of which can damage your wok's seasoning.

WOK DOS AND DON'TS

- **Do** cook with oil regularly to build patina.
- **Don't** use soap, abrasive scrubbers, or the dishwasher.
- **Don't** soak or expose to moisture for long periods.
- **Do** remember, a well-maintained wok improves with age, developing guō qì 锅气 or "wok hei"—the desirable seasoned flavor we want!

INGREDIENTS

KATHY: When I talk to our customers, they tell me that their biggest hurdle when it comes to cooking Chinese food at home is the unfamiliar ingredients—seasonings, dry goods, produce, and more.

This makes me so sad, because one of my favorite things about Chinese cuisine is the beautiful diversity of its ingredients, especially produce and greens. Honestly, I could write an entire book about Chinese vegetables. (Maybe that will be our next book!)

But rest assured, you do not need to have an encyclopedic knowledge, or even my passion for Chinese ingredients, to cook Chinese food. In fact, to cook most of the recipes in this book, you only need a small handful of kitchen staples, all of which you can find in Western grocery stores.

On page 281, you'll find a complete alphabetical glossary of the ingredients called for in the book. That is for the people like me, who want to go deep. But if you are ready to just start cooking, take a look at the list of the essential ingredients below. I'm guessing you have most of them at home already!

Garlic (dà suàn 大蒜 / daaih syun): Garlic is the aromatic backbone of so many Chinese dishes. Our greatest piece of advice is to work quickly when you add it to a wok. Minced garlic can go from golden to burnt in a matter of seconds, and if you burn garlic, its bitterness will ruin a dish. Store garlic cloves in a cool, dry place with good airflow.

Ginger (jiāng 姜 / gēung): Ginger is another core aromatic in Chinese cooking. In Cantonese dishes, it might be steamed to create an elegant fragrance, or julienned and used raw as a garnish. Young ginger is more tender and less fibrous than mature ginger, which is more pungent and most commonly used in Chinese cuisine. Mature ginger is also more widely available in Western grocery stores. If your ginger is unpeeled, store it at room temperature (as long as your kitchen doesn't get extremely hot) for up to a week. For longer storage, or if your ginger is cut or peeled (in which case you should pat it dry, wrap it in a paper towel, and toss it in a ziplock bag), store it in the fridge.

Scallions (cōng 葱/ chūng): Scallions, aka green onions, are ubiquitous in Chinese cooking. They are the foundation of our signature onion cakes (page 85). We julienne them (see page 50) to use as a garnish. We slice them thin to use in sauce (page 59). They are used in marinades, soups, stir-fries, and as a filling. When scallions are called for in this book, use both the white and green parts, unless otherwise specified.

White pepper (bái hú jiao 白胡椒 / baahk wù jīu): Peppercorns come from the small, dried fruits of a tropical vine. Depending on how the fruit is processed, it might be black, green, rose-colored, or white. White pepper is more frequently used than black in Chinese cooking; it has a sharp, slightly fermented heat. The aromatic floral spice is what gives hot and sour soup its distinctive peppery kick. It also adds heat to light-colored dishes without adding black specks, which gives the finished dish a nice, clean appearance.

Cornstarch (yù mǐ diàn fěn 玉米淀粉 / yuhk máih dihng fán): Cornstarch (called "cornflour" in the UK) is a neutral-tasting thickening agent with a silky texture when dissolved. (In our kitchen, where we speak Cantonese, and at home, we call it "sāang fán," a reference to "raw starch.") Cornstarch plays a crucial role in Chinese cooking, particularly in marinades and for tenderizing meat. We use it for:

- *Velveting* (see page 53), which creates a silky tender texture in meats.
- *In marinades* (see page 53), to help the flavors adhere to the meat. It also creates a protective coating, like a jacket, that seals in moisture during cooking.
- *Quick cooking.* The cornstarch coating allows for quick cooking at high temperatures without drying out the meat, which is why it's crucial to

always marinate meats in cornstarch before stir-frying in a wok or saute pan.

- *Tenderizing.* A cornstarch coating helps prevent protein fibers from tightening too much during cooking, resulting in more tender meat.
- *Thickening sauces.* When mixed into a slurry (see page 53) and added to sauces, it creates the characteristic glossy thickness you associate with many Chinese dishes.

Soy sauce (jiàng yóu 醬油 / sih yàuh): Here's another ingredient you likely already have in your pantry. This salty, umami-rich, dark brown condiment is used as a seasoning, marinade base, or dipping sauce; it is found in the sauce aisle of Asian markets, in bottles or large jugs. Variations include light, dark, and low-sodium versions. Chinese brands are often labeled as "light soy sauce" to differentiate from dark soy sauce (see below). We typically use the Japanese brand Kikkoman or the Chinese brand Lee Kum Kee. If you are gluten intolerant, Japanese tamari or Bragg's Liquid Aminos are wheat-free options. We store soy sauce in a cool, dark place.

Dark soy sauce (lǎo chōu 老抽 / lóuh chāu): This is a thicker, sweeter soy sauce aged with molasses, resulting in a rich, complex flavor. Dark soy sauce is used to add color and depth to dishes and is found in the soy sauce section, typically in glass bottles or plastic containers. We store dark soy sauce in a cool, dark place.

Shaoxing wine (shào xīng jiǔ 紹兴酒 / Siuh hīng jáu): This rice wine is a specialty of the eastern coastal region of Zhejiang, south of Shanghai. It is amber colored and smells a bit like cooking sherry. We use it to add depth and minimize gaminess in marinades and sauces, or add a deeper flavor to stir-fries. Look for it in the sauce or alcohol sections of Asian markets in glass bottles. You can buy cooking-quality or drinking-quality versions; we often use Qian Hu or Poiget brand. We store ours in our pantry (at room temperature); however, if you don't use it often and want to extend the shelf life, you can store it in the fridge.

Chinkiang vinegar (zhèn jiāng xiāng cù 镇江香醋 / jan gōng chou): Often labeled as "Zhenjiang-style vinegar." This is Chinese black rice vinegar from a specific place: Zhenjiang (often Anglicized as Chinkiang), in Jiangsu province. It is black in color and its flavor is rich and complex, with a mellow acidity and slightly sweet aftertaste. It is used in dipping sauces, marinades, stir-fries, and braises to balance flavors in dishes. Look for it in the vinegar section, typically in glass bottles. Do not use sweetened black vinegar (often labeled as "diluted sweetened black vinegar"), as this is a different product and cannot be used interchangeably.

Neutral oil (zhōng xìng yóu 中性油 / jihk maht yàuh): Most of the recipes in this book call for a "neutral oil" for stir-frying and deep-frying. You could use any number of refined vegetable oils, such as canola, soybean, or corn. In the restaurant, we use soybean oil. At home, we like to use avocado oil, which is great but pricey. For deep-frying, an affordable option like vegetable or canola works. It is essential to use an oil with a high smoke point.

Toasted sesame oil (ma yóu 香油 / màh yàuh): Most of the sesame oils you'll find in markets are toasted, which gives them a darker color and nuttier flavor and aroma. It is used as a finishing oil or in marinades and sauces. Look for it in glass bottles in the oil section of Asian and Western markets; we often use Kadoya brand. Light (untoasted) sesame oil is more often sold in large plastic bottles and has a less aromatic finish—we do not recommend it for the recipes in this book.

Chili oil (là yóu 辣油 / laaht yàuh): For our House of Nanking recipe, see page 274. If you prefer to use store-bought chili oil, look in the condiment or oil aisle of an Asian or Western market—the Lee Kum Kee brand is easy to find, and we also like Kadoya. Different brands have different levels of spice, and might have additional flavoring agents like Sichuan peppercorn. Whatever you buy, look for something with nice clarity; cloudy oils in plastic rather than glass tend to be lower quality.

White rice (bái mǐ 白米 / baak mai): At home and at the restaurant, we use long-grain jasmine rice as our everyday rice for steaming. Some of our favorite brands include Three Ladies, Golden Phoenix, Elephant, Royal Umbrella, and AAA Jasmine Rice, which offer good quality at bulk prices. At home we use Three Ladies or Elephant and purchase fifteen-pound bags because we steam rice five to six days a week, every week. However, for households that don't prepare rice as often as we do, five- or ten-pound bags will do. For more on the types of rice used in this book, see page 290.

李錦記
LEE KUM KEE
特級老抽
HONDASHI
PREMIUM BOUILLON POWDER FLAVORED WITH CHICKEN
NET WEIGHT 8 oz (227 g)
辣椒油
CHILI OIL
辣豆瓣醬
CHILI BEAN SAUCE (TOBAN DJAN)
NET WT. 13 oz (368 g)
鮮味生抽
SOY SAUCE
NET 16.9 fl oz (1.05 pt)
spicer
KINGSFORD'S
CORN STARC
玉米澱粉
NET WT. 1 LB
SALTED BLA
PICKLED CAB
雪菜大王
拌飯剁辣椒
冠珍醬園
海鮮醬
ROASTED SESA
5.5 FL.OZ (163ml)
SHAOXING COOKING WINE
紹興厨用酒
Pickled Sour Mustard

TECHNIQUES

This section focuses on the most common and fundamental cooking techniques used in Chinese restaurant kitchens, particularly methods frequently used in day-to-day cooking.

Knife Cuts

What follows is a list of the essential knife and preparation methods used in Chinese restaurant kitchens. That said, there are many more cuts than what's listed below in Chinese cuisine, including many cuts that are specifically for aesthetics. But for the recipes in this book, you just need to know these basics.

Batons (gùn bàng qiē 棍棒切): The translation from Chinese is "stick cut," which we use for firmer vegetables such as daikon and eggplant. To cut batons, cut long rectangular strips, typically about ¼ inch (6 mm) wide and 2 to 3 inches (5 to 7.5 cm) long.

Bias cut (xié qiē 斜切): When we call for ginger in this book, it is often cut on the bias (less than 45-degree angle) into thin (about ⅛ inch/3 mm) long (often 2 inches/5 cm) ovals. We

don't like to waste anything, so we don't really trim the ginger before slicing—it's all edible and usable! We also often bias cut our scallions, as in the photo above.

Coin cut (yuán piàn qiē 圆片切): Thin, circular slices for ingredients like cucumbers, carrots, lotus root, or ginger.

Cube (kuài 块): Larger square cuts for meats and root vegetables.

Dice (ding 丁): Small cubes for vegetables and meats.

Julienne (sī 丝): For vegetables like ginger or scallions, which will be gently steamed or enjoyed raw as a garnish. To julienne ginger, start with bias-cut ginger. Slice the ovals into thin, ⅛-inch (3 mm) strips. To julienne scallions, cut the scallions (both white and green parts) into 3-inch (7.5 cm) segments. Then,

slice those segments into very thin strips, lengthwise. If you don't plan to use it right away, submerge julienned scallion in ice water to keep it fresh and firm.

Mincing (duò 剁): Finely chopping ingredients such as garlic, ginger, and meat. Mincing is crucial for creating fine textures and releasing flavors, and is often used in combination with pounding (see below) for dishes like steamed minced pork and steamed beef patty (page 239).

Oblique cut (xié qiē 斜切): In Chinese cuisine, the oblique cut (also translated as bias cut) is used for beef, pork, or chicken that will be stir-fried. By slicing the meat at a 45-degree angle against the grain, you create wider, thinner pieces that will cook quickly and evenly. It also increases tenderness by shortening muscle fibers, thus improving texture and allowing for better absorption of marinades and sauces. Typically we cut meat into equal slices about ⅛ to ¼ inch (3 to

6 mm) thick. In the chicken and snow peas recipe on page 220, we oblique cut chicken to ensure each piece cooks quickly and evenly.

Roll-cut (gŭn dāo qiē 滚刀切): Diagonal cuts for cylindrical vegetables like carrots, asparagus, and snow peas that will be stir-fried. Roll-cutting creates irregularly shaped pieces with angled edges, which cook evenly and add visual interest to your dish. Start by holding the vegetable on your cutting board and make a diagonal slice at a 45-degree angle. After cutting, roll the vegetable a quarter turn toward you. Make another diagonal cut at the same angle and thickness. Continue this pattern of rolling a quarter turn and cutting at a 45-degree angle until you've worked your way through the entire vegetable.

Pounding (pāi 拍): Often used to tenderize meat or crush aromatics like ginger and garlic to release their oils. Pounding involves crushing ingredients to break fibers, which significantly impacts the final texture and flavor of dishes. It's used in combination with mincing to make "ground" protein. When pounding aromatics like garlic or ginger, we use the flat side of our cleaver to smash the veg until flattened and the juices are released. Then, we chop it with a cleaver to mince it even finer. For meats, pounding requires chopping with a cleaver over and over in a rhythmic pattern to break down fibers, creating a crosshatch pattern. This is our equivalent to using a meat mallet.

Scoring (piàn huā 片花): Making shallow cuts on the surface of meat or seafood.

Shred (sī 丝): In dishes such as the Nanking Noodles on page 117, you will "shred" pork tenderloin, which means cutting it into small, matchstick-size strips to allow for rapid heat penetration and quick, even cooking in the wok. To do this, first cut the tenderloin crosswise into thin medallions. Now cut those medallions into thin, matchstick-size strips. The result should be slightly thicker than julienne but still quite thin.

Slice (piàn 片): Thin, flat cuts for meats and vegetables.

THE RAW DEAL

KATHY: When my father first arrived in the United States, he encountered a culinary concept that left him bewildered: the idea of eating meat that wasn't fully cooked. In China, the sight of pink or red in meat is a no-no; if a piece of meat shows any sign of being undercooked, it's considered poorly prepared and would likely be returned to the kitchen. "You want me to eat that?" he'd exclaim, eyeing a medium-rare steak with a mix of curiosity and apprehension. For him, and many Chinese cooks, meat should be cooked until no trace of blood remains. It took time, but gradually, my parents began to appreciate the flavors and textures of a perfectly seared, pink-centered steak. However, this Western approach to meat remains foreign to traditional Chinese cooking. In fact, one of the major pillars of Chinese cuisine is the art of making meat tender while cooking it completely through.

Deep-Frying (zhà 炸)

At the restaurants, we have dedicated deep fryers. You'd have to be pretty passionate about deep-frying to have a setup like this at home. So our suggestion for the recipes in this book is to deep-fry in a heavy-bottomed pot, Dutch oven, or wok (stabilized with a wok ring, if it has a round bottom).

- Always choose a neutral oil with a high smoke point (e.g., peanut, canola, or vegetable oil).
- Fill your pot no more than halfway with neutral oil, to prevent overflow.
- Use a deep-fry thermometer to check the temperature of the oil, which should typically be around 350 to 375°F / 175 to 190°C.
- Pat food dry before adding to the oil, to prevent splattering.
- Do not overcrowd.
- Prepare a landing zone: a wire rack with paper towels underneath, where you can transfer fried ingredients with a spider skimmer.
- Be cautious of water and hot oil interaction!

Steaming (zhēng 蒸)

There are many ways to achieve beautifully steamed vegetables, dumplings, and proteins. If you'd like, you can invest in elegant bamboo steamer baskets like you'd see at a dim sum restaurant. In one instance in this book (the fish on page 256), we're even letting you "steam" in a microwave. Any way you do it, steaming is a great way to gently cook ingredients while emphasizing their natural flavors.

When steaming delicate things such as dumplings, you should line the steamer with cabbage, wax paper, or a thin layer of oil to prevent sticking. This can also extend the life of a bamboo steamer by minimizing the direct contact of food to the surface.

Passing Through Water (guò shuǐ 过水)

This is the process of quickly swishing or passing ingredients through hot or boiling water to clean or partially cook them. This allows for greater control over doneness, ensuring the right texture and tenderness. It's a fast step and usually happens right before you toss the ingredient into a wok.

Passing Through Oil (guò yóu 过油)

Briefly passing ingredients through hot oil seals in flavors and/or partially cooks the ingredient, removes impurities, and locks in natural juices.

Thickening Sauces with Cornstarch Slurry

Many dishes in this book call for a cornstarch slurry, which is simply a 1:1 combination of cornstarch and water. You can prepare it in advance of cooking, as part of your mise en place (or bèi cài 备菜), but make sure to give it a stir before adding it to the wok, since the cornstarch tends to sink to the bottom and you want to make sure it's well-incorporated.

When you add it to the wok, drizzle the slurry in a circular motion so that it spreads evenly over all the ingredients. Immediately stir with your wok spatula to incorporate it and prevent clumping. Keep stirring until thickened and well combined. You might not need to use all of the slurry, and keep in mind that the sauce will thicken up further once it's off the heat.

If your sauce seizes up, there are typically two culprits. If the entire sauce seizes, you added too much slurry. If only parts of the sauce seize up and become clumpy, then you probably didn't work and stir quickly enough. (Unfortunately, there's no good way to save a seized sauce . . . You can try to add water to dilute it, but your best bet is to start over.)

Velveting (huá 滑)

This is the term for coating meat in a mixture of cornstarch, sometimes egg whites, baking soda, and Shaoxing wine before cooking, for example in the chicken and snow peas recipe on page 220. This creates a protective layer that seals in moisture and ensures tenderness.

ON TENDERIZING & MARINATING

KATHY: A lot of the dishes in this book call for quickly marinating meats before cooking—often in a mixture of cornstarch, soy sauce, dark soy sauce, and/or Shaoxing wine. Typically in Chinese households, we'll add all the marinade ingredients directly to the bowl with the protein and then mix with chopsticks to combine—although you could certainly use a fork. We tend not to premix the marinade ingredients before adding the protein. (The exception to this is brines.) If you're new to cooking Chinese food, you should feel free to premix marinade ingredients before adding them to a protein, if that makes you more comfortable.

In Chinese cooking, the marinades tend not to be as wet as some American marinades. When I cook American dishes, it seems like there's always a lot of leftover marinade that gets discarded. By contrast, you'll add the entire contents of the marinating bowl—protein and seasonings—directly to the wok.

It's for this reason that our marinades and sauces aren't particularly wet. A very wet marinade would prevent the high-heat searing we're looking for—it's this searing that seals in the juices and flavors of the protein. The cornstarch is there to help coat the meat (we like to think of it as a "cornstarch jacket") and further seal in the flavor, sauces, and juices.

Think about Chinese marinating as a way of seasoning, tenderizing, and treating the meat before a stir-fry.

Stir-Frying in a Wok (chǎo 炒)

- Preheat your wok over the highest heat possible before adding oil. Your wok should be smoking and as hot as it can get.
- Don't overcrowd the wok—cook in batches if necessary. If you add too much meat at once, it will steam instead of brown. As you're getting started, don't add more than ½ cup (120 ml) of an ingredient to the wok at a time.
- Keep in mind, when you're cooking in a wok, you can't just double a recipe and expect the same results. When you overfill a wok, not only do you get less contact with the surface of the wok (which results in less searing and sealing in of flavor and moisture); you also reduce the overall temperature inside the wok, which is no good. Cooking in batches is the solution here.
- Add aromatics like scallions, ginger, and garlic first to season the oil and wok, which will impart flavor to the meat or vegetables that will be added shortly thereafter.
- When you're working with vegetables, add firmer root vegetables first, delicate or leafy vegetables last.
- Keep ingredients moving to prevent burning.
- Use a combination of the wok spatula and the "wok toss" to move ingredients around. A wok spatula is specially designed to work around the curve of the wok, and has the capacity to lift and toss more ingredients than a wooden spoon. The "wok toss" is what it sounds like: a motion you use to toss ingredients in the wok without the aid of a spatula. The wok toss is a fluid, rhythmic motion. Hold the wok's handle with one hand and a spatula or ladle in the other. Start with the wok tilted slightly toward you, ingredients settled at the bottom center. Push the wok forward and slightly upward, using your wrist and arm to flick ingredients into the air. As the ingredients fall, you pull the wok back toward you, catching them in the center. This entire motion is repeated rapidly, often several times in quick succession. The goal is to keep the ingredients moving constantly, ensuring even cooking and preventing sticking.
- The Maillard reaction is crucial for developing the complex flavors and appealing brown color we're looking for in wok-cooked proteins. To check if your meat is cooked properly, look for an even, golden brown sear across the exterior with no raw or gray areas visible. The pieces should appear glossy and vibrant from the oil and sauce, rather than dry or shriveled, and the sauce should cling to the protein without pooling excessively. While a slight char on the edges can be desirable for some dishes, the protein shouldn't look burnt. Some pieces may have a slight curl or fold from the high heat.

MASTERING THE WOK

KATHY: Mastering wok cookery begins with understanding the intense heat required. In professional kitchens, wok burners can reach a whopping 50,000 BTU or more, heating the wok to a temperature of 700 to 850°F (370 to 450°C). While home stoves typically max out around 12,000 to 15,000 BTU, you can still achieve good results by preheating your wok thoroughly—to the point where it's smoking even without oil. Aim for temperatures around 400 to 450°F (200 to 230°C) at home.

When it comes to cooking oil, choose a high-heat, neutral-tasting option like soybean, canola, avocado, or rice bran oil. These oils can withstand intense heat without breaking down or imparting strong flavors, allowing the true taste of your ingredients to shine through. Avoid using oils with low smoke points such as extra-virgin olive oil, sesame oil, or unrefined nut oils. Steer clear of butter, which burns quickly at high temperatures. You'll be surprised by how many times customers ask us if we use butter or cream in our food—the answer is always no. Butter is not a traditional ingredient in Chinese cuisine and should never be used as a fat for wok cooking.

Proper preparation is crucial. Your mise en place must be ready to go, and the sequence of cooking steps should be clear in your mind before you begin. My dad always tells our new chefs in the kitchen to think about their plan of attack before they step up to the wok. If you don't have a plan in place for every step, the dish will fall apart and you will have to start over again. In professional kitchens, wok chefs have internalized every move, resulting in a fluid, fast process that's pure muscle memory. This level of preparation and focus is what elevates a dish from good to exceptional.

The hallmark of superior wok cookery is the elusive "wok hei" (guō qì), which translates to "breath of the wok." This concept is central to Chinese cuisine, particularly Cantonese cooking. Wok hei refers to the distinct flavor and aroma imparted to food by cooking in a wok at very high heat. It's characterized by a subtle smoky taste and a certain "essence" that's difficult to describe but immediately recognizable.

Here's where the magic happens: You can experience wok hei before the food even touches your lips! As soon as a dish is served, lean in close and take a deep breath. That initial whiff is like a preview of culinary fireworks—a tantalizing blend of caramelization, smokiness, and the essence of your ingredients, all amplified by the intense heat of the wok. This aromatic symphony is your first clue that you're about to taste something extraordinary.

Achieving wok hei requires precise control of heat, timing, and technique. The presence (or absence) of wok hei can make or break a dish in the eyes of discerning diners and is often used to judge a chef's skill level. It's this elusive quality that separates a good stir-fry from a truly exceptional one, elevating simple ingredients into a dish that dances on your palate.

That said, don't be intimidated if you're new to wok cooking. Wok hei is something that not all Chinese people can even discern, and thus certainly is not required from a dish that is made at home. So relax and enjoy this book as a way to explore Chinese cookery with a new piece of equipment in the kitchen. Like any skill, it can be learned with practice and patience. While many of the dishes in this book were developed in the House of Nanking kitchen, others are dishes created at home by home cooks: grandparents, aunts, and uncles, who don't have the expertise of a Chinese restaurant chef. They were able to create mouthwatering dishes from the most basic of tools! Just start with simple stir-fries and gradually work your way up.

Here are some practical tips to get you started. Remember, even professional chefs started as beginners. Happy wokking!

THE ART OF COLD DISHES

KATHY: I was a patient child, but there was one gathering that tested even my admirable forbearance: the elaborate banquets my restaurant grandfather would bring me to annually, hosted by his benevolent association at the Empress of China.

The issue wasn't the countless gān bēi (toasts), or the din of adult chatter as grownups roamed around the room. As the hours crawled by, my small frame would fidget in oversized chairs, stomach growling, eyes darting between animated faces and empty table spaces. The air was thick with anticipation and the aroma of dishes yet to come. I wanted to eat.

Then, like the opening notes of a symphony, the feast would begin. Platters laden with delicious food appeared, and the first course was always the cold dishes.

Jellyfish salad, translucent, tender, and crunchy; marinated beef shanks, sliced thinly with tendon in a garlic soy sauce; and more, a preview of the culinary performance to come.

These childhood banquets are where my love affair with cold dishes began. I consider cold dishes to be the unsung heroes of Chinese cooking, with a history as rich and complex as their flavors. Dating back to the Zhou Dynasty more than two thousand years ago, these dishes were born from a blend of culinary artistry and traditional Chinese medicine. Our ancestors believed in balancing the body's energies through food, and cold dishes were their delicious solution to counteract heavier, "warmer" foods.

In Shanghai, where my father was born, cold dishes are elevated to an art form. They present an opportunity for chefs to showcase intricate knife skills, artistic presentations, and a masterful balance of flavors. These dishes are our way of honoring seasonal ingredients, demonstrating hospitality, and setting the stage for the meal to come. Yet, beyond their artistic origins, cold dishes have also become staples in humble settings. For example, in the sweltering Shanghai summers of my dad's childhood, my grandmother

DISHES

would prepare simple but beautiful cold dishes to nourish her large family in their cramped, hot living quarters, without having to light a cooking fire.

Liáng cài is more than just food—it's a social experience. In Chinese dining, whether at a family dinner or a formal banquet, you might be presented with cold dishes before you are even seated, as a way to welcome you and encourage instant conversation. They represent abundance, prosperity, and the host's warmth and generosity. In my aunt's home, the lazy Susan became a wheel of fortune. With each spin, a new adventure greeted us—little, beautiful plates of sweet, spicy, sour, savory, crunchy, or soft cold dishes sitting happily on that round glass tray.

The cold dishes in this chapter embrace both tradition and innovation. You'll find classics that have graced our family's dinner tables for generations, as well as contemporary dishes my father and I created for our restaurants. With each dish we try to focus on texture, flavor, and even nutrition. Our goal is to awaken your palate or complement the heavier dishes that follow.

They're perfect for health-conscious diners, wonderful as light meals on hot days, and the answer to the question "What should we eat?" when you can't be bothered to turn on the stove.

So, whether you're new to Chinese cuisine or a longtime fan, I invite you to explore the art of liáng cài. These dishes are more than just starters; they're a window into Chinese culture, a celebration of ingredients, and a delicious

MARINATED CHINESE CELTUCE STEM WITH SCALLION OIL

葱油莴笋
CŌNG YÓU WŌ SŌN

Serves 2

PETER: Celtuce stem, which is native to China, was one of my favorite vegetables growing up. Both the leaves and the stem can be stir-fried and eaten—but to me, the stem is the best part. It has a firm crunch, and a very clean and refreshing aroma ("qīng xiāng") and taste to it. My favorite way to enjoy the stem is raw, marinated in a light seasoning. Even after you let it sit overnight, it retains its crunch and color.

When I first immigrated to the United States, I missed this vegetable very much. It wasn't until the last decade that celtuce started to appear in Chinatown markets (occasionally, and confusingly, translated as "lettuce stem"). Usually when a new native vegetable shows up in Chinatown, the pricing is rather high. I didn't care about the price, though; I was just so happy to get a taste of home again. Today, celtuce is a pretty common sight when it comes into season in spring, summer, and fall.

The scallion oil my family uses for this dish is actually a very common dressing for cold marinated root vegetables in Shanghai. You can use it on thinly sliced white radishes, carrots, and cucumbers. Alternatively, drizzle it over plain white rice, toss it with noodles, or use it to finish steamed egg custard. Drizzle some over boiled eggs and add a dash of Maggi sauce. Think of it as an alternative to toasted sesame oil.

---

1 whole celtuce stem

½ teaspoon kosher salt

½ cup (120 ml) neutral oil

3 scallions, chopped

1 teaspoon sugar

Use a chef's knife to remove the fibrous and tough skin of the celtuce stem until you see the light green, translucent flesh. Slice the flesh thinly into coins and place it in a bowl, then toss with the salt. Cover with plastic wrap and place in fridge for 30 minutes. Wash the scallions, pat them dry, and let air dry on a paper towel for 15 minutes, or until they are completely dry.

Heat the oil in a small stockpot over medium heat. Fry the scallions, turning occasionally, until they turn light brown. This should take 10 to 12 minutes—if they're browning too quickly, reduce the heat. Once the scallions are done, transfer the scallions and scallion oil to a bowl to cool to room temp.

Remove the celtuce from the fridge and drain the liquid from the bowl. Taste the celtuce first to check saltiness. If it feels salty, rinse with water and drain. If it tastes underseasoned, add just small pinch of salt. Season with the sugar and 3 tablespoons of the scallions and scallion oil, or to taste. Any remaining scallions and scallion oil can be stored airtight in the fridge for up to 3 days.

KATHY'S SERVING TIP: I like to keep this in the fridge and enjoy it on its own as a light, refreshing appetizer or snack. To turn it into a complete vegan's delight, serve with white rice and Crispy Tofu with Nanking's Famous Peanut Sauce (page 270). Crispy hot tofu with a soft interior, mixed with sweet rich peanut sauce, and crunchy cold scallion celtuce—it's so many flavors and textures in one.

GRANDPA FANG'S BEER NUTS

爷爷的啤酒花生
YÉ YE DE PÍ JIǓ HUĀ SHENG

Serves 6

KATHY: When Grandpa Fang moved to the United States, he adapted rather quickly to his new life in America. He started wearing baseball caps, watched American movies like *Independence Day* and *Beverly Hills Cop* on his home television, and, more importantly, discovered Budweiser. Every night for dinner, he would pour himself a huge coffee mug of Shaoxing wine or a glass of beer for his "happy hour." When it felt like a beer kind of night, he always pulled out his version of beer nuts: peanuts in the shell boiled with soy, spices, sugar, and salt. When we had juice from xián cài in the fridge, my grandmother would add that to the brine, too. It was simple to make and lasted for days in the fridge, and there is nothing more satisfying than biting into a cold whole peanut, breaking the shell, and releasing some of the juice into your mouth. Then you pick out the peanuts and enjoy with your Bud.

This makes a large serving, since I usually make a jar for myself and one to give to my parents. Feel free to cut it in half.

- 1 pound (455 g) raw peanuts in their shell
- 2 tablespoons soy sauce
- 1 tablespoon salt
- 1 teaspoon sugar
- 3 bay leaves
- 4 star anise

Soak the peanuts in water for 10 minutes to help remove dirt. Drain and rinse a few times, until the water runs clear. Place into a medium pot and pour in enough water to cover the peanuts by at least 2 inches (5 cm). Add the soy sauce, salt, sugar, bay leaves, and star anise and bring to a boil over high heat. Reduce the heat to low and simmer for 1 hour, or until the peanuts are soft. Turn off the heat, allow to cool to room temperature, then transfer the peanuts and their brine into glass containers. Store in the fridge for up to 1 week, so long as you don't eat directly from the jar!

SPICY GARLIC CUCUMBERS

凉拌青瓜
LIÁNG BÀN QĪNG GUĀ

Serves 2 to 4

KATHY: This dish was born of necessity, when House of Nanking had to pivot to takeout-only during the pandemic. We knew we needed menu items that sat well in a box, so I decided to create $5-a-pop cold dishes, just like the little cold appetizers my Shanghainese grandmother and aunts would lay out on the table to accompany our meals at home. We featured five different cold dishes, and they were a hit—some orders would come in with every single cold app on the ticket. While we eventually switched back to our regular menu, we still kept a few of our top-selling cold dishes, the spicy garlic cucumber being one of them.

---

5 Persian cucumbers, cut crosswise into 4 equal pieces

1 garlic clove, smashed and then minced

1½ teaspoons sugar

½ teaspoon MSG

¼ teaspoon salt

½ teaspoon Chinkiang vinegar

1 tablespoon toasted sesame oil

1 teaspoon duò jiāo (Chinese salted chopped chilis, see page 285) or sambal oelek

Sesame seeds, for garnish (optional)

Using the flat side of your cleaver, lightly smash the cucumbers so they flatten a bit and the inside flesh is exposed. This allows for better absorption of flavors. Place into a medium bowl. Add the garlic, sugar, MSG, and salt and toss the cucumbers with your hands or a spoon until they're evenly coated with the seasoning. Add the vinegar, sesame oil, and duò jiāo and toss again to coat. Cover with plastic and chill in the fridge for at least 5 minutes before serving. The cucumbers can marinate overnight and will be extremely flavorful the next day. Store in the fridge in an airtight container for 2 to 3 days.

SERVING TIP: Try paring this with . . .

- *Crispy Tofu with Nanking's Famous Peanut Sauce (page 270) and steamed white rice.*
- *A bowl of steamed white rice and an over-easy egg.*
- *A bowl of white porridge (page 156) for a cleansing meal, especially after traveling and overeating.*

PRESERVED MUSTARD GREENS WITH EDAMAME

咸菜毛豆
XIÁN CÀI MÁO DÒU

Serves 4

PETER: By the time my parents immigrated to the US, House of Nanking was up and running and had afforded me financial stability. There was nothing more gratifying than driving my parents to my house upon their arrival, then showing them what I was able to build after leaving China more than ten years prior.

The origins of this humble dish are connected to our Ningbo heritage; it's meant to accompany rice or congee and help people fill up when they can't afford meat. But as it turns out, it also goes hand-in-hand with beer and Shaoxing wine, which my father loved to drink out of a coffee mug for his daily "happy hour." Years after my parents immigrated to the US, my father would still ask my mom to prepare this for him. He wouldn't eat it for the congee or rice; he liked it alongside his adult beverages. The salty, savory, delicious bite of edamame punctuated by crunchy mustard stems is very good on its own, but even better with an icy-cold beer. If you are a fan of salted edamame as a starter with your beer and sake, try this instead. On days when I think about my dad, I make the unshelled version for Nanking and Fang as a cold starter. A lot of the food I ate in my childhood finds its way into the dishes at my restaurants now.

---

1 pound (455 g) frozen shelled edamame

1 tablespoon neutral oil

4 cloves garlic, minced

3 slices ginger, julienned

6 ounces (170 g) preserved mustard greens (xián cài, see page 62)

1 tablespoon Shaoxing wine

1 teaspoon toasted sesame oil

1 teaspoon sugar

¼ teaspoon ground white pepper

1 pinch of salt

1 teaspoon duò jiāo (Chinese salted chopped chilis, see page 285) or sambal oelek (optional)

Steamed white rice or plain congee (page 156; optional)

Run warm water over the frozen edamame until defrosted. Drain.

Heat a wok over high heat, add the neutral oil, and swirl to evenly coat. When the oil begins to smoke, add the garlic and ginger and stir-fry for 5 seconds, just to release the aroma. Add the edamame and stir-fry for 2 minutes, then add the preserved greens and stir-fry for 1 minute more. Add the Shaoxing wine and let it cook for another minute, then add the sesame oil, sugar, white pepper, salt, and duò jiāo, if using, and stir-fry for 3 minutes, or until all the moisture has evaporated. Plate and serve immediately with congee or steamed rice, if you like, or let it cool down and chill overnight in the fridge, then enjoy it the next day with some beer.

SERVING TIPS: The best way to enjoy this dish is cold—it has maximum flavor when it's been chilled in the fridge. Leftovers are also great on top of a salad. To turn this into a finger food, substitute unshelled edamame and prepare it the same way. That way you can pick it up and eat it with your hands as a bar snack.

TOFU AND KALIMERIS SALAD

马兰头
MĂ LÁN TÓU

Serves 4

PETER: Whenever I make this dish at home, it makes me think about my childhood years in Shanghai. On those sweltering summer days, my younger brother and I would spend hours sprawled out on the concrete floors in the hallway of our home, which felt like the coolest place in the building. Our mom would summon us to the dining room for lunch, where she treated us to an array of cold dishes she'd prepared. One of the most refreshing things she would make was mă lán tóu, marinated five-spice bean curd tossed with Kalimeris indica.

Kalimeris indica (see page 283), also known as Indian aster, is a green with a very herbaceous, almost grasslike flavor profile. To some, it tastes slightly bitter. When you boil it, the vegetable resembles spinach, but texturally it's far more interesting. When you squeeze Kalimeris indica, it holds its shape well and doesn't tear. It can be a little tough to chop, so be sure to go over it with a cleaver a few times. I love its texture combined with bean curd, and the resulting flavors are light and fragrant, with a pop of herby grassiness. Mă lán tóu is incredibly easy to make and perfect on a hot day. This dish and its simple seasoning inspired many of my seasonal cold dishes at House of Nanking over the years: Whenever the weather would get hot in San Francisco, which is not as often as I would like, I would toss seasonal vegetables from the Chinatown market in this seasoning and think of my mom preparing her mă lán tóu for us.

- 1 pound (455 g) marinated tofu (see page 281)
- 1 pound (455 g) frozen Kalimeris indica (see page 283), partially defrosted at room temperature for 1 hour
- ¼ cup (60 ml) toasted sesame oil
- 1 teaspoon salt
- 1 teaspoon sugar
- ¼ teaspoon ground white pepper

Finely mince the tofu and place it into a large bowl.

Bring a medium pot of water to boil, then add the Kalimeris indica. Once the vegetables are all freely floating and there are no frozen bits, turn off the heat. Drain the vegetables in a colander and rinse under cold water, then, using your hands, squeeze out all the water.

Keeping the vegetable in a tightly packed bundle, transfer it to a cutting board. Start by slicing the bundle thinly, then go back over it with your cleaver or knife. You may find it's easiest to work in batches, as Kalimeris indica can be tough to mince. Once it's finely minced, add to the bowl. Season with the sesame oil, salt, sugar, and white pepper, then use a spoon to toss and incorporate evenly. Wrap with plastic wrap and chill in the fridge for at least 1 hour before serving.

SERVING TIPS: The dish is traditionally enjoyed as a cold appetizer alongside other cold dishes on a hot day. It also pairs well with a bowl of hot plain white congee (page 156).

COLD TOSSED TOFU WITH PORK FLOSS AND THOUSAND-YEAR-OLD EGG

凉拌豆腐配肉松皮蛋
LIÁNG BÀN DÒU FU PÈI RÒU SŌNG PÍ DÀN

Serves 4 as an appetizer

TIP: If this is your first time trying thousand-year-old egg, start with one. My mother's version calls for two, but start slow.

PETER: Liáng bàn dòu fu is a classic cold tossed tofu dish that every family and restaurant serves, most commonly with pí dàn (thousand-year-old egg). Well, in case you haven't had it before, thousand-year-old egg (also known as preserved or alkalized egg) has a very distinctive flavor to it. The egg, preferably duck egg, is preserved in clay, ash, alkaline salt, quicklime, and other ingredients for several weeks or months—not one thousand years, as the name suggests. During the preserving process, the egg yolk becomes dark green and creamy in texture, and the egg whites become dark and translucent. When you look at the final product, the shell has a gray hue and sometimes the egg whites have a pattern in it, making it look like it's been aged for more than a thousand years (see photo on page 288). The eggs give off an aroma of ammonia and have a rather pronounced flavor. It's an acquired taste; either you like it or you don't. My mother loved pí dàn and she had a unique way of eating it: quartered, with sugar sprinkled on top. The sugar was her own unique flourish, and she applied it to liáng bàn dòu fu, too. To elevate the dish another notch, she added light, fluffy, crispy pork floss (ròu sōng), which is sweet, savory, and full of umami. A bite of cold silken tofu mixed with fresh scallions, creamy yolks, sweet crispy pork floss, and crunchy zhà cài (aka preserved radish), was an explosion of flavors and textures. It's so good, it can make you forget about even the hottest of summers in Shanghai.

- 1 pound (455 g) silken tofu
- ¼ cup (35 g) preserved mustard stem (zhà cài, see page 285), roughly chopped
- 1 or 2 thousand-year-old eggs (see Note)
- 1 teaspoon sugar
- ⅓ cup (20 g) chopped scallions
- 2 tablespoons soy sauce
- 2 tablespoons toasted sesame oil
- 1 tablespoon chili oil (homemade, page 274, or store-bought) and/or diced red Thai bird chilis (optional, if you like it hot)
- ⅓ cup (15 g) pork floss
- 1 teaspoon toasted sesame seeds

Remove the seal from the container of tofu. To drain the tofu without breaking it, place a large paper towel over the tofu and flip the container over while holding the tofu in your hand to prevent it from falling. Allow excess liquid to drain, then place the tofu in a shallow bowl. Slice crosswise into ½-inch (12 mm)–thick slices, then fan the slices out a bit to expose them. Spread the chopped zhà cài evenly over the top of the tofu. Quarter the egg; then you have two choices: You can cut it into wedges, as in the photo at right, or do as my mother did and chop it into roughly ¼-inch (6 mm) pieces. The yolk will be creamy and jammy and might stick to your knife, so make sure to scrape any off the knife and onto your tofu. Place the egg on top of the tofu and season the egg with the sugar. Top with the scallions and drizzle with the soy sauce, sesame oil, and chili oil or chilis, if using. To finish, top off with the pork floss and toasted sesame seeds and serve.

SERVING TIP: You can mix everything up and serve it over steamed rice, or enjoy it as a cold dish appetizer to accompany cold porridge or hot congee.

THREE-TIERED BABY PEA SHOOT SALAD

三层豆苗沙拉
SĀN CÉNG DÒU MIÁO SHĀ LĀ

Serves 2 as a main or 4 as a side

KATHY: I still remember the day my dad first created his famous pea shoot salad, a delicious mix of baby pea shoots, shredded napa cabbage, cucumber, and apple tossed in a tangy sweet and sour dressing with a touch of spice, topped with hot crispy julienned sweet potatoes. I was honestly surprised my dad pulled it off, considering Chinese people don't eat salads. Growing up, the closest we got to eating salad was the coleslaw from KFC and the complimentary iceberg lettuce and shredded carrots drenched in Thousand Island dressing we'd get at Hong Kong Western-style cafes.

But my dad listens to his customers, and when we kept getting requests for "a fresh green salad," Dad started tinkering.

One day, boom, he brought something green, leafy, and fresh to the counter. The pea shoots popped beautifully, with the color and even aroma of freshly cut grass. Then there were layers of crunch from cucumbers, apples, and napa cabbage, fused with the richness of toasted sesame oil and tartness from the vinegar. And then, finally, the clutch move: crispy julienned sweet potatoes coated in hoisin. The hot and cold combination in one bite, with multiple layers of texture, was divine!

DRESSING

- 1 tablespoon sugar or agave nectar
- ¼ teaspoon Dijon mustard
- 1 garlic clove, smashed and minced
- 2 tablespoons rice wine vinegar
- 1 teaspoon lemon juice
- 1 teaspoon soy sauce
- ¼ teaspoon salt
- 1 pinch of ground white pepper
- 1 pinch of powdered ginger
- 2 tablespoons toasted sesame oil
- 1 teaspoon chili oil (homemade, page 274, or store-bought)

- 1 cup (240 ml) neutral oil
- 1 cup (4 ounces / 115 g) julienned (unpeeled) sweet potato
- 1 tablespoon hoisin sauce
- 1 tablespoon chili oil (homemade, page 274, or store-bought)
- 3 cups (2 ounces / 55 g) baby pea shoots, washed, trimmed, and cut in half if long
- 2 cups (4 ounces / 115 g) thinly sliced napa cabbage or romaine lettuce
- 1 Persian cucumber (unpeeled), julienned
- ½ small Fuji apple (unpeeled), julienned
- Red chili flakes (optional)

Make the dressing: In a small bowl, whisk together the sugar and mustard until fully incorporated. Add the garlic, vinegar, lemon juice, soy sauce, salt, white pepper, and powdered ginger and whisk vigorously. While whisking, slowly add 1 tablespoon of the sesame oil, then add the remaining 1 tablespoon sesame oil and the chili oil and whisk to emulsify. Set the dressing aside.

Heat a wok or large, heavy-bottomed pot or Dutch oven over high heat. Add the oil and swirl to coat. When the oil begins to smoke, add half of the sweet potatoes and fry, stirring with a wok spatula to ensure they get even color, until they are golden and crispy, 2 to 3 minutes. Use a spider to transfer the sweet potatoes to a bowl, then repeat with the remaining sweet potatoes. Add the hoisin sauce and chili oil and toss to evenly coat.

In a separate bowl, combine the pea shoots, cabbage, and cucumber and pour about half of the dressing over the top. Toss to fully incorporate, then transfer to a serving plate stacked in a tall mound. Top with more dressing, if desired, then the apples and, last, the crispy fried sweet potatoes. Sprinkle chili flakes on top, if using, and serve.

QUICK SERVING TIP: If you don't have the time to fry up sweet potatoes, hand-shred leftover roasted chicken and coat it in the same hoisin and chili oil sauce. Use this to top the salad for a twist on Chinese chicken salad! For extra crunch, add toasted almonds, crushed peanuts, or crumbled pita chips.

ASIAN TOFU "CAPRESE" TOAST

意大利式豆腐番茄烤面包
YÌ DÀ LÌ SHÌ DÒU FU FĀN QIÉ KǍO MIÀN BĀO

Serves 1 as a light lunch or 2 as a starter

KATHY: This is my twist on a tomato caprese sandwich, for anytime I have a craving but don't have mozzarella. Tofu is a staple in my fridge because it's incredibly versatile, healthy, and has a long shelf life—and it turns out, texturally and flavor-wise, it's the perfect complement to a juicy slice of tomato and crispy toast. The addition of hoisin adds a surprising element of caramelized sweetness. (Hoisin has become a go-to condiment for me as an adult. Try it on avocado toast and thank me later.) I liked this tofu caprese so much, I added it to Fang's very first private event menu as a passed hors d'oeuvres. At home, you can make mini toast points and serve it as a cocktail bite, or serve it on a nice thick piece of toasted shokupan as an open-faced lunch sandwich.

- Medium-firm tofu (from a 14- or 16-ounce [400 or 455 g] package)
- 1 slice shokupan (Japanese milk bread), Pullman loaf, or brioche bread
- 2 tablespoons olive oil
- 1 teaspoon minced garlic
- ½ cup (90 g) quartered cherry tomatoes
- 4 leaves hand-torn Thai basil
- ⅛ teaspoon sea salt
- 1 pinch of ground black pepper
- 2 teaspoons hoisin sauce
- 1 teaspoon toasted sesame oil
- ½ teaspoon chili oil (homemade, page 274, or store-bought)

Remove the tofu from its container and slice a piece that is roughly the same size of the bread slice and ½ inch thick. Pat dry. (Store the rest of the tofu for up to 3 days in the fridge for another use.)

Drizzle 1 tablespoon of the olive oil over both sides of the bread and toast in a toaster oven for about 4 minutes, until crispy and golden brown. (Alternatively, you can toast it in a preheated 350°F (175°C) oven.)

In a small saucepan, heat the remaining 1 tablespoon olive oil and the minced garlic over medium heat. Cook for 45 seconds, or until the garlic turns a light golden hue. Turn off the heat and set aside. Place the tomatoes in a small bowl and pour the garlic and garlic oil over it. Add the basil, season with salt and pepper, and toss with a spoon to fully incorporate.

Spread 1 teaspoon of the hoisin sauce on the toast, place the sliced tofu on top, then spread the remaining 1 teaspoon hoisin sauce over the tofu. Drizzle the sesame oil over the tofu and add the tomato-basil mixture over the top. Finish by drizzling with the chili oil. Enjoy with a fork and knife or pick it up with your hands and eat.

GLUTINOUS RICE–STUFFED LOTUS ROOT WITH OSMANTHUS FLOWER SYRUP

桂花糯米莲藕
GUÌ HUĀ NUÒ MǏ LIÁN ǑU

Makes 8 pieces to serve 2

KATHY: This dish originates from the Jiangnan region of China, referring to the lands south of the Yangtze River, an area that includes my family's hometown of Shanghai. According to Shanghainese custom, this sweet, syrup-glazed lotus root is eaten as part of a multicourse feast that begins with assorted cold dishes. It may sound odd to pair savory cold dishes like sesame oil–tossed jellyfish and cold-smoked fish with sweet, dessert-like dishes. But trust me, it's not.

I still remember the very first time my aunt Jean made this. My a niáng (our nickname for my father's mother) was due to arrive in the States for the first time, and since the proper way to welcome your parents is to cook up a very elaborate feast, to show your love and respect, my aunt (the eldest and first daughter) got cooking in the kitchen. I have an image in my mind of her hovering over her sink with a pink plastic bucket filled with soaked rice, the kitchen dark except for two overhead lights directly over the sink. She used her hands to scoop the rice onto the lotus root and push it down into the holes. Then she'd issue a few heavy taps of the lotus root against a small cutting board, to shift the rice so it fell down the tiny holes inside. The taps would cause her reading glasses to slide down her nose, so after each one she'd have to push her glasses back up. But she insisted that the success of this dish relies on how well-stuffed the holes are—you cannot have air pockets, and god forbid someone ends up with an empty slice—so my saint-like aunt sat over the sink, completing this laborious, dare I say torturous, task. When, the next night, she presented the finished dish on our glass lazy Susan, every face around that dinner table, including mine, lit up. That's how I knew it was worth the effort. This was a taste of home for my grandma and relatives—a sense of comfort—and for me, it was another joyful discovery of what it means to be Shanghainese.

continued

Wash the lotus root to remove any dirt, then use a Y-peeler to remove the skin. Cut off only one end of the lotus root, about 2 inches (5 cm) from the end, but do not discard it. Drain the glutinous rice, then stuff the lotus root with the soaked rice, using a chopstick to push the rice into the holes of the root and tapping it to make sure the rice is forced down to the very bottom. Continue this process until the holes are all tightly filled to the top (you may have extra rice, which you can use to make congee, page 156). Return the cut end of the lotus root to its original place and secure it with 4 toothpicks. This is to ensure the rice does not fall out of the lotus root during cooking. Place the lotus root in a large stockpot and add enough water to cover by 3 inches (7.5 cm). Cover the pot with a lid and bring to a boil, then reduce the heat to medium and simmer for 2 hours, replenishing the water if it gets too low, or until you can easily pierce the root with a toothpick. Remove from the heat, remove the lid, and allow to cool to room temperature. Remove the lotus root from the water (but do not discard the water if you want to use it for congee!), then wrap it in plastic and place in the fridge to chill overnight. To serve, remove and discard the toothpicks and the previously cut end. Slice the root crosswise into ¼- to ½-inch (6 to 12 mm) circular slices, then arrange the slices on a serving plate.

Make the osmanthus syrup: In a small pot, combine the agave, dried osmanthus flower, and cornstarch slurry and bring to a boil over high heat. Reduce the heat to medium and cook, stirring, for 30 seconds. Remove from the heat and let the syrup cool to room temperature. Generously pour the syrup over the lotus root, glazing it completely in the syrup, then serve.

1 whole lotus root (10 to 12 inches / 20 to 30 cm) long) or 2 small (6-inch/15 cm) lotus roots

1 cup (225 g) glutinous rice, soaked in cold water for 2 hours

OSMANTHUS SYRUP

2 tablespoons agave nectar

2 teaspoons dried osmanthus flower

1 teaspoon cornstarch whisked with 1 teaspoon water into a slurry

HEART TOO SOFT, AKA RED DATES STUFFED WITH SWEET GLUTINOUS RICE BALLS

心太软
XĪN TÀI RUǍN

Serves 12

KATHY: The first time I had xīn tài ruǎn, it was in Shanghai, during a twenty-course, banquet-style meal. Go to a nice, traditional Shanghainese restaurant and sit in one of their private rooms, and you will be treated to one of these elaborate dinners—you start with six to eight little cold dishes, then six to eight hot dishes, ranging from steamed, braised, stir-fried, and deep-fried, and end with soup, dim sum (diǎn xīn), and dessert. When I heard the name of the dish, I thought it was so cute—even though I'm not someone who likes sweets. But this was different. The chewy, soft, mochi-like texture tucked inside a sweet red date was delightful, so much so that I started making my own version when I got home to the States. In Shanghai this might be served with osmanthus syrup (see page 72); I think the dates are sweet enough on their own, but feel free to add it or agave if you like. Enjoy as a delicious snack, a healthy dessert, or an appetizer with cold dishes.

NOTE: If you can't find jumbo-sized jujubes, you'll want to use less filling (about ½ teaspoon per jujube). If you have extra filling, you can always stuff more jujubes, or roll the filling into small mochi balls, which you can steam and then simmer in agave nectar or osmanthus syrup.

½ cup (60 g) glutinous rice flour

12 jumbo jujubes (Chinese red dates), split in half lengthwise and pitted (see Note)

Neutral oil, for steaming

Place the glutinous rice flour in a small bowl. Slowly drizzle in ¼ cup (60 ml) warm water, mixing with your hands or a fork until the dough can form a smooth, elastic ball without being too sticky or dry. Add more flour if the dough is too sticky and wet, and add more water, a tablespoon at a time, if it's too dry to roll into a ball. Roll the dough into a long cylinder and rip off a 1-inch (2.5 cm) piece. Roll that piece into a ball and stuff it into the cavity of the date, squeezing the date so the rice ball is encased but a sliver is still showing, almost like a jujube whoopie pie. Repeat with the remaining dates.

Set up a medium steamer (see page 42) and bring the water to a boil. Brush the steamer with oil to prevent sticking, then place the dates on top. Steam for 10 minutes, or until the white filling is puffy and moist to the touch. (For a softer texture more reminiscent of Japanese mochi, steam for longer—however, in Shanghai, we like to have a little texture and chew to it.) Remove from the heat and let it sit for an additional 5 minutes before serving.

HOT
APPET

PRELUDE TO THE FEAST

KATHY: Hot appetizers have a rich history in Chinese culinary tradition. As far back as the Tang Dynasty (618–907 AD), small, hot dishes were served as "fun foods" during casual drinking gatherings. These evolved into more refined appetizers during the Song Dynasty (960–1279 AD), where they became an integral part of formal banquets.

In traditional Chinese cuisine, hot appetizers serve multiple purposes: They stimulate the appetite, showcase the chef's skills, and demonstrate the host's hospitality. They also reflect the Chinese philosophy of balance in dining, offering a variety of flavors, textures, and cooking methods to start the meal.

At House of Nanking, we've taken this centuries-old tradition and given it a modern, San Francisco twist. We like to think our hot appetizers are a bridge between traditional Chinese cuisine and the innovative spirit of Chinese American cooking.

When I picture my childhood, I often see myself seated at the wooden counter at Nanking that my dad helped build and sadly no longer exists. More often than not, I'd be snacking on a piece of shrimp cake, hot off the fryer, with thick sweet peanut sauce dripping down my hands. Or maybe a soft, pillowy chicken dumpling with toasted sesame seeds. These were the go-to snacks when I was a kid—no string cheese or peanut butter crackers, which made me pretty lucky.

This section features recipes for our cult classics: dishes like onion cakes, dumplings, and buns, which seem familiar at first but all have the big, bold flavors and distinctive Nanking twists that put us on the map in the late 1980s.

We've carefully adapted these recipes for the home cook to ensure you can recreate the Nanking experience in your own kitchen. We've simplified some of our techniques so you can get similar results without specialized equipment . . . and so the flavors and essence of each dish remain true to what you'd experience in our restaurant.

IZERS

EXPLOSIVE SHANGHAI EGG ROLLS WITH NAPA CABBAGE, SHIITAKE, PORK, AND BAMBOO SHOOTS

上海春卷
SHÀNG HǍI CHŪN JUǍN

Makes 14 to 20 egg rolls

KATHY: "Shanghai egg rolls are the best in the world," my a niáng would always say. "Not a single egg roll out there is comparable"—and I would have to agree with her. That's because we take our egg rolls very seriously, from appropriate wrapper to filling ratio to the expensive, high-quality ingredients. Whereas most dim sum–style egg rolls use canned bamboo shoots, we opt for fresh winter bamboo shoots, which have a slightly sweet crunch. It's a rather pricey ingredient to put into an egg roll, but the taste of fresh is far superior to canned, which can be stringy, tough, and slightly sour. We also splurge on pork tenderloin, so the meat is tender, napa cabbage, which makes it sweet and juicy, and dried shiitake mushrooms, for extra flavor and texture.

And then there's the amount of the filling. Our well-fed egg rolls are downright fat compared with the skinny, stingy ones you find elsewhere. Nothing is worse than when the fillings seem to disappear into the skin when fried. The shape of ours might not be what you're used to—they're flatter, less round—but this allows us to maximize the filling.

The art of eating the egg roll is also important. We call it explosive for a reason: The filling is not dry like in most egg rolls; it's incredibly juicy and saucy. In fact, it's so juicy, you have to be careful not to burst the egg roll from behind when you bite into it. Oh, and no sweet and sour sauce, please. Only Worcestershire sauce and a side of straight hot sauce if you like it spicy. If you want to eat it the Fang family way, you must dig in as soon as the egg roll comes out of the fryer, to ensure proper juiciness. Yes, you heard me right. You are not to leave these on the table to sit till room temp. Steam needs to come out of the filling when you take the first bite. We like our food HOT, to the point where we are willing to sacrifice the membrane of our hard palates to do these egg rolls justice.

NOTES: To prep the bamboo shoot, peel off the hard exterior skin until you see the white shoot. Cut off the dark part, about ½ inch (12 mm) from the end. Julienne the center flesh of the bamboo and place into a large bowl. Cover with water and soak for 20 minutes to release the bitterness and bite.

Look for Wei-Chuan egg roll skins at Chinese markets and online, where they come in packs of about 32. You won't need that many for this recipe, but it never hurts to have extra. Egg roll skins are about 7 by 7 inches (17 by 17 cm). Note that it is important to use these egg roll skins rather than the kind sold in many Western-style stores (which are actually wonton skins). Wei-Chuan egg roll skins are thin and result in a lighter, crispier skin.

continued

Marinate the pork: In a medium bowl, combine the pork with the sugar, Shaoxing wine, cornstarch, dark soy sauce, sesame oil, dashi powder, and white pepper. Let marinate for 5 minutes.

Make the fillings: Pour 2 tablespoons of the neutral oil into a large nonstick skillet and heat over medium heat. Add the ginger and pork and stir-fry until 80 percent done, 2 to 3 minutes. Remove the ginger and pork from the wok and add the sliced shiitakes. Stir-fry for 1 minute to release the aroma, then reduce the heat to low. Drain the bamboo shoots and dry with a paper towel. Add the bamboo shoots to the wok and increase the heat to high. Add the remaining 2 tablespoons neutral oil and stir-fry for 1 minute. Add half of the napa cabbage and allow it to wilt down a bit before adding the remaining cabbage. Stir-fry for 3 to 5 minutes, until the cabbage has melted down.

In a small bowl, whisk together the salt, sugar, soy sauce, Shaoxing wine, dashi, and white pepper along with 2 cups (475 ml) water. Pour the sauce into the skillet, toss to incorporate, and cook for 5 minutes over medium heat. This will allow the napa cabbage to melt down into a soft, juicy mixture. After 5 minutes, increase the heat to high and add the pork and ginger back to the wok. Give the slurry a quick whisk and drizzle it into the filling while stirring to distribute it evenly. Cook, stirring, until the sauce thickens into a paste-like or pudding consistency. Transfer the filling to a shallow bowl and let it cool to room temp, then cover with plastic wrap and chill in the fridge for 30 minutes. (The filling can be made up to 3 days in advance.)

To shape the egg rolls, lay an egg roll skin out like a diamond on a clean, dry work surface. Make a glue for the wrappers by mixing the flour with about 2 tablespoons water. It should be a little thicker than Elmer's glue.

Place ⅓ to ½ cup (75 to 120 ml) of filling just off the center of the skin, toward one of the corners. (If you're a beginner, start with less filling—the fuller the egg roll, the more explosive! But harder to wrap.) Wrap the bottom corner up and over the filling. Continue rolling until the egg roll is halfway rolled, then tuck the side corners in toward the center of the roll to encase the filling on three sides. Continuing rolling up. Once you've rolled up most of the egg roll and only a small triangle of skin remains, use your finger or a brush to paint that triangle with the flour glue. Continue rolling the wrapper to close it fully, then press lightly to seal the edges. Continue wrapping egg rolls until no more filling remains.

Fill a large cast-iron skillet halfway with neutral oil. Heat over high heat until it reaches 350°F (175°C) on a deep-fry thermometer. Working in batches so you don't overcrowd the pan, fry the egg rolls for 3 to 4 minutes on each side, until golden brown. If the egg rolls brown too fast, the heat needs to be turned down to medium or low to ensure the filling is cooked through and does not burn. Use a spider or slotted spoon to transfer the egg rolls to a paper towel–lined plate to drain. Serve hot! And only with Worcestershire sauce and hot sauce.

SUBSTITUTION TIP: If you can't find fresh bamboo and napa cabbage, you can use half a bag of coleslaw mix (cabbage and carrots) and half a bag of bean sprouts. Simply add the cabbage-carrot-bean sprout mix when instructed to add the napa cabbage, and continue as directed.

PORK MARINADE

8 ounces (225 g) pork tenderloin, thinly sliced and then cut into thin strips

1 teaspoon sugar

1 teaspoon Shaoxing wine

1 teaspoon cornstarch

1 teaspoon dark soy sauce

1 teaspoon toasted sesame oil

1 pinch of dashi powder

1 pinch of ground white pepper

¼ cup (60 ml) neutral oil, plus more for deep-frying

FILLINGS

1 tablespoon minced ginger

8 dried shiitake mushrooms, soaked in cold water for 30 to 40 minutes, until soft, then drained and thinly sliced

1 large winter bamboo shoot, peeled, julienned, and soaked (see Notes)

2 pounds (910 g) napa cabbage, sliced into ½-inch (12 mm) strips

1½ teaspoons salt

1 tablespoon sugar

2 tablespoons soy sauce

3 tablespoons Shaoxing wine

1 tablespoon dashi powder

1 pinch of ground white pepper

¼ cup (30 g) cornstarch whisked with ¼ cup (60 ml) water into a slurry

1 pack Wei-Chuan egg roll skins (see Notes)

1½ tablespoons all-purpose flour

Worcestershire sauce and hot sauce, for serving

FANG

FANG

FANG

FANG

FANG

FANG

NANKING'S ONION CAKES WITH PEANUT SAUCE

葱油饼配花生酱
CŌNG YÓU BǏNG PÈI HUĀ SHĒNG JIÀNG

Serves 2

KATHY: Nanking's onion cakes with peanut sauce have been one of our most popular vegetarian appetizers for thirty years and counting. Onion cakes, called scallion pancakes at many Chinese restaurants, are flaky pancakes made with flour, water, oil, and scallions. The texture, size, and flavor vary depending on what region of China you are from: Northern-style pancakes are thinner and chewier, oftentimes used as a vessel to wrap around proteins and vegetables, almost like a flour tortilla flecked with scallions. Down south, the pancakes get thicker, crispier, and more flavorful, meant to be enjoyed on their own. Being Shanghainese, we like to eat onion cakes on their own, dipped in hot sauce (or our customers' favorite peanut sauce) and, ideally, paired with hot sweet soy milk. This at-home version is inspired by the famous version from Nanking, except it uses a quick, freezer-aisle hack that lets you whip it up in less than ten minutes.

NOTE: Look for frozen puff paratha at markets specializing in Indian and South Asian ingredients. However, many Chinese markets and even some Western markets sell them. Or you can buy them on my favorite website for Asian ingredients, Weee! (sayweee.com). Most brands come separated by layers of wax paper. I prefer to leave the wax paper on while I'm working, as the dough can be quite sticky and this makes it easier to work with.

- 2 pieces frozen puff paratha (see Note) with wax paper still on
- 2 tablespoons neutral oil
- 1½ cups (85 g) chopped scallions
- 2 tablespoons minced preserved mustard stem (zhà cài, see page 285)
- 1 tablespoon toasted sesame oil
- ¼ teaspoon salt
- ¼ teaspoon sugar
- ¼ teaspoon ground white pepper
- Nanking's Famous Peanut Sauce (page 270), to serve
- Sambal oelek, to serve

Preheat the oven to 375°F (190°C). Line a sheet pan with parchment paper. Remove the paratha from the freezer and set aside to thaw slightly (figure about 5 to 10 minutes) while you work on the scallions.

Heat a medium nonstick skillet over medium heat. Add 1 tablespoon of the neutral oil, then add the scallions, mustard stem, sesame oil, salt, sugar, and white pepper. Cook until the scallions soften and no longer have a raw bite, about 2 minutes. Transfer to a small bowl and set aside.

Heat a large nonstick skillet over medium heat and add the remaining 1 tablespoon neutral oil.

While the pan is heating, assemble the onion cake. Remove one piece of wax paper from a paratha and spread the scallion mixture evenly over the exposed dough, leaving a ½-inch (12 mm) border around the edge (eventually, this is where you'll seal the onion cake). Remove one side of wax paper from the other piece of paratha. Place the exposed side of the second piece of dough over the side with the scallion mixture on the other piece of dough—you're essentially sandwiching the onion mixture between two layers of paratha. Use your fingers to press down on the ½-inch (12 mm) edge to tightly seal. (If you have trouble sealing it, you may just need to let the dough thaw out a bit more.)

Remove the remaining two layers of wax paper, then transfer the onion cake to the pan and fry until lightly golden brown, about 1 minute. Flip the cake and cook until the other side is golden, about 1 minute more. Transfer the cake to the prepared sheet pan and pop it into oven. Bake for 8 minutes, or until it's evenly golden brown on both sides and warmed through. Cut into 4 equal slices and serve with peanut sauce and sambal oelek.

NANKING'S CHICKEN DUMPLINGS

鸡肉水饺
JĪ RÒU SHUǏ JIAO

Makes 12 dumplings

KATHY: I still vividly remember the first night my dad made these dumplings. A regular customer asked for chicken dumplings on a whim—our customers know Chef Peter can always whip something up for them within minutes. Of course, prior to immigrating to the US, my dad had never eaten a chicken dumpling in his life—pork, vegetables, and lamb are far more common in China.

That night, my dad minced up his velvet chicken and added sesame seeds rather than vegetables for texture. He wanted his customer to really taste the chicken. The best part of growing up in a kitchen like Nanking is I get to taste everything out of the wok. When I tried the unassuming chicken dumpling, I was yet again blown away by one of my dad's simple, tasty creations.

My shortcut version uses Bachan's Japanese BBQ Sauce rather than the sweet soy sauce he always had on hand at the restaurant. The swap tastes like the original except it can be made much faster.

DUMPLINGS

3 chicken breast tenders (about 6 ounces / 170 g total), finely minced

2 teaspoons cornstarch

1 pinch of salt

1 pinch of sugar

1 generous pinch of ground black pepper

2 tablespoons toasted sesame seed

2 tablespoons Bachan's Japanese BBQ Sauce

12 round dumpling skins (see page 287)

SAUCE

2 tablespoons soy sauce

2 teaspoons toasted sesame oil

½ teaspoon Chinkiang vinegar

½ teaspoon chili oil (homemade, page 274, or store-bought)

½ teaspoon toasted sesame seeds, for garnish

2 tablespoons julienned scallions, for garnish (optional)

Make the dumplings: Bring a medium pot of water to a boil over high heat.

Meanwhile, in a small bowl, combine the chicken, cornstarch, salt, sugar, and black pepper and marinate for 5 minutes.

Boil the chicken for 1 minute, then drain and rinse under cold water to stop the chicken from cooking. Once it's cool to the touch, transfer to a medium bowl and add the sesame seeds and Bachan's BBQ sauce. Mix thoroughly.

Fill a small bowl with water to use as glue to seal the dumplings.

Place a tablespoon of filing into the center of each dumpling skin, then dip your finger in the water and run it along half of the edge of the skin. Bring one side over and press down to create a half circle. Seal the edges and repeat. Once all the dumplings are assembled, boil for 2 to 3 minutes, until they all float. Do not overcook the dumplings; the skin should still have a slight chew to them. Use a spider or slotted spoon to transfer the dumplings to a shallow soup bowl.

Make the sauce: In a small bowl, whisk together the soy sauce, toasted sesame oil, Chinkiang vinegar, and chili oil. Pour over the dumplings, garnish with the toasted sesame seeds and chopped scallions, if desired, and enjoy right away!

PAN-FRIED VEGETARIAN BUNS WITH NANKING'S FAMOUS PEANUT SAUCE

素煎包配花生酱
SÙ JIĀN BĀO PÈI HUĀ SHĒNG JIÀNG

Makes 8

KATHY: When Nanking started to get incredibly popular within the first few years, my dad noticed many customers lining up specifically for his dry-fried green beans and garlic eggplant. Word had spread that Chef Peter Fang made the best eggplant and green beans in the city—the smell of beans hitting the wok would waft down the street and cause people to stop and line up. A ton of vegetarians started to come to our restaurant, which my dad noticed right away. He started to add more vegetarian dishes to his menu, so he could offer them more than just stir-fried vegetables.

One of the most beloved of these were the pan-fried veggie buns filled with zucchini and peas, which seemed to blow everyone away. They featured a pop of fresh green vegetables wrapped in a soft, yeasty bun with a crisp bottom. Traditional vegetarian buns are filled with bok choy, mushroom, and cabbage, which, when steamed, turn to mush that is almost brown in color. Not appetizing and also not great texturally. Juicy, fresh green vegetables with a bit of snap in a soft bun with a crunchy bottom was the solution! It's as if a vegetarian potsticker fused with a steamed bun. It became such a hit, he was selling out before dinner shift would even begin, and night after night, customers would complain when the buns weren't available. So one day after a late shift, my dad drove me and my mom to Safeway. He picked up a carton of Pillsbury biscuit dough and started using that to meet demand. I love this creative hack, which you can also do at home to make easy and foolproof buns.

continued

In a medium bowl, toss the zucchini and peas with the sesame oil, salt, sugar, black pepper, and white pepper. Set aside.

Take each of the 4 pieces of biscuit dough and, using a sharp knife, slice them in half crosswise (through the equator) to yield 2 thinner dough circles. You should end up with 8 dough circles.

On a clean and lightly floured surface, with a floured rolling pin, roll out each dough circle from edge to center, rotating the dough as you roll. Keep rolling until the dough becomes thin (no more than ⅛ inch (3 mm) at the center, and as thin as possible on the edges) and is close to 4½ inches (11 cm) in diameter. Be sure to keep the edges thinner than the center. Repeat with the remaining dough pieces, adding more flour to your rolling pin and work surface each time.

Wrap the buns by using the pleating method: Hold a piece of dough in your nondominant hand and place 2 tablespoons of the zucchini-pea filling in the center. Using your dominant hand, grab a segment of the edge of the dough with your thumb and index finger and pull it up and toward the center of the dumpling. Pinch the dough together to form a pleat, then, using one of your fingers, grab another segment of dough, pull it toward the pleat you're holding with your thumb and index finger, and pinch it to the first pleat to form a second pleat. Moving counterclockwise, repeat this folding and pleating process until the filling is completely enclosed, making sure the dough is nicely sealed when you are pleating. Place the buns pleat-side down onto a lightly floured sheet pan.

Once all the buns have been wrapped, heat a 12-inch (30 cm) nonstick skillet over medium heat, then drizzle in neutral oil and swirl to evenly coat the bottom. Reduce the heat to low, then place the buns, pleat-side down, onto the pan, 1 inch (2.5 cm) apart from each other (the buns will expand as they cook). Fry the bottom slowly for 3 to 5 minutes, until they are light golden brown. Keep in mind that you will NOT flip these buns—they will cook with the pleat side down for the whole duration, so you don't want them to brown too quickly.

Add enough water to come halfway up the sides of the buns, then cover the pan and cook over medium-low heat (or low, if the bottoms are browning too quickly) for 16 minutes. Check the water level throughout: If the water has evaporated, add a touch more. After 16 minutes, garnish the buns by sprinkling the scallions and sesame seeds on top, if desired. Re-cover the pan and cook for an additional 4 minutes, or until the water has mostly evaporated. Remove the lid and cook for 1 minute more, or until the bottoms are nice and crispy.

Using a flat rubber spatula, gently lift the buns from the pan and transfer to a serving plate, pleat side up. Serve with the peanut sauce on the side.

1 cup (125 g) small diced zucchini (from 2 to 3 small zucchini)

1 cup (135 g) frozen petite peas, lightly thawed at room temperature for 10 minutes

1 tablespoon toasted sesame oil

1½ teaspoons salt

¾ teaspoon sugar

¾ teaspoon ground black pepper

1 pinch of ground white pepper

4 pieces (½ of a pack) of Pillsbury brand Grands biscuit dough, chilled

All-purpose flour, for dusting

1 tablespoon neutral oil

¼ cup (15 g) minced scallion (green parts only), for garnish (optional)

1 tablespoon toasted black sesame seeds, for garnish (optional)

Nanking's Famous Peanut Sauce (page 270), for serving

NANKING'S VEGGIE WONTONS

素菜馄饨
SÙ CÀI HÚN TÚN

Makes 24

PETER: We have a very large following of vegetarians and vegans who always say they love coming to Nanking and Fang because they can enjoy so many different dishes with different flavors and textures. When combined with our tender, spicy garlic eggplant (page 168), these veggie wontons become a complete vegetarian entrée—a dish that was so unique and successful that it drew the attention of the most popular food show in China, *A Bite of China*, which has garnered more than two hundred million viewers. When we found out *A Bite of China* had chosen us to be the ONLY American Chinese restaurant to be featured in their fourth season, we were in disbelief. That the biggest food show in China chose us out of the forty-five-thousand-plus Chinese restaurants across the United States . . . It is truly the greatest honor for my wife, daughter, and me. Now people in the country I left, love, and miss so dearly have the opportunity to learn about a restaurant I frugally built with my wife and daughter more than thirty-five years ago. Moments like this make me wish my parents were still alive to see it and taste my veggie wontons and garlic eggplant.

---

1 cup (125 g) small diced zucchini (from about 1 large)

1 cup (135 g) frozen petite peas, lightly thawed at room temperature for 10 minutes

1 tablespoon toasted sesame oil

1½ teaspoons salt

¾ teaspoon sugar

¾ teaspoon ground black pepper

1 pinch of white pepper

24 round dumpling skins (see page 287)

Nanking's Szechuan Eggplant (page 168; to turn it into an entrée)

Chinatown Chili Black Bean Sauce (page 275), Chili Oil (page 274), or chili crisp, to serve

In a medium bowl, toss the zucchini and peas with the sesame oil, salt, sugar, black pepper, and white pepper. Set aside.

Set up a small bowl filled with water by your workstation. This will be the glue for sealing the wonton edges.

Place 1 teaspoon of filling into the center of a dumpling skin. Dip your index finger into the water bowl and run your wet finger along the edge of the dumpling skin. Fold the skin in half, sealing the filling inside to form a semicircle. Dab water on the right corner of the semicircle and bring the left corner over to the right. Press down and seal to create what resembles tortellini. Repeat until all the filling has been used. (For step-by-step photos of folding wontons, see page 155.)

Bring a large stockpot of water to a boil over high heat. Add all the dumplings into the pot and cook for 3 to 4 minutes, until the wontons float and the skin is translucent. Immediately remove from the water with a spider and set aside.

If you will be plating this as an entree, place the garlic eggplant on a serving plate and top with the wontons.

Drizzle chili black bean sauce, chili oil, or chili crisp over the top and serve.

WONTONS IN JALAPEÑO-SOY SAUCE

青辣椒酱油拌馄饨
QĪNG LÀ JIĀO JIÀNG YÓU BÀN HÚN TÚN

Serves 2

PETER: This is my version of the classic wontons in chili oil, dialed down a few notches in spice. After three days in the fridge, the soy and garlic brine I use to marinate jalapeños develops a rich, umami flavor that I love to use as a dumpling or wonton sauce. You could also use it to cook with or drizzle over steamed fish or eggs as a finishing sauce. I eat all my dinners at home in the late evening, and by then I want something fast, easy, and light. I always have frozen homemade Shanghai wontons in my fridge or freezer, so I boil them, drizzle the jalapeño garlic soy sauce over the top, and add some marinated peppers from the jar. A dash of Sichuan pepper oil is optional to add that tingly, má là spice.

- 8 wontons (Shanghai Wontons, page 150; Veggie Wontons, page 92; or store-bought)
- 3 tablespoons brine from Soy-Marinated Jalapeños (page 265)
- 3 to 6 slices Soy-Marinated Jalapeños (page 265)
- ¼ cup (15 g) finely chopped scallions
- ¼ teaspoon toasted sesame seeds
- 1 teaspoon chili oil (homemade, page 274, or store-bought)
- 1 tablespoon minced cilantro (optional)
- ¼ teaspoon Sichuan pepper oil (see page 289, optional)

Bring a small pot of water to a boil over high heat. Add the wontons, stirring so they don't stick to the bottom of the pan, and cook until the skin is translucent, 4 to 6 minutes for fresh wontons or 8 to 10 minutes for frozen. Drain the wontons and transfer them to a serving bowl. Pour the brine over the top, then add the scallions, sesame seeds, chili oil, cilantro, and Sichuan pepper oil, if using. Serve immediately.

NANKING'S STUFFED MUSHROOMS WITH SWEET CHILI SAUCE

蘑菇酿肉
MÓ GŪ NIÀNG RÒU

Makes 12 to serve 2 to 4

KATHY: This is probably one of the easiest recipes to make out of this book, and a great one to recreate with your kids. Juicy mushrooms with moist pork on the inside and crispy pork on the top will win everyone over. It became my regular order soon after it hit the House of Nanking menu (when I was a kid, one of my favorite things was to sit at the counter and pretend to be a customer). I would spread a bowl of hot steamed rice on my plate, place the mushrooms on top, and then spoon sweet chili over everything. Now that I know how easy it is to make at home, this dish has entered our family rotation. I hope it will become a regular in your home as well.

- 12 small to medium white button mushrooms (try to find even-sized ones)
- 8 ounces (225 g) ground pork
- Salt
- 1 tablespoon neutral oil, or as needed
- 5 tablespoons (75 ml) Sweet Chili Sauce (page 271)
- Toasted sesame seeds, for garnish
- 1 scallion, julienned, for garnish
- Steamed white rice, to serve

Tear off and discard the stems of the mushrooms. Using your pointing finger, clean the pocket by scraping it smooth so you can stuff the ground pork inside. Using your fingers, fill each mushroom with ground pork until it's nicely stuffed and you have a smooth round mound on the top. (If your mushrooms are on the small side, you might not use all the pork.) Season the pork side of the mushrooms with salt.

Heat a large nonstick skillet over high heat and add the neutral oil. Once the oil is hot, sear the stuffed mushrooms, pork side down, for 2 minutes, or until golden brown. Flip the mushrooms over and sear the other side for 1 minute. If the mushrooms seem to be sticking, add a bit more oil.

Add 2 tablespoons water to the pan and cook until the water has evaporated and the mushrooms are warmed through, 1 to 2 minutes. Add 3 tablespoons of the sweet chili sauce and toss to glaze the mushrooms, about 30 seconds. Transfer the mushrooms to a serving plate, then add the remaining 2 tablespoons sweet chili sauce to the pan. Once hot, pour it over the mushrooms. Garnish generously with toasted sesame seeds and scallions and serve with a side of steamed white rice.

SHRIMP CAKES WITH PEANUT SAUCE

虾饼配花生酱
XIĀ BǏNG PÈI HUĀ
SHĒNG JIÀNG

Makes 12 to serve 4

NOTE: If you'd like to make the Nanking version, sub in peas and small diced zucchini (as in the recipes on pages 89 and 92) for the celery and scallions.

KATHY: Hanging on Nanking's wall is a clipping from a column by the Pulitzer Prize–winning San Francisco journalist Herb Caen. It reads, "At the House of Nanking, writer Edwin Heaven was making a pitch to Francis Ford Coppola about his script, 'The Lobster & the Mobster.' Francis, between bites of fiery-hot shrimp cakes and gulps of Chinese beer: 'Well, mobsters, they are always in season, but try to find a good lobster when you need one!'"

It wasn't unusual to see Francis Ford Coppola perched on a barstool at Nanking; he owns the famous flatiron building across from our restaurant and would eat at our counter so regularly that when I was a kid, he became one of my favorite people to chat with. Not realizing that what I was about to ask was incredibly offensive, I once asked him why he was so big. He had a witty answer to all my questions, and this time, he said, "Well, it's because I'm always eating your father's delicious food."

Shrimp cakes were a particular favorite of Mr. Coppola, and many other HoNK fans and regulars. What most people don't know is, these crispy little triangles filled with zucchini and peas are actually a riff on my dad's mom's dish. My grandmother used celery and scallions in her filling; my dad swapped in peas and zucchini because they were readily available in the Nanking kitchen. But the biggest difference is that my grandmother would dip hers into Worcestershire sauce, whereas my dad uses our signature peanut sauce. The recipe below is for the mini versions that my grandmother would make, since they're a lot faster and easier to fry at home. It's important to use thin, wheat-based spring roll skins (see page 289) to achieve that light, airy, crispy skin.

continued

In a medium bowl, mix the shrimp, celery, scallions, Shaoxing wine, soy sauce, salt, white pepper, sesame oil, dashi powder, sugar, and cornstarch until combined.

Wrap the cakes: Place your wrappers on a plate covered with a damp towel so they don't dry out while you work.

Cut the spring roll wrappers in half to make 12 rectangles.

Near the bottom of each strip of spring roll wrapper, spoon 1 heaping teaspoon of filling. Use a spoon to spread a bit of your flour-water paste along the two outer edges of the wrapper. Fold the bottom left corner of the wrapper strip over to the right, to meet the long edge of the wrapper and form a triangle that encompasses the filling. Spread more of the flour-water paste on the top edge of the triangle, then fold the triangle with the filling onto the wrapper twice, adding more flour-water paste as needed and patting with your fingers to seal. You'll end up with a small triangle. Repeat with the remaining filling and wrappers.

Fill a large, heavy-bottomed skillet halfway with neutral oil and heat over medium-high heat until it registers 350°F (175°C) on a deep-fry thermometer.

Working in two batches, fry the shrimp cakes for 1 to 2 minutes, until golden brown, turning once halfway through. Use a spider or slotted spoon to transfer to a paper towel–lined plate to drain. Serve immediately with peanut sauce or Worcestershire sauce.

6 medium shrimp, shelled and minced into a paste-like consistency

¼ cup (30 g) minced celery

¼ cup (15 g) minced scallions

1 teaspoon Shaoxing wine

1 teaspoon soy sauce

1 pinch of salt

1 pinch of ground white pepper

½ teaspoon toasted sesame oil

½ teaspoon dashi powder

¼ teaspoon sugar

¼ teaspoon cornstarch

6 (8-inch/20 cm) square spring roll wrappers (see page 289)

Neutral oil, for frying

½ cup (65 g) flour mixed with ½ cup (120 ml) water until it resembles a sticky, Elmer's glue-like paste

Nanking's Famous Peanut Sauce (page 270) or Worcestershire sauce, to serve

I DREAM OF NANKING'S CHICKEN LETTUCE CUPS

鸡肉生菜卷
JĪ RÒU SHĒNG CÀI JUǍN

Makes about 8

Note: For perfect lettuce cups, use iceberg lettuce only!

PETER: Prior to moving to the United States, I had never had a lettuce wrap before. In fact, I had never even seen iceberg lettuce until I moved to San Francisco. I first noticed it at Cantonese restaurants, where it was used as a filler in dishes like Hong Kong–style wonton noodle soup, beef brisket noodle soup, or clay pot pork. But the most common way I saw lettuce used was as a wrap. This is not something Chinese people typically order, but it was incredibly popular among Americans, and enough Americans started requesting it at House of Nanking, that I of course decided I needed to create my own version. But first I had to try it at other restaurants.

My first thought was, *Not bad. I can see why people would like this.* Cold crisp lettuce, hot sauteed chicken, vegetables . . . It sounded good in theory, but the execution was always off. The texture of the ground chicken was always dry, the vegetables were minced into an unrecognizable pulp, and the only vegetable I could taste was horrible, canned water chestnuts, which always leave a lingering sour taste. (Back then, every Chinese restaurant used canned water chestnuts, canned straw mushrooms, and canned bamboo shoots in everything. I hated it! When I opened Nanking, I knew canned vegetables would never make it past my front door.)

I wanted Nanking's chicken lettuce wrap to be exploding with freshness. I wanted tender, velvety chicken breast meat stir-fried with diced FRESH vegetables to give it a juicy pop, with a pungent sauce of garlic, soy, vinegar, and just a hint of hoisin. The raw onions with Thai basil added another level of freshness. When I served this, people went crazy for it. Regulars would come a few times a week and tell me, "Peter, I dream about your chicken lettuce cups." (See photo on pages 104–105.)

Remove and discard the outer two layers of leaves. Hold the head of lettuce about 8 inches (20 cm) above a cutting board, with the core facing down, toward the board. Drop the lettuce onto the board. The impact should loosen the core. Now grab the core of your lettuce with your hands, twist, and pull to remove and discard. To create a clean edge, cut away and discard ½ inch (12 mm) from the bottom. Run cold water down through the center of the lettuce and all the crevices—this will make it easier to separate the leaves. Separate the leaves to form your individual lettuce cups.

Make the marinated chicken: In a medium bowl, combine the diced chicken, neutral oil, cornstarch, Shaoxing wine, salt, and sugar. Stir to coat the chicken, then set aside to marinate.

Make the fried noodles: Use a knife to cut the noodles in half crosswise so they are shorter, then use your hands to separate the noodles so they come apart a bit. Cut them in half again to create noodles that are 4 inches (10 cm) in length. Heat a wok over high heat and add the neutral oil. Test the oil by adding one piece of noodle. If the noodle starts to puff up immediately, the oil is ready. Working in batches, fry the noodles until they puff up, 30 seconds to 1 minute. Use chopsticks to move the noodles around to ensure even frying. Transfer to a paper towel–lined plate to drain while you repeat with the remaining noodles. Set aside.

To finish: Bring a medium pot filled with water to a boil over high heat. Add the zucchini and frozen peas and boil for 1 minute, then strain the vegetables into a bowl. Allow the water to come back to a boil, then add your marinated chicken to the water. Stir and cook over high heat for 45 seconds, or until slightly pink. Strain the chicken into the same bowl with the vegetables (you can discard the cooking water now). Tilt the bowl with the chicken and vegetables over the sink to pour out any excess water.

In a medium bowl, stir to combine the hoisin sauce, soy sauce, garlic, sugar, fish sauce, white pepper, black pepper, and MSG. Set the sauce aside.

Heat a wok over high heat. Once it begins to smoke, add the neutral oil and swirl the wok to evenly coat the cooking surface. Once the wok is smoking again, add the chicken-vegetable mixture to the wok along with the pre-mixed sauce. Stir-fry for 1 minute, then add the dark soy sauce, red onions, and chopped basil and stir-fry for another minute, allowing the sauce to coat the ingredients and develop color. While stirring in a circular motion to avoid clumping, drizzle in the slurry. The sauce should begin to glaze the ingredients so there is no sauce on the bottom of the pan. Remove from the heat.

To serve, arrange the lettuce cups, fried noodles, and hot chicken filling in three separate serving plates or bowls. Place the basil leaves in a separate small bowl. Encourage your guests to assemble their own lettuce cups by spooning some chicken filling into the center of a lettuce cup, then topping with crispy noodles and basil leaves for garnish. They can add some sriracha or chili sauce, if they like it spicy, on top.

1 head of iceberg lettuce

MARINATED CHICKEN

1 cup diced (½-inch/12 mm cubes) chicken breast meat, from about 8 ounces (225 g) white-meat chicken (5 tenders or 1 breast)

1½ teaspoons neutral oil

1½ teaspoons cornstarch

1½ teaspoons Shaoxing wine

½ teaspoon salt

½ teaspoon sugar

FRIED NOODLES

4 ounces (115 g) dried rice stick noodles (mei fun)

1 cup (240 ml) neutral oil, for frying

TO FINISH

1 large zucchini, diced (about 2 cups / 230 g)

½ cup (90 g) frozen petite peas (do not defrost)

1 tablespoon hoisin sauce

1 tablespoon soy sauce

1½ teaspoons minced garlic

1½ teaspoons sugar

1½ teaspoons fish sauce

1 pinch of ground white pepper

1 pinch of ground black pepper

1 large pinch of MSG

1 teaspoon neutral oil

1 tablespoon dark soy sauce

½ cup (75 g) diced (½ inch / 12 mm) red onion

½ cup (20 g) chopped Thai basil leaves, plus a few basil leaves for garnish

1 tablespoon cornstarch whisked with 1 tablespoon water into a slurry

Sriracha or chili sauce (homemade, page 271, or store-bought; optional)

RICE &
NOOD

KATHY: In Chinese, we often greet each other with "nǐ chī fàn le ma?" Literally, "Have you eaten rice?" It's our way of checking in to see if you've had a meal, since a meal without rice isn't really a meal at all. The centrality of rice in Chinese culture makes sense once you understand how far back our connection with it really goes: Rice cultivation in China dates back more than ten thousand years.

More recently, I had a personal epiphany when I realized how lost I feel without the constant, comforting fragrance of rice cooking in a room nearby. During my first year at USC, far from the comforts of home, I found myself yearning for that aroma, so fundamental to my upbringing that its absence felt like a vital element was missing from the air I breathed. The sweet, nutty smell of cooking rice had always permeated our home, seeping into every corner and crevice, and its absence left a void that no amount of campus cuisine could fill. It was more than just a smell; it was the embodiment of home, family, and comfort.

Noodles, while a more recent addition to the Chinese culinary canon, still boast an impressive four thousand–year history. In fact, the world's oldest known noodles, discovered in northwestern China, date back to 2000 BCE! They've since evolved into a versatile canvas for flavors, adapting to regional tastes across China's vast landscape. From the hearty wheat noodles of the north to the delicate rice noodles of the south, they reflect China's diverse culinary traditions.

Together, rice and noodles are more than just food; they are the backbone of Chinese civilization. During the Han Dynasty (206 BCE–220 CE), the government established granaries and regulated grain prices, recognizing that a well-fed population meant a stable empire. The saying "mín yǐ shí wéi tiān" ("food is the first necessity of the people") highlights this fundamental truth. Nutritionally, rice and noodles provide the carbohydrates needed to power long days of work. In traditional Chinese medicine, they're considered essential for maintaining balance in the body, which is why a meal without them often feels incomplete to Chinese diners.

In this chapter, we will share some of our household favorites, from House of Nanking cult classics like our Nanking Noodles with Shredded Pork (page 117) and soothing Cold Sesame Noodles (page 114) to dishes that have been on our family dinner tables for generations, such as Clay Pot Rice with Cured Pork Belly, Salted Duck, and Chinese Sausage (page 110) and Cài Fàn (page 113). Some of the dishes carry the weight of tradition and promise of sustenance, while others are an opportunity for us to show a bit of our Fang family flair.

CLASSIC SCALLION AND EGG FRIED RICE

蛋炒饭
DÀN CHǍO FÀN

Serves 2

KATHY: Fried rice, one of the most classic staples in Chinese cuisine, also happens to be one of the most underappreciated. Many people think of it as a way to get rid of old rice—in concept, an easy dish anyone can prepare at home. But executing perfect fried rice is actually harder than you think.

I grew up watching my dad and Uncle Tong order fried rice at Chinese restaurants. They had a habit of ordering the fried rice first, which is unusual. They claimed that you can judge the quality of the chef by their fried rice. If the fried rice is bad, then forget about ordering any main dishes; get something light, save your money, and move on. They even had a process for analyzing the rice. They would look at it, spoon some into the rice bowl, smell it, and finally taste. When you look at the rice, it should be fluffy, with glistening grains that don't stick together into clumps. You should be able to smell the wok hei, or "breath of the wok," in the rice. When you take a bite, there should be both slivers of scrambled egg and bits of egg coating the grains of rice, which should have just the right amount of dryness and oil. After many lessons on how eat and rate fried rice, I finally got to learn how to make it. It was one of the first things my dad taught me how to make out of the wok at Nanking. Now, I make the same classic scallion egg fried rice for my kids at home.

- 2 cups (320 g) day-old white rice (preferably jasmine or another long-grain variety)
- 2 eggs, whisked
- ¼ teaspoon salt, plus more to season the eggs
- 1 tablespoon neutral oil
- 2 scallions, minced
- 2 teaspoons soy sauce
- 1 teaspoon minced ginger (optional)
- 1 teaspoon oyster sauce (optional)
- 1 teaspoon MSG or dashi powder
- ¼ teaspoon sugar
- ¼ teaspoon ground white pepper

Place the rice in a microwave-safe bowl and microwave it on full power for 35 seconds, just to warm it. This will allow the rice to soften up a little but not fully reheat. In a separate bowl, combine the eggs, a pinch of salt, and a teaspoon of water, then whisk to mix.

Heat a wok over high heat, then add the neutral oil and swirl to coat. When the oil begins to smoke, add the eggs and cook undisturbed for about 5 seconds, to allow it to puff up on the edges. Start to gently scramble the eggs by folding the eggs over each other but not breaking it apart into smaller pieces. Add the rice and start folding the eggs into the rice by using your wok spatula to flip the eggs over the rice and pressing down to break the eggs into the rice. Stir to incorporate the eggs evenly into the rice.

Spread the rice and eggs into a flat, even layer on the bottom of the wok and toast for a few seconds before stirring the rice again. Repeat this so the rice gets toasted on all sides. Continue stir-frying until you can hear the rice start to pop off the wok, which means the moisture has been cooked out and the rice is fragrant and dry, 2 to 3 minutes.

Add the scallions, soy sauce, ginger and oyster sauce, if using, the MSG, ¼ teaspoon salt, sugar, and white pepper and stir to incorporate, always making sure the rice keeps moving so it does not burn or stick to the bottom of the wok. Taste the rice and season with more salt if necessary. The fried rice should be light and not overly salty, where you can taste the rice and eggs itself. Turn the heat off and serve.

SERVING TIP: Serve this with any protein and/or vegetables dishes as a replacement for steamed white rice. Or enjoy on its own with a dollop of Chinatown Chili Black Bean Sauce (page 275) or chili crisp. It also works great as a packed lunch; simply add protein and vegetables to the wok when you add the other seasonings.

CLAY POT RICE WITH CURED PORK BELLY, SALTED DUCK, AND CHINESE SAUSAGE

腊肉咸鸭腊肠煲仔饭
LÀ RÒU XIÁN YĀ LÀ CHÁNG BĀO ZǍI FÀN

Serves 2

KATHY: I thought I knew everything there was to know about clay pot rice . . . until my mom and I discovered Lei Garden in Hong Kong's Central district. When our server lifted the lid, I immediately noticed the cured meats came whole, not sliced up like at many of the dai pong dong joints in Mong Kok, one of the most celebrated street-food rows in the world. The server lifted the meats and choy sum from the rice, sliced them tableside, and plated it beautifully. They drizzled part of the seasoned soy into the rice, then mixed and scooped it to release the faahn jīu—the charred, crispy rice from the bottom of the clay pot. I took a bite of the juicy, flavorful cured meat, followed by a bite of the fragrant rice, some fluffy, some crispy, with each grain coated by the meats' oils and seasoned soy. It was a revelation: Steaming the meat whole and not thinly sliced keeps it as juicy and flavorful as possible and allows you to truly savor each individual meat.

Ever since this experience, I always try to make clay pot rice the unrushed, refined way at home. However, if you want to go the dai pong dong route and slice your meats beforehand, you can certainly do that—it's a little less work for you on the back end.

SEASONED SOY

2 tablespoons neutral oil

3 scallions, each cut into 4 pieces

3 tablespoons soy sauce

2 teaspoons sugar

Pinch of ground white pepper

2 tablespoons neutral oil, plus more to coat the clay pot

1½ cups (280 g) jasmine rice, rinsed, soaked, and drained (see Notes)

1½ cups (360 ml) warm, previously boiled water

3 ounces (85 g) cured pork belly (là ròu/laap yuhk; see page 281), cut into 3 equal parts, rinsed

1 salted duck leg (see page 281)

2 Chinese sausages (lap cheong; see page 281), cut in half crosswise and rinsed

NOTES: For tips on buying and caring for a clay pot, see page 43.

Rinse the rice until the water runs clear, then place it in a large bowl and cover with water. Soak for 30 minutes, then drain thoroughly.

Make the seasoned soy: Heat the neutral oil in a small pot over medium heat. Add the scallions and cook until they turn light brown, 2 to 3 minutes. Let cool, then add the soy sauce, sugar, pepper, and 1 tablespoon water and whisk to combine. Set aside.

Using a paper towel soaked in neutral oil, rub a medium or large clay pot to coat the interior evenly. Heat the clay pot over medium heat to warm it slightly. Add the rice to the clay pot and drizzle with 1 tablespoon of the neutral oil. Stir with a spatula to coat, then add the warm water. Increase the heat to medium-high and stir with the spatula to incorporate the oil and water into the rice.

When the water reaches a light boil, stir again a couple of times to release the rice from the bottom of the pot. Then reduce the heat to medium-low and cover with a lid. Check the rice after 3 to 4 minutes, and once the water level has become even with the rice, arrange the meats on top. Re-cover with the lid and reduce the heat to low. Cook for 10 minutes, or until you hear some crackling, which means the rice is starting to toast. Open the lid and drizzle the remaining 1 tablespoon neutral oil evenly down the sides of the clay pot. Put the lid back on and increase the heat to medium so the rice will continue to toast. If you want to crisp up the rice on the sides of the pot, you will need to use oven mitts to hold the clay pot by its handles and tilt it to expose the sides to the flame. (If you're a newbie, I suggest skipping this step and just having the bottom of the clay pot toasted.) If you're just toasting the bottom, expect to cook for about 2 to 4 minutes. Use a spatula to lift the bottom of the rice to check for doneness. Aim for a light golden brown your first time around; better that then burned rice, which will permeate the aroma of your entire dish and ruin it.

Remove the meat from the pot, slice it, and arrange it on a serving platter. Pour some of the seasoned soy into the clay pot with the rice and mix. Present the clay pot at the table, and serve the remaining seasoned soy, along with the sliced meats, on the side.

CÀI FÀN WITH CHINESE CURED PORK BELLY AND BOK CHOY

腊肉菜饭
LÀ RÒU CÀI FÀN

Serves 4

PETER: Cài fàn, which literally translates to "vegetable rice," is a humble local food—a way to stretch your ingredients with lard, small scraps of salted pork, and diced vegetables to add a boost of flavor. You can find cài fàn on the menu at any Shanghainese restaurant, but it's never as good as the way my mother made it. At restaurants, they focus on presentation, so the vegetables are tossed in much later in the cooking process to maintain the bright green color. But this means the rice never gets the chance to absorb all the sweet vegetable juices. If I see cài fàn at a restaurant, I don't want it. I call it fake cài fàn—it's just steamed rice tossed with vegetables.

When my mother made it, she folded the vegetables into raw rice at the beginning, allowing them to melt into the rice and coat the grains. This dish—with Shanghai bok choy, fresh fava beans, homemade salted pork (or, if we got lucky, Chinese cured pork belly, là ròu), and, of course, lard—is my childhood. The smell makes me think of our kitchen in Shanghai and the life we had back then. I think of how my mother used the simplest ingredients to make even the most frugal meals the best-tasting ones. And I think of how her cooking philosophy influenced me when we first opened House of Nanking, when we used every hard-earned dollar to survive and succeed. I believe that for food to be amazing, it does not need to be fancy, look pretty, or be overcomplicated; it simply needs to taste good.

1½ cups (280 g) jasmine rice

1½ tablespoons lard or neutral oil

1 pound (435 g) Shanghai bok choy (see page 282), chopped

½ cup (70 g) cured pork belly (là ròu/laap yuhk, see page 281), cut crosswise into ¼-inch pieces

½ cup (120 g) shelled and skinned fresh fava beans (optional but delicious!)

1 teaspoon salt

1 teaspoon dashi powder

½ teaspoon sugar

Rinse the rice until the water runs clear to remove the sugars and starches. Heat a wok over high heat, and when it starts to smoke, add the lard. Add the bok choy and stir-fry for 2 minutes to release some of the moisture. Add the cured pork belly and fava beans, if using, and stir-fry for 1 minute, just to release some of the oils from the pork belly. Remove from the heat and transfer the vegetables into your rice cooker or a medium pot. Add the rice and 2 cups (480 ml) water. Season with the salt, dashi powder, and sugar and stir to fully incorporate.

Cook the rice and vegetables on the white rice setting of your rice cooker, or, if cooking on your stovetop, bring everything to a boil over high heat, then cover with a lid, reduce the heat to low, and cook for 10 to 15 minutes, until the water is fully absorbed. Remove from the heat and let it sit with lid on for 12 minutes. Stir to incorporate before serving.

KATHY'S NOTE: The technique of folding vegetables into the raw rice is one that you can apply in many different ways. You can play around with the ratio of rice, pork, and bok choy—go heavy on the veggies, if you'd like—or you can swap in another type of leafy greens. Or try a Southern twist with andouille sausage, collard greens, and even cooked red beans.

COLD SESAME NOODLES

冷面
LĚNG MIÀN

Serves 2

PETER: I consider cold sesame noodles a common folk food in Shanghai. It's easy to make, affordable, and accessible to all. In Shanghai there was one spot that always had the longest line. I would often wait in that infamous line, but I didn't mind it because I loved watching the man, maybe he was the owner, build a noodle plate for each customer. He had a really good system and never seemed rushed or off his rhythm, no matter how crazy the line was or how impatient his customers became. When I first opened Nanking, I would get flashbacks to the cold sesame noodle guy and it would relax me. I would think, *If he can do it every day and not crack from pressure, so can I.*

Back then, the old-school way to chill noodles was to use a hand fan. At this joint, the owner didn't have the time to hand-fan his noodles, so he used an electric fan. Whatever you do, placing the cooked noodles in the fridge is a no-no; you'll end up with cold, hard, lifeless noodles with a horrible texture. If you don't want to chill your noodles by fanning them, you can run them under cold water (as I suggest in the method below). But you must make sure they are thoroughly dried by patting excess water with a paper towel. If the noodles are wet, the sauce will not grab onto the noodles. The noodles should be cool, not cold, and light, springy, and soft—never stiff and hard. Toss the noodles in the sauce right before you serve and enjoy right away! You can double or even triple it to feed a crowd.

- 4 ounces (115 g) thin dried wheat noodles
- 3 tablespoons Sesame Sauce (page 271)
- 2 tablespoons toasted sesame oil
- 2 tablespoons soy sauce
- 1 tablespoon chili oil (homemade, page 274, or store-bought)
- ½ teaspoon salt
- ¼ cup (15 g) chopped cilantro or scallions
- 1 tablespoon toasted black or white sesame seeds
- 1 teaspoon Chinatown Chili Black Bean Sauce (page 275; optional)
- Julienned cucumber (optional)

Bring a large pot of water to a boil. Cook the noodles until soft according to the package directions, then drain and run under cold water until cold to the touch. Use a paper towel to further dry the noodles and absorb excess water. Toss into a medium bowl.

Add the sesame sauce, sesame oil, soy sauce, chili oil, and salt and toss to incorporate. Divide between 2 serving bowls and garnish with the chopped cilantro and sesame seeds. Add Chinatown chili sauce on top if you like it spicy and julienned cucumbers if you'd like additional crunch.

NANKING NOODLES WITH SHREDDED PORK

肉丝炒面
ROÙ SĪ CHĂO MIÀN

Serves 2 to 4

PRO TIP: In Shanghai, we like to set out extra Chinkiang vinegar to drizzle into the noodles as we eat it.

PETER: My first experiences with chow mein in the US left me feeling very dissatisfied. I remember looking down at my plate and thinking, *The person making this doesn't really care*. The noodles were soft and lifeless with overcooked vegetables, nothing like the Shànghăi cū chăo miàn ("thick chow mein") I grew up with in Shanghai.

When I decided to add chow mein to the menu of House of Nanking, I had to custom design the thickest Shanghai noodle that Chinatown or San Francisco had ever seen. I needed noodles as thick as udon, maybe even thicker, but less chewy, with a softer, smoother bounce that comes from high-protein flour. The extra gluten in the high-protein flour results in a denser, bigger chew, plus greater surface area for the sauces to grab onto. The fragrant smell—xiāng wèi—of the soy sauce, sugar, and vinegar hitting the wok is very powerful. I'm convinced the reason my Nanking noodle became such a hit is because the smoke and smells would waft out the door, down the line, and into people's noses. After one bite, they were hooked—just like I was as a kid tasting my first plate of Shanghai cū chăo miàn.

MARINATED PORK

5 ounces (140 g) pork tenderloin

2 teaspoons cornstarch

1½ teaspoons toasted sesame oil

½ teaspoon soy sauce

½ teaspoon dark soy sauce

½ teaspoon Shaoxing wine

⅛ teaspoon sugar

1 pinch of salt

1 pinch of ground white pepper

NOODLES

8 ounces (225 g) fresh Shanghai noodles

1 tablespoon plus 4 teaspoons neutral oil

3 cups (210 g) sliced cabbage (1 inch / 2.5 cm wide and 3 inches / 7.5 cm long)

1 cup (110 g) sliced red onions (½ inch / 12 mm wide and 3 inches / 7.5 cm long)

1 tablespoon Shaoxing wine

1 tablespoon soy sauce

1 tablespoon dark soy sauce

1 tablespoon Chinkiang vinegar, plus more for serving

1 teaspoon duò jiāo (Chinese salted chopped chilis, see page 285) or sambal oelek

1 teaspoon MSG

1 teaspoon sugar

3 cups (120 g) Taiwanese spinach with roots (see page 284), cut into 3-inch (7.5 cm) lengths

Marinate the pork: Slice the pork into thin (¼ inch / 6 mm) slices with the grain. Now cut those slices into thin threads, resulting in 2-inch (5 cm)-long, ¼-inch (6 mm)-wide matchsticks. Transfer the pork to a medium bowl and add the cornstarch, sesame oil, soy sauce, dark soy sauce, Shaoxing wine, sugar, salt, and white pepper. Stir with chopsticks or a fork to integrate, then set aside to marinate for 10 minutes.

Make the noodles: Bring a large pot of water to a boil over high heat. Add the noodles and cook for 4 minutes, or until al dente.

Meanwhile, while the noodles are cooking, heat a wok over high heat and add 2 teaspoons of the neutral oil. When the oil is smoking, add the pork and stir-fry for 30 seconds, or until slightly pink and about 80 percent cooked. Transfer the pork to a bowl or plate and add 2 more teaspoons neutral oil to the wok. Add the cabbage and onions and stir-fry over high heat for 30 seconds. Add the Shaoxing wine and stir-fry for 1 minute. Add 2 tablespoons water to the wok and continue to stir-fry for another 2 minutes, or until slightly wilted but still with a slight raw crunch.

Add the cooked noodles to the wok, then immediately add the soy sauce, dark soy sauce, vinegar, chili sauce, MSG, sugar, and the remaining 1 tablespoon neutral oil. Wok toss the noodles to incorporate all the seasoning for 30 seconds, then add the spinach and pork. Continue to wok toss for 1 minute to allow the pork to finish cooking and the seasoning to fully absorb and caramelize into the noodles. Serve immediately!

SCALLION OIL–TOSSED NOODLES WITH DRIED SHRIMP

虾米葱油拌面
XIĀ MI CŌNG YÓU BÀN MIÀN

Serves 1

PETER: Scallion oil–tossed noodles in a Shanghainese family is probably the equivalent of spaghetti aglio e olio for a Neapolitan family. Both are simple, affordable yet satisfying noodle dishes that use an infused oil—scallion in Shanghai, garlic in Naples. It's one of those dishes that we never ordered at a restaurant, because it's such a home-cooking staple. The running joke is that every Shanghainese person claims that they make the best . . . and no restaurant can make it better. God forbid you pay money for something as simple as scallion oil tossed noodle!

The most traditional form of this dish is made with just dark soy sauce, regular soy sauce, MSG, and scallion oil. But, of course, our home version has to be a tad different. A very common thing you see people do in Shanghai is add a splash of Chinkiang vinegar to stir-fried noodles. The acid from the vinegar helps cut through the grease and brings out another layer of umami, balancing out the flavors of wheat and salty soy. Once you go black vinegar on noodles, you can't go back. Then there was my dad's affinity for food with a slight sweetness, thus the addition of sugar. Last we added dried shrimp soaked in Shaoxing wine, to give it a salty umami pop.

---

10 small pieces dried shrimp (the smallest you can find!)

1 tablespoon Shaoxing wine

¼ cup (60 ml) neutral oil

5 scallions, white and green parts separated, then cut into 3-inch (7.5 cm) lengths and thinly sliced

3 ounces (85 g) dry Chinese wheat noodles (or substitute spaghetti)

1 tablespoon dark soy sauce

1 tablespoon soy sauce

2 teaspoons sugar

1 teaspoon Chinkiang vinegar

½ teaspoon MSG

Sriracha (optional), for serving

In a small bowl, soak the dried shrimp in the Shaoxing wine for 30 minutes, or until soft. Remove the shrimp from the wine (save the wine for future use, or discard it). If you could find nice, small shrimp (like those pictured), you can leave them whole. If they're on the larger side, roughly mince them.

Heat the neutral oil in a medium saucepan over high heat. The oil shouldn't be so hot that it's smoking, but hot enough that you feel the heat when you hold your hand above it. Reduce the heat to medium, then add the white portion of the scallions and cook for 2 minutes, stirring occasionally, to slowly char. Reduce the heat to medium-low, then add the green part of the scallions to the pan with the white parts, and cook slowly for 6 to 7 minutes, until light golden brown. Turn off the heat and use a spider skimmer or slotted spoon to remove the scallions from the oil. Set the scallions aside in a bowl.

Turn the heat back up to high, and when the oil is hot, add the shrimp. Toast for 30 seconds, or until fragrant, then turn off the heat and set aside. Bring a medium pot of water to a boil over high heat and follow the package instructions to cook the noodles until slightly chewy and al dente, usually around 4 to 7 minutes.

In a deep noodle serving bowl, combine the dark soy sauce, soy sauce, sugar, vinegar, and MSG. Drain the noodles and add them to the bowl on top of the seasoning. Top the noodles with the fried scallions and pour the scallion oil and shrimp over the noodles and scallions.

To enjoy, toss the noodles from bottom to top using a pair of chopsticks to incorporate the seasoning, scallions, and oil until the noodles pick up a beautiful light brown hue. For an extra spicy kick, drizzle sriracha on top and give it a nice big toss before you inhale the noodles.

SCRAPPY NOODLES

香炒面包碎拌面
XIĀNG CHĂO MIÀN BĀO SUÌ BÀN MIÀN

Serves 1

PETER: As a teenager, I used to bring home a plastic bag filled with free batter scraps from the pork chop noodle house up the street (see page 146), and I'd feel like I'd hit the jackpot. In those days, affordable and filling staples like rice and noodles were the basis of all our meals. We had very little produce and protein, and since lunch was usually a free-for-all, with all of us kids fending for ourselves, I was always trying to find ways to make rice and noodles more interesting. One day I seasoned my noodles with soy, sugar, Chinese black vinegar, MSG, sesame oil, and, last, some of the batter bits. I tossed it and took a bite. It was incredible! Exactly what I had imagined it would be. These crispy bits were like biting into bacon fat. They added crunch and depth to an otherwise pretty sad bowl of noodles. From that day forward, I would visit the man every few days and store all the bits in a jar, which I shared with my family. We started using them with our noodles, and even added them to our wontons when we didn't have any protein for filling. The best part was it didn't cost us anything.

NOTE: This recipe assumes that you don't have several bags worth of pork-batter scraps already. Instead, we are showing you how to make a delicious panko topping from scratch. But if you've saved your scraps from the pork chops on page 146, use them instead!

TOASTED BREADCRUMBS
- 2 tablespoons neutral oil
- 1 cup (80 g) panko breadcrumbs
- 2 teaspoons sugar
- 1 teaspoon salt
- 1 teaspoon MSG
- 2 teaspoons soy sauce

NOODLES
- 3 to 4 ounces (85 to 115 g) thin Chinese wheat noodles (1½ cups cooked), or substitute spaghetti
- 1 tablespoon soy sauce
- 2 teaspoons toasted sesame oil
- 1 teaspoon Chinkiang vinegar
- ½ teaspoon sugar
- 1 pinch of salt
- 1 pinch of ground white pepper
- 1 pinch of MSG
- ¼ cup (15 g) minced scallions (green parts only)
- 1 teaspoon chili sauce (homemade, page 271, or store-bought; optional, if you like it spicy)

Make the toasted breadcrumbs: Heat a 12-inch (30 cm) nonstick skillet over medium heat. Add the neutral oil, then swirl the pan to coat. Add the panko and spread it in an even layer. Toast for 1 minute, just until the oil coats the panko evenly, then add the sugar, salt, and MSG. Toast, stirring occasionally with a rubber or silicone spatula, until light golden brown, about 7 minutes. Add the soy sauce and stir to distribute evenly. Toast for another 2 minutes, or until the panko is fragrant, crisp, and a nice golden. Transfer to a shallow bowl and set aside. Do not wash out the pan.

Make the noodles: Bring a medium stockpot filled with water to a boil over high heat. Add the noodles and cook according to the package instructions. Drain the noodles, then add them to the pan that you used to toast the panko. Add the soy sauce, sesame oil, vinegar, sugar, salt, white pepper, and MSG. Toss the noodles in the pan to pick up any leftover panko bits and oil and fully incorporate all the seasoning.

Transfer the noodles to a serving bowl and top with ¼ cup (20 g) of the toasted panko (save the rest in an airtight container at room temperature—it's great on noodle soups, over steamed rice, or over salad like a "crouton") and scallions. To kick it up a notch, add chili sauce.

SPAGHETTI "BOLOGNESE" CHOW MEIN

肉酱意大利炒面
RÒU JIÀNG YÌ DÀ LÌ CHǍO MIÀN

Serves 2

KATHY: My teenage years were defined by a weird mix of freedom and loneliness. I was finally old enough to be home alone . . . yet the empty house felt so quiet and lonely. On weekends when my parents were working, I started visiting my relatives, mostly to avoid sad, solo dinners. I'll never forget one particular night I spent with my dad's little sister, my frugal aunt. She lived in this tiny SRO, where the dinner table was squeezed so tight between the kitchen and her bed that we had to use the bed as a bench. She'd drag out a couple stools for other guests, and somehow, we'd make it work.

One night, I'd plopped myself on the bed for dinner when she presented us with yì dà lì miàn: "Italian noodles," her take on spaghetti Bolognese. She'd chopped cabbage and onions, thrown in some tomatoes, and cooked it all down till it was super soft. Then she mixed in ground beef, ketchup, soy sauce, Chinkiang vinegar, and a dash of MSG. It was freaking delicious, with a subtle, smoky wok hei flavor, as if spaghetti bolognese and chow mein had a love child.

Later that night, she opened the tiny cabinet above her stove, and I saw it was stuffed with boxes of dry spaghetti. Her face lit up as she told me: She'd discovered community centers in Chinatown that gave out free food to folks who needed it. Every time I make this dish now, I see my aunt's proud, beaming face.

MARINATED BEEF
8 ounces (225 g) ground beef
1 tablespoon soy sauce
1 tablespoon toasted sesame oil
1 teaspoon dark soy sauce
1 teaspoon Shaoxing wine
1 teaspoon cornstarch
½ teaspoon salt
1 pinch of sugar

½ teaspoon salt, plus more for the spaghetti
8 ounces (225 g) spaghetti
3 tablespoons neutral oil
2 cups (140 g) minced cabbage
1 cup (125 g) minced yellow onion
1 garlic clove, minced
1 teaspoon Shaoxing wine
1 medium vine-ripened tomato, diced
1 tablespoon ketchup
1 tablespoon dark soy sauce
1 tablespoon Chinkiang vinegar
1 teaspoon MSG
Freshly grated Parmesan cheese, to top (optional)
Red chili flakes, to top (optional)
Duò jiāo (Chinese salted chopped chilis, see page 285) or sambal oelek, to top (optional)

Marinate the beef: In a medium bowl, combine the beef, soy sauce, sesame oil, dark soy sauce, Shaoxing wine, cornstarch, salt, and sugar. Set aside to marinate.

Bring a large pot of salted water to a boil and cook the pasta to al dente according to the package instructions.

Meanwhile, heat a large nonstick skillet over medium-high heat. Add 2 tablespoons of the neutral oil, then the marinated beef. Saute for 30 seconds, then transfer to a plate.

Add the remaining 1 tablespoon neutral oil and the onions and saute for 1 minute. Add the cabbage and saute for 2 minutes, or until it has softened and shrunk down, then add the garlic and Shaoxing wine and saute for 1 minute. Add the tomatoes, salt, and a ladleful of pasta cooking water and cook for 2 minutes, or until saucy. Return the beef to the pan and stir to fully incorporate.

Drain the spaghetti and add it to the pan, along with the ketchup, dark soy sauce, vinegar, and MSG. Toss to fully incorporate, then taste and adjust the seasoning as needed. Stir-fry the noodles for an additional 1 to 2 minutes to allow the pasta to absorb flavors, then transfer to serving bowls. Top with Parmesan cheese, chili flakes, and/or duò jiāo as desired.

SOUPS

湯和粥

& CO

COMFORT IN A BOWL

KATHY: In our family, as in many Chinese households, soups and congees have always been more than just food. They're a way to show love, to care for one another after a grueling day of work. I can still hear the soft clink of a ladle against the well-worn pot and gentle, rhythmic bubbling of liquid as my a niáng (our Shanghainese nickname for my father's mother) or pó po (Cantonese for grandmother, my mother's mother) stirred her latest creation. The aroma would waft through our small apartment, a promise of nourishment to come. That first sip of broth, fragrant and soothing, was like a warm embrace. Today, I find immense joy in introducing my own children to these traditional soups, watching their faces light up as they taste the same flavors that have comforted our family for decades.

Soups and congees have been part of Chinese culture for millennia. They embody the Chinese philosophy of food as medicine, with different ingredients chosen not just for flavor, but for their perceived health benefits. A hearty bone broth to strengthen the body, a light vegetable soup to cleanse the palate, or a warming congee to soothe a troubled stomach—there's a soup or congee for every need and occasion.

Economically, these dishes have long been a way to stretch ingredients and feed many mouths on a tight budget. A small amount of meat or vegetables can flavor a large pot of soup, while congee can make a little rice go a long way. This practicality has made these dishes staples in times of both scarcity and plenty.

As you simmer these soups in your own kitchen, I hope they'll fill your home with the same warmth, love, and comfort they've brought to ours.

NGEES

LOTUS ROOT, PEANUT, AND PORK BONE SOUP

莲藕花生猪骨汤
LIÁN ǑU HUĀ SHĒNG ZHŪ GǓ TANG

Serves 4 to 6

PETER: My mother-in-law used to make this soup for Lily and me. Every time she would see us, she would scold us for not taking better care of ourselves. We had a very unhealthy lifestyle when we first opened House of Nanking. Mornings were always busy, so we skipped breakfast. We would go to Chinatown to shop for produce for the day, go to the restaurant, begin prep, and open shop. Once the doors opened, there was no time to eat or take a break. And because we were open all day, we would often get stuck working until we closed shop, usually 10 or 11 p.m. On some weekends, we would drop off Kathy with my mother-in-law while we worked, and when we picked her up close to midnight, my mother-in-law would always have a hot bowl of lotus root soup waiting for us.

According to Chinese traditional medicine, lotus root is considered "cool" in nature, which means it can help reduce the heat in one's body. And since we work in a restaurant, constantly near heat and fire, we need to balance out the "fire breath" in our body by eating more "cool" ingredients such as lotus root. The root is also high in fiber, iron, and calcium, which helps promote digestive health, invigorates the spleen, and nourishes the blood. But this tonic, essentially a bone broth, is great whether or not you work in restaurants. It is also beneficial if you've recently had deep-fried dishes, spicy dishes, or heavy, greasy meals.

NOTE: For the tonics in this chapter, you can use either pork neck bones or pork ribs. At Asian supermarkets, pork ribs are usually sold cross-cut into long strips that are between 1 and 1½ inches (2.5 and 4 cm) wide, or already cut into riblets and shrink-wrapped (which would also work for this recipe—you won't have to do any additional prep to the riblets). If you go to a Western butcher and can only find racks of ribs, ask the butcher to remove any silverskin and then cut the rack into thirds lengthwise (across the bones rather than in between the bones). Don't try to do this at home, unless you have a butcher saw! When you get home, you will use a knife or cleaver to separate the long strips into riblets.

- 1 pound (455 g) pork neck bones or cross-cut pork ribs (see Note), cut in between the bones into roughly 2-inch (5 cm) riblets
- 2½ pounds (1.2 kg) lotus root (see page 284), peeled and sliced into 1-inch (2.5 cm)-thick half circles
- 2 large carrots, peeled and bias-cut into 2-inch (5 cm) pieces
- 2 bias-cut slices ginger (⅛ inch / 3 mm thick and 2 inches / 5 cm long)
- 1 cup (150 g) raw shelled peanuts

Place the pork in a large stockpot with enough water to fully submerge the pork. Bring to a boil over high heat and cook for 5 minutes, until scum rises to the surface. Remove from the heat and drain the pork, discarding the water. Rinse the pork with cold water to remove all impurities. Clean the pot and add 10 cups (2.4 L) fresh, cold water, along with the pork, lotus root, carrots, ginger, and peanuts. Bring to a boil over high heat and cook for 30 minutes. Then reduce the heat to low and simmer for 1½ hours. Serve hot. Cool leftovers and keep in the fridge for up to 3 to 5 days.

KATHY'S TIP: I love to use leftovers to make savory oatmeal in the morning. Simply replace whatever water you'd normally use with the soup (peanuts and lotus root included), and drizzle with soy sauce or ponzu before serving.

PAPAYA, FIG, AND PORK BONE SOUP WITH DRIED CHINESE ALMONDS

木瓜无花果杏仁猪骨汤 MÙ GUĀ WÚ HUĀ GUǑ XÌNG RÉN ZHŪ GǓ TANG

Serves 6 to 8

NOTE: Rinse all dry ingredients with water a few times, like you would wash rice, prior to cooking.

PETER: When you walk into a Cantonese restaurant, especially a smaller one that caters to locals, it is very common to be served a complimentary bowl of lòuh fó tōng, a Cantonese style of soup made from simmering fresh or dried vegetables, fresh or dried fruits, meat, herbs, and grains, at the start of the meal. The direct translation for "lòuh fó tōng" is "old fire soup," referring to the traditional way of cooking soup on low heat for several hours, a method that is believed to better extract nutrients and flavors from the ingredients. The soup is good for your health, and Chinese people from Hong Kong, Guangdong, and elsewhere down south believe it's crucial for maintaining balance in the body. Most households brew their own soups/tonics every week so they can have it every single day. I never tried this type of soup until I immigrated to the US. In Shanghai, there is no such thing as lòuh fó tōng ("slow soups") or bōu tōng ("brew soups").

Now I have noticed the benefits of having tonics on a regular basis, and my wife, Lily, makes them at home. Some tonics have bitterness, some have strong herb finishes, and some are sweet. This soup errs on the sweeter side, as it has both papaya and dried figs. It's great for someone experiencing cold symptoms such as a dry cough or phlegm or who feels their qi (energy) is too hot, perhaps from eating too many greasy or fried foods. Once they're fully cooked, you can consume all the ingredients in the soup, or you can just enjoy the broth. The pork is best with a dipping sauce on the side: Try ponzu, or soy sauce mixed with toasted sesame oil.

---

1 pound (455 g) pork neck bones or cross-cut pork ribs (see Note on page 127), cut in between the bones into roughly 2-inch (5 cm) riblets

1 bias-cut slice of ginger (⅛ inch / 3 mm thick and 2 inches / 5 cm long)

0.8 ounces (23 g) dried south almonds (see page 287), rinsed

0.4 ounces (11 g) dried north almonds (see page 287), rinsed

2½ pounds (1.2 kg) ripe papaya (see page 284), peeled, seeded, and cut into 2-inch (5 cm) cubes

8 dried white figs, rinsed

Place the pork in a large stockpot with enough water to fully submerge the pork. Bring to a boil over high heat and cook for 5 minutes, until scum rises to the surface. Remove from the heat and drain the pork, discarding the water. Rinse the pork with cold water to remove all impurities. Clean the pot and add 10 cups (2.4 L) fresh, cold water, along with the pork, ginger, and south and north almonds, then bring to a boil over high heat. Boil for 3 minutes, then reduce the heat to achieve a simmer. Simmer, covered, for 45 minutes. Add the papaya and figs, re-cover, and continue to simmer for an additional 30 minutes. Serve hot. Store any leftovers airtight in the refrigerator for up to 3 days.

KATHY'S TIP: If you have leftover broth, use it to cook oatmeal—it's perfect for breakfast or a light dinner!

WATERCRESS PORK BONE SOUP WITH FIGS AND DRIED CHINESE ALMONDS

西洋菜无花果杏仁猪骨汤
XĪ YÁNG CÀI WÚ HUĀ GUŎ XÌNG RÉN ZHŪ GǓ TĀNG

Serves 6 to 8

KATHY: Growing up in a very traditional Chinese household, it seemed like there was a soup for every single ailment and condition out there. This watercress pork neck soup, which has a distinctive and herbaceous flavor and aroma, was what we'd make to alleviate dry coughs. It moistens the lungs and throat, which makes it great for anyone overcoming a cold, suffering from allergies, or who has asthma. It's particularly popular among chefs and line cooks in Chinese restaurants because it's considered "cooling." I'll leave it to you to decide whether it truly works or not. All I know is it can't hurt, and I do feel really good after having a bowl.

If you've never had watercress in soup, it almost tastes like the broth has a ton of celery steeped into it. There is an underlying bright bitterness to it that isn't strong but rather clean tasting. You feel healthy drinking this soup, just like how you would feel if you drank a bottle of pressed vegetable juice.

- 2 pounds (910 g) pork neck bones or cross-cut pork ribs (see Note on page 127), cut in between the bones into roughly 2-inch (5 cm) riblets
- 3 coin-size slices of ginger
- ¼ cup (30 g) dried south almonds (see page 287), rinsed
- 2 tablespoons dried north almonds (see page 287), rinsed
- 10 dried Turkish figs
- 2 medium carrots, peeled and cut on a bias
- ½ cup (40 g) dried lily bulbs, soaked in water for 30 minutes
- 1 bunch watercress, rinsed
- 1 dried tangerine peel (see page 289)
- Soy sauce, for serving
- Toasted sesame oil, for serving

Place the pork in a large stockpot with enough water to fully submerge the pork. Bring to a boil over high heat and cook for 5 minutes, until scum rises to the surface. Remove from the heat and drain the pork, discarding the water. Rinse the pork with cold water to remove all impurities. Clean the pot and add 10 cups (2.4 L) fresh, cold water, along with the pork, ginger, dried south and north almonds, the figs, and carrots. Add 8 cups (1.9 L) water and bring to a boil. Once boiling, reduce the heat to low and simmer, covered, for 1 hour. Drain the dried lily bulbs and add them to the pot, along with the watercress and tangerine peel. Simmer for an additional 1 hour. Turn off the heat, discard the tangerine peel and ginger, and ladle into serving bowls. Make a dipping sauce by mixing soy sauce with a dash of toasted sesame oil and dip the pork meat into the sauce before you take a bite.

SERVING TIP: Although I'm not a fan of food waste, and the traditional way to serve this is with the simmered ingredients, you can treat this soup like a bone broth, if you wish, and discard the watercress, almonds, fig, and carrots. But I do encourage you to leave them in. The pork neck bones are difficult to eat but worth it; the meat is incredibly tender and tasty in the soy dipping sauce.

FIVE-MINUTE SOUP WITH TOMATO, EGG, AND SEAWEED

紫菜番茄蛋花汤
ZǏ CÀI FĀN QIÉ DÀN HUĀ TANG

Serves 4

PETER: This soup combines two of my favorite frugal, five-minute soups, soups that kept my family fed for decades when we had limited resources: tomato egg soup and egg flower soup. We have a lot of Chinese tourists who come visit Fang and Nanking, and after eating so many of their meals at Western restaurants, they are always hankering for a proper Chinese meal, something to soothe the soul. Do you know what their most-requested dish is? Tomato egg soup! They say, "I want something simple and light," and I know exactly where they are coming from. Of course, my version has to be a little different, with a little extra pop. Dried seaweed, which we call zǐ cài ("purple vegetable") because of its dark purple hue, is commonly used in egg flower soup to add umami and a lovely texture. Seaweed is also rich in nutrients, loaded with calcium, iron, and iodine. My parents always told us kids to eat a lot of seaweed to prevent thyroid problems as adults. To this day, the flavors in this soup—umami from the seaweed, mild sourness from the tomato, richness from the egg and sesame oil—make me think of home. Not just Shanghai, but also the various SROs and tiny apartments my wife and daughter drifted into and out of over time.

- 1 tablespoon neutral oil
- 2 large vine-ripened tomatoes, diced
- 3 coin-size slices ginger
- 1 tablespoon dashi powder
- 1½ teaspoons sugar
- ½ teaspoon salt
- ½ teaspoon ground white pepper
- ½ teaspoon soy sauce
- 2 eggs, whisked
- ½ disc of dried laver or zǐ cài (Chinese dried seaweed, see page 290), broken into 2-inch (5 cm) pieces
- 1½ teaspoons toasted sesame oil
- Chopped scallions and toasted sesame seeds, for garnish (optional)

In a medium pot, heat the neutral oil over high heat. Add the tomatoes and ginger and stir-fry for 1 minute, or until the tomato breaks down and releases its juices. Add 3 cups (720 ml) water and bring to a boil. Add the dashi powder, sugar, salt, white pepper, and soy sauce and stir to incorporate. Taste and adjust the salt if needed. Without stirring, drizzle the eggs into the pot in a circular motion to create a flowering effect. Let the eggs set for 30 seconds before stirring so you get ribbons and don't cloud up the soup. Add the dried seaweed and stir until the seaweed softens, about 20 seconds, then drizzle in the sesame oil. Ladle into soup bowls, then garnish with the scallions and sesame seeds, if using.

SERVING TIP: For a light, cleansing meal after heavy indulging, serve this soup with a plain bowl of steamed rice and side of kimchee or Chinese pickles.

A NIÁNG'S CURRY CHICKEN SOUP

咖喱鸡汤
GĀ LÍ JĪ TANG

Serves 8

NOTE: Feel free to halve this recipe if, unlike my mom, you aren't feeding a large family of hungry kids!

PETER: This curry chicken soup is a one-pot wonder my mom created when our family was going through hard times. Typically in Shanghainese cuisine, curry chicken is braised alongside potatoes, carrots, and onions. The result is a thick sauce with large chunks of tender chicken and vegetables. My mom's version used chicken bones, lots of vegetables, and just a small bit of meat. She cooked it in a curry broth, which is not traditional, but by making it a soup rather than a curry, she ended up with a giant meal for five people rather than two.

Part of her genius was knowing how to extract the most flavor possible from her ingredients. She marinated the chicken bones in turmeric powder, salt, Chinese wine, and flour. Then she'd brown the chicken meat and bones in oil to extract more flavor and fat from the chicken and turmeric. Only then would she add the rest of the ingredients and water. She simmered the hell out of the chicken bones and vegetables for a generous amount of time, until they fell apart, then seasoned everything with Worcestershire sauce, her secret weapon in the kitchen.

Even during the darkest days, we always looked forward to our meals together—and Chicken Curry Soup Night was one of my favorites. I can still picture all of us with our bowls of rice, sitting around a large pot of soup in the cold. It's strange how the food somehow always tasted better then than it does now. Maybe we were just so hungry, or maybe there wasn't much to look forward to beyond a meal that filled our stomachs.

continued

Place the chicken pieces in a large bowl and pour the Shaoxing wine over the top. Add the curry powder, turmeric, and 1 teaspoon of the salt and use your hands to toss and massage the wet and dry ingredients into the chicken meat and bones. Set aside to marinate for 10 minutes.

Place the flour in a shallow pan or baking dish. Remove the chicken from the marinade, allowing any excess to drip off, then coat each piece in the flour, refreshing the flour as needed.

In a large stockpot, heat the neutral oil over high heat. Working in batches as necessary (you don't want to crowd the pan), brown the chicken drumsticks and thighs until the fat renders, 5 to 8 minutes. Add the chicken back to the pot along with the onion, potatoes, carrots, and ginger. Add enough chicken stock to cover all the ingredients, then cover the pot and bring to a boil.

Reduce the heat to low to achieve a gentle simmer, then add the tomatoes. Simmer until the chicken meat is tender and falling off the bone, about 1 hour and 15 minutes.

Season the soup with the sugar, Worcestershire sauce, and remaining 2 teaspoons salt. Stir to combine, then turn off the heat, cover with the lid, and allow to sit so that the flavors meld for 10 minutes.

To serve, scoop white rice into soup bowls. Ladle the soup over the rice. Make sure to get pieces of chicken and vegetables, then remove and discard any bones or cartilage. But really, the broth is the star of the dish. Store any leftovers covered in the fridge. I think it tastes even better the next day.

OTHER SERVING IDEAS: Instead of white rice, serve over rice noodles with fresh mint, Thai basil, and a squeeze of lemon for a Southeast Asian twist. Or, top the soup with shredded cheddar cheese, diced red onion, and saltine crackers and serve with Tabasco sauce. For a Mexican riff, top with crispy tortilla strips, diced avocado, cilantro, and sour cream. Last, you can never go wrong with pào fàn (see page 156).

3 skin-on chicken drumsticks

3 skin-on, bone-in chicken thighs

¼ cup (60 ml) Shaoxing wine

⅓ cup (30 g) curry powder (S&B Oriental Curry Powder preferred)

¼ cup (40 g) turmeric powder

3 teaspoons salt

2 cups (250 g) all-purpose flour, or as needed

¼ cup (60 ml) neutral oil

1 large yellow onion, quartered

1 large russet potato, peeled and cut into large (about 1½-inch / 4 cm) pieces

2 large carrots, peeled and cut on the oblique into large pieces

4 slices ginger

6 cups (1.4 L) chicken stock, or as needed

2 large tomatoes, quartered

2 teaspoons sugar

¼ cup (60 ml) Worcestershire sauce

Steamed white rice, for serving

A NIÁNG'S SHANGHAINESE RUSSIAN BORSCHT WITH BEEF

上海罗宋汤

SHĀNG HǍI LUÓ SÒNG TANG

Serves 4 to 6

KATHY: I first visited Shanghai, the city my parents and grandparents are from, when I was in middle school. Prior to that, I always loved listening to my a niáng describe her love for the city and everything she missed about her home, which she called the Paris of the East. She painted a picture of romance: stunning architecture along the Bund (Wàitān), the waterfront area of the historic old town, and jazz clubs inside glitzy hotels.

As a kid, I thought my a niáng knew nothing about the Western world because she couldn't speak English. But Shanghai, even back then, was such a cosmopolitan city. When she told me she would have coffee, toast with butter, Russian borscht, and potato salad in Shanghai, I was blown away. She just chuckled and said, "I know how to appreciate all kinds of foods. In fact, your a niáng can make the best Russian borscht, the Shanghainese way." She then recounted in detail her first meal at the Red House Restaurant, Hóng Fáng zi. It's one of the oldest Western-style restaurants in Shanghai, and a favorite among political dignitaries. This is where she tasted her first bite of potato salad and borscht. Since beets were not a common ingredient in Shanghai, my a niáng used tomatoes instead. And since there was no ketchup or tomato paste, she stir-fried the tomatoes in oil with onions to release flavors and create her own tomato sauce, resulting in a much lighter but still flavorful version. She also added a secret ingredient that made it that much more distinctive than any other borscht: a touch of milk. To me that was perfection—a light, vegetable forward beef broth that I can drink for days without it feeling too heavy. (See photo on page 142.)

---

1 pound (455 g) beef shank or boneless beef chuck roast, cut into 1½-inch (4 cm) chunks

4 large tomatoes, diced

1 large onion, chopped

¼ cup (60 ml) neutral oil

2 carrots, peeled and cut on the bias into 2-inch (5 cm) pieces

1 large russet potato, peeled and cut into 8 pieces

½ head cabbage (about 1 pound / 455 g), chopped into 2-inch (5 cm) pieces

3 tablespoons Worcestershire sauce

4 teaspoons salt

2 teaspoons sugar

2 teaspoons MSG

½ cup (120 ml) whole milk

Chili oil (homemade, page 274, or store-bought) and freshly cracked black pepper, to serve (optional)

Place the beef shank in a stockpot and add water to cover. Bring to a boil and cook for 2 minutes to purge impurities. Drain the shank, then run it under cold water to rinse off the scum and clean out the pot. Add the shank back to the clean pot, cover with 8 cups (2 L) water, and bring to a boil.

Meanwhile, heat a large nonstick skillet over high heat and add the neutral oil. Add the tomato and onion and cook, stirring occasionally, for 5 to 7 minutes, until the tomatoes and onion soften to a sauce-like consistency. Add the tomato-onion sauce to the boiling pot of beef shank. Boil for 5 minutes, then reduce the heat to medium, cover with lid, and simmer for 30 minutes. Uncover, stir, then add the carrots and potatoes. Cover again and simmer for 40 minutes more. Add the cabbage, increase the heat to high, and boil with the lid off for 5 minutes. Season with the Worcestershire sauce, salt, sugar, and MSG. Turn off the heat, add the milk, and stir with a ladle to fully incorporate. To serve, ladle into bowls and enjoy with chili oil and/or black pepper, if using.

SAVORY SOY MILK

咸豆浆
XIÁN DÒU JIĀNG

Serves 1 to 2

PETER: Shanghainese breakfast in my opinion is one of the best in the world. Our version of going into Starbucks to grab a coffee and pastry is to buy a bowl of savory soy milk with a side of shāo bǐng yóu tiáo, a sesame flatbread filled with fried dough stick. This is the dream breakfast set for me: In a few bites, you will find, crispy, crunchy, soft, spicy, sweet, salty, and umami.

Think of this savory soy milk as a slightly creamy soup that has a subtle umami flavor to it, along with a nutty aroma from the soybeans and a little kick of spice at the finish. The dried baby shrimp and dried seaweed add another layer of umami; the crunchy salted mustard stems, scallions, and fried yóu tiáo add a crisp element. After a few minutes, the yóu tiáo will soak up the soy milk and soften into a flavorful sponge that melts in your mouth, just like the crostini that melts into your French onion soup. Over the course of a few minutes, the soup changes with every bite.

---

2 tablespoons dried baby shrimp (xiā mǐ, see page 289)

1 tablespoon minced preserved mustard stem (zhà cài, see page 285)

6 torn pieces of dried laver or zǐ cài (Chinese seaweed, page 290)

Half of a yóu tiáo (Chinese donut, see page 290), sliced crosswise into ½-inch (12 mm) pieces

1 tablespoon chopped scallions

2 tablespoons soy sauce

1 tablespoon chili oil (homemade, page 274, or store-bought)

1½ teaspoons Chinkiang vinegar

1 teaspoon toasted sesame oil

1 pinch of ground white pepper

1½ cups (360 ml) unsweetened soy milk

Arrange all the ingredients except the soy milk in 1 medium soup bowl or 2 small bowls. In a small pot over medium-high heat, heat the soy milk until it begins to boil. Pour the hot soy milk over the ingredients in the bowl and enjoy immediately!

PAIRING IDEAS: Since this recipe only calls for half of a yóu tiáo, you can dip the second in the savory milk and eat it like a piece of bread. Or toast a frozen piece of shāo bǐng (a sesame-coated flatbread you can find at Asian supermarkets). Slice open the toasted shāo bǐng, sprinkle it with a generous amount of sugar, then stuff the yóu tiáo inside and eat it like a sandwich with the savory milk on the side. You can even pair the savory soy milk with a sweet, Western-style pastry. Kathy likes pairing it with a kouign-amann, which she says reminds her a little of the sweet shāo bǐngs from Shanghai.

HEALTHY TWIST: Skip the Chinese dough stick and add 2 tablespoons minced raw celery, which adds a refreshing crunch.

YÁNG CHŪN NOODLE SOUP

阳春面
YÁNG CHŪN MIÀN

Serves 1

KATHY: Yáng chūn miàn is a plain bowl of noodle soup, meant to be an accompaniment to a main dish such as beef shank, braised pig's intestines, or the pork chop on page 146. The noodles are usually thin fresh wheat noodles, cooked till al dente and served in a very simple soup, garnished with finely chopped scallions. It's often found at small restaurants and street stalls, where it might take the place of a bowl of steamed rice. The broth we make at home is on the simpler, cleaner side, but it's not meant to be super flavorful—the bold flavors come from whatever main dish is accompanying the yáng chūn miàn.

NOTE: We like to use fresh thin wheat noodles you can find at Chinese supermarkets. However, a package of dried thin wheat noodles from the grocery store will do as well. Wu-Mu Dry Noodle is a good alternative to fresh noodles.

- 1 tablespoon finely chopped scallions
- ½ teaspoon powdered chicken bouillon
- 1 generous pinch of ground white pepper
- 1 pinch of salt, or to taste
- 1 teaspoon toasted sesame oil
- 3 to 4 ounces (85 to 115 g) fresh or dried thin Chinese wheat noodles (see Note), cooked until al dente according to package instructions

In a small pot or tea kettle, bring 1¾ cups (420 ml) water to a boil. Place the scallions in a soup bowl, then add the chicken bouillon, white pepper, salt, and sesame oil. Add the boiling water to the bowl and stir to mix the seasoning completely. Immediately add the cooked noodles to the center of the bowl and serve.

SHANGHAI "HOT SAUCE NOODLES"

上海辣酱面
SHÀNG HǍI LÀ JIÀNG MIÀN

Serves 1

KATHY: *Là jiàng* directly translates to hot sauce, but là jiàng miàn is so much more than just hot sauce with noodles. First of all, là jiàng is actually hot sauce on steroids, loaded with delicious bits of pork, marinated tofu, dried shrimp, and peanuts. You fry these ingredients in oil until they're dry and crisp, then simmer them in broad bean sauce, chili sauce, hoisin sauce, and MSG. The end result has pops of sweet, savory, salty, and spicy.

When I came home after my first semester of freshman year at USC, my mom saw how much I missed my family and our food. Panda Express and Cup O' Noodles just weren't cutting it. So my mom, being the loving and observant parent she is, prepared là jiàng the night before I went back for my second semester. She wrapped the jar in plastic, then in old T-shirts, and stuffed it in my suitcase. Just like that, my mom sent me back to LA with a piece of home.

¼ cup (60 ml) Là Jiàng (page 267)

Yáng Chūn Noodle Soup (page 142)

Chopped scallions, for garnish

In a medium soup bowl, spoon the là jiàng over the noodles and top with scallions. Serve piping hot!

SHE DI LE PORK CHOP NOODLE SOUP

鲜得来排骨汤面
XIĀN DE LÁI PÁI GǓ TĀNG MIÀN

Serves 2

NOTE: If you don't have a meat tenderizer, you can pound the pork with a rolling pin or mallet (pound it lengthwise, then go back over it crosswise, working around the bone). After it's pounded thin, use a fork or a chef's knife to prick shallow holes all over the surface.

PETER: I was always interested in learning how to cook. Apart from watching my mother cook and reading cookbooks, I would walk down the alleys of Shanghai and watch the chefs cook in their street stalls. There was a pork chop noodle shop near our house that made the most incredible pork chops ever. To this day, I can still remember the smell and the taste of them. You can't find anything like it in Shanghai anymore. What was so special about this pork chop was the batter. It had a mix of egg, flour, cornstarch, soy sauce, Shaoxing wine, sugar, MSG, and white pepper. The pork would sit in this seasoned batter and marinate all day long. When the chef fried it, the coating would puff and crisp up. Usually this was served with a side of yáng chūn miàn (page 142), simple noodle soup with chopped scallions.

I would watch the chef every week, mesmerized by his swift movements, feeding a long line all by himself. In fact, after watching him do this week after week, I started to notice all the batter bits he'd fish out of the oil and toss. I thought to myself, *This is the best part; what a waste to throw it away!* So one day I asked him if I could take the batter bits. He looked bothered and perplexed: "Why do you want it, son? It's scraps. I toss it out." I said, "Don't worry about it. If you don't want them, I'll take them." In this way, the chef gave me two dishes—this pork chop, which I was able to re-create from my memories of watching him, and the Scrappy Noodles on page 121, which were my own invention.

- 4 bone-in pork rib chops
- ⅓ cup (80 ml) Shaoxing wine
- ⅓ cup (80 ml) light soy sauce
- 3 eggs, whisked
- 1 tablespoon dark soy sauce
- ½ cup (65 g) cornstarch
- 2 teaspoons sugar
- 1 teaspoon MSG (optional)
- ½ teaspoon ground white pepper
- ½ teaspoon salt
- ½ cup (65 g) all-purpose flour
- Neutral oil, for frying
- Yáng Chūn Noodle Soup (page 142), for serving

Place each pork chop in between layers of wax or parchment paper and, working from the middle of each chop to the edges, pound with the flat side of a meat tenderizer (see Note) until the chops are an even ¼-inch (6 mm) thickness. Remove the top layer of paper and pound again, this time using the spiky side of your tenderizer. Flip the pork chops and pound the other side with the spiky side of your tenderizer. Place the chops in a bowl or shallow pan.

In a small bowl, whisk the Shaoxing wine, light soy sauce, eggs, dark soy sauce, cornstarch, sugar, MSG, if using, the white pepper, and salt until smooth. Pour the marinade over the pork chops and use your hands to massage it into the chops.

Pour the flour into a shallow bowl. Lift each pork chop from the marinade, allowing any excess to drip off, and dredge in the flour to coat evenly. Place the dredged pork chops in a ziplock bag, then pour the remaining marinade into the bag, close, and shake the chops to evenly coat. Transfer to the refrigerator to marinate overnight.

Fill a shallow cast-iron skillet with ¾ inch (2 cm) of oil and heat over high heat until it registers 375°F (190°C).

Make 2 cuts (you're not scoring here; go all the way through!) into each pork chop, perpendicular to the bone and stopping as close to the bone as you can get without the meat coming off. This should make the meat fan out into 3 even pieces.

Fry the pork chops in the oil for 2 minutes per each side, or until the thickest part of the chop registers 140°F (60°C) on a meat thermometer. Serve over bowls of yang chūn miàn and make sure to save any fried batter bits for scrappy noodles (page 121)!

FORTY-DEEP WONTON BOWL

上海猪肉青菜馄饨
SHÀNG HǍI ZHŪ RÒU QĪNG CÀI HÚN TÚN

Serves 2 to 4

PETER: One of my favorite pastimes with my younger brother, Jason (Xiǎo Dì), was to wrap small Shanghai wontons for lunch. It would be hot as hell, and we would sit on wooden stools in the kitchen wearing sleeveless undershirts and track shorts, wrapping packets of pork, lard, and bok choy. Our mouths would water as we worked, eager to eat them as fast as possible. We would often inhale forty wontons each! To give you an idea of how many wontons this is, a normal porcelain bowl that serves soup for a family does not fit that many wontons. We had to use metal bowls that were used to wash vegetables and dishes to serve our wontons in. We would sweat completely through our shirts while eating them. But boy was it worth it.

KATHY: Chinese people like even numbers and find them to be auspicious. In our household, we always serve food in even-numbered quantities, no matter how small or large the serving. This recipe makes about forty wontons, which is enough for four people with lighter appetites, or two with larger appetites. When my dad and uncle used to make this, they doubled the recipe and made forty for each of them.

continued

Make the Shanghai wontons: Bring a large pot of water to a boil. Blanch the bok choy just until the leaves and stems are slightly softened—it should still be bright green—45 to 60 seconds. Transfer to a colander and run cold water over the bok choy. When it's cool enough to handle, use kitchen towels to squeeze out any excess water from the bok choy, then finely mince. Season the minced bok choy with a pinch of sugar and salt and mix by hand to incorporate. Let sit for 4 minutes.

Grab the bok choy by the handful and squeeze it again in kitchen towels to remove excess water. When dry, put the bok choy in a clean, dry bowl.

Add the ground pork, scallions, sesame oil, soy sauce, Shaoxing wine, lard, if using, cornstarch, MSG, white pepper, the remaining 1 teaspoon sugar, and remaining ½ teaspoon salt to the bowl with the bok choy. Mix by hand until fully incorporated. Add 2 tablespoons water and hand mix again for about 5 minutes, until the mixture has a pastelike texture.

Set up a small bowl filled with water by your workstation. This will be the glue for sealing the wonton edges.

Place 1 teaspoon of filling into the center of a wrapper. Dip your index finger into the water bowl and run your wet finger along the edge of the wonton skin. If using square wonton skins, fold the skin in half by bringing the right bottom corner of the square to the top left corner of the square. Seal the filling inside to form a triangle. Dab water on the right corner of the triangle and bring the left corner over to the right. Press down and seal to create what resembles a pointed tortellini. If using round dumpling skins, follow the shaping instructions on page 92. Repeat until all the filling has been used.

Bring a large stockpot of water to a boil over high heat. Add all the dumplings to the pot and cook for 8 to 10 minutes, until the pork is cooked through. (If you don't have a pot large enough to boil all of the dumplings, work in batches. And if you don't want to cook all the dumplings, you can freeze uncooked dumplings: Arrange them on a baking sheet and wrap tightly with plastic wrap. Transfer to the freezer; then, once frozen, transfer the dumplings to ziplock bags for easier storage.)

To serve: In each serving bowl, add a pinch of white pepper, chopped scallions, 1 teaspoon of lard, a pinch of salt, and 1 tablespoon of soy sauce. Ladle the dumplings into the bowls, along with enough of the boiling liquid to make the wontons float in the bowl (figure about a cup / 240 ml), depending on the size of your bowl). Add chili sauce, if using, and serve immediately. Any leftover boiled dumplings can be pan-fried the next day to be enjoyed as a delicious breakfast or snack.

SHANGHAI WONTONS

6 ounces (170 g) Shanghai bok choy (see page 282)

1 teaspoon sugar, plus more for seasoning the bok choy

½ teaspoon salt, plus more for seasoning the bok choy

8 ounces (225 g) ground pork

3 tablespoons minced scallions

2 tablespoons toasted sesame oil

1 tablespoon soy sauce

1 tablespoon Shaoxing wine

1 tablespoon melted lard (optional)

1 teaspoon cornstarch

½ teaspoon MSG or dashi powder

¼ teaspoon ground white pepper

1 pack square wonton wrappers (see page 289) or round dumpling skins (see page 287)

TO SERVE

White pepper

Chopped scallions

Lard or toasted sesame oil

Salt

Soy sauce

Chili crisp or chili oil (homemade, page 274, or store-bought; optional)

VARIATIONS

Try serving these dumplings in chicken bone broth instead of the seasoned boiling liquid.

For a fully loaded Shanghai wonton soup, add dried baby shrimp, dried seaweed, dried shallots, and egg ribbons.

WHITE RIVER SOUP WITH WONTONS AND TOFU PUFF

馄饨鱼汤
HÚN TÚN YÚ TANG

Serves 6

NOTE: If you don't feel up to spending 1½ hours making a pork bone broth, you can substitute 1 quart of chicken broth. But the pork bone broth is worth the effort for the authentic Cantonese flavors, and it makes a big difference!

KATHY: "Eat more fish. Eating fish will make you smart." That is what my pó po would always say to me and all the grandkids. Pó po was well versed in Cantonese cuisine, which meant she cooked up a lot of fish for us, but our favorite was always this soup. It was the inspiration for the famous white river soup we serve at Fang restaurant, which is particularly popular among our Asian clientele. I can't tell you how many times we've had people traveling from Asia tell us that, after eating steaks and pasta throughout the trip, all they want is this comforting, satisfying bowl of soup that makes them feel like home. When I was at a Fintech cocktail party in Danang, Vietnam, a guest of the event spotted me and proceeded to tell everyone at the party that she had enjoyed the most amazing fish soup at my restaurant. Well, all I can say to that is, this dish would not be what it is if it wasn't for my pó po, who loved her family so dearly that she would spend four hours making fish soup for us, so we would be smart. Is it safe to say it worked?

1½ pounds (680 g) pork bones (see Note)

2 bias-cut slices ginger (⅛ inch / 3 mm thick and 2 inches / 5 cm long)

½ cup (80 g) raw shelled peanuts

2 tablespoons neutral oil

1 (1-pound / 455 g) whole tilapia, patted very dry

1 pound (455 g) white daikon (1 medium), cut into 4-inch (10 cm)-long batons

12 wontons, homemade (see Shanghai wontons, page 150) or store-bought

2½ ounces (70 g) rice stick noodles (mei fun), soaked in water to cover by a few inches (1½ cups once soaked; see page 286)

1 tablespoon fish sauce

1½ teaspoons salt

⅛ teaspoon ground white pepper

6 pieces tofu puff, sliced in half

⅓ cup (20 g) chopped scallions or cilantro leaves

Chili oil (homemade, page 274, or store-bought), for drizzling

Place the pork bones in a large stockpot with enough water to cover the bones. Bring to a boil over high heat and boil for 3 minutes to purge impurities. Drain the bones (discard the water), then rinse the bones and pot to clean it. Return the pork bones to the pot along with the ginger and enough water to come 4 inches (10 cm) above the bones. Bring to a boil over high heat. Once boiling, reduce the heat to medium-low, cover, and simmer for 1 hour and 25 minutes. Remove and discard the pork bones, then add the peanuts to the pork bone broth. Increase the heat to high until boiling, then reduce the heat to low, cover, and simmer for another 45 minutes.

While the soup is simmering, heat a large nonstick skillet over high heat. Add the oil, then carefully lay the fish down in the oil (it may splatter). Pan-fry for 5 to 8 minutes, until one side is a nice golden brown, then flip the fish and cook the other side for another 5 to 8 minutes. Transfer the fish to the pork bone broth and add the daikon. Bring to a boil over high heat, then reduce the heat to medium-low, cover, and simmer for another 45 minutes.

Meanwhile, bring a medium pot of water to a boil over high heat. Once boiling, add the wontons and watch for the wontons to float to the surface. After that, cook for 1 minute longer. Use a slotted spoon or spider to transfer the cooked wontons to a plate or bowl for later. Add the mei fun to the pot and boil until soft, 1 to 2 minutes. Drain the noodles and divide them among 6 soup bowls. Add 2 wontons to each bowl.

When the soup is done, season it with fish sauce, salt, and white pepper. Use a large sieve to scoop out the whole fish—your goal is to get it out in one piece, so you don't have any bones floating in the soup. Traditionally, we discard the flesh of the fish, but if that feels wasteful, you can certainly eat it (I often do, with some jalapeño soy [page 95] for dipping). Then use chopsticks to remove the ginger. The peanuts and radishes should remain in the soup. Add the tofu puffs and cook until the puffs are warmed through. Divide the soup among the 6 serving bowls, making sure everyone gets 2 tofu puffs. Garnish with scallions and a drizzle of chili oil, then serve.

FRIED OMELET SOUP WITH PORK MEATBALLS

煎蛋肉丸粉丝汤
JIĀN DÀN RÒU WÁN FĚN SĪ TANG

Serves 4

PETER: My mom used to make dàn jiao: a half-moon-shaped dumpling where the skin is made from fried eggs, wrapped around ground pork, sort of like a baby pork omelet. The egg dumplings are then simmered inside a casserole filled with vermicelli noodles, tofu puff, and napa cabbage. This style of dumplings is incredibly laborious: I would watch my mom standing over the stove with a flat ladle (which was the perfect size and shape for making dumplings), drizzle a little oil in the ladle, spread the oil, then pour whisked egg into it. She'd cook the egg slowly until she could flip it over without tearing, add the raw pork filling, then fold the egg over and drizzle a little more whisked egg to seal, sometimes flipping the egg over several times to ensure it was slightly golden brown on both sides. Imagine how many she had to make to feed our whole family of seven. There's a lot of food that excites me, but this has been permanently sealed in my brain as one of the top five dishes my mom made for us. When she immigrated to the United States, she made it for Kathy a few times, but with old age, her dexterity and patience began to wane.

In this version, we cut the egg into ribbons and drop the pork filling directly in the soup to form little meatballs. It gives the flavor and satisfaction of my mother's version, minus the work.

Make the meatballs: In a large bowl, use your hands to mix all the meatball ingredients together until fully incorporated and set aside.

Make the soup: Heat a 12-inch (30 cm) nonstick skillet over medium heat, add 1 teaspoon of the neutral oil to the pan, and swirl to evenly coat. Season the eggs with a pinch of salt. Pour into the hot pan and fry for 2 minutes on each side, or until the eggs are golden brown and fully set—this makes the eggs easier to flip, and well-done eggs will taste even better once they're simmered in broth. Transfer the fried eggs to a cutting board and slice into ½-inch (12 mm)-wide strips, about 3 inches (7.5 cm) long.

Drain the shrimp. Heat a medium pot over high heat and add the remaining 1 teaspoon neutral oil. Add the ginger and dried shrimp and toast for 30 seconds to release the ginger's aroma and flavor. Add the napa cabbage to the pot along with the chicken stock and preserved vegetables. Bring everything to a boil, then add your egg ribbons. Start rolling your pork meatballs by hand into balls slightly smaller than a golf ball. If you're Kathy or Peter, you'll toss them into the broth as you roll them—but you can also roll them all out ahead of time if that's your preference. Layer the meatballs evenly across the soup and not on top of each other. Once all the meatballs are in the pot, bring to a boil, then turn the heat down to medium and cover with a lid. Cook for 5 to 8 minutes, until the pork is cooked through. Season the broth with ¼ teaspoon salt, the soy sauce, and sesame oil. Stir to incorporate. Taste and add extra salt if needed. If you're adding vermicelli noodles, drain them, add them to the soup now, and cook for 1 to 2 minutes, just until soft.

To serve, ladle the soup into a large bowl and garnish with scallions. Serve with rice on the side (or, alternatively, serve the soup in a shallow bowl over the rice).

MEATBALLS

1 pound (455 g) ground pork

1 scallion, finely minced

1 egg

1 tablespoon soy sauce

1 tablespoon Shaoxing wine

1 tablespoon toasted sesame oil

1 teaspoon oyster sauce

1 tablespoon cornstarch

⅓ cup (25 g) panko breadcrumbs

¼ teaspoon salt

¼ teaspoon sugar

1 pinch of powdered ginger

1 pinch of ground white pepper

SOUP

2 teaspoons neutral oil

5 eggs, whisked

Salt

8 medium-size dried shrimp, soaked in cold water for 10 minutes, or until soft

3 bias-cut slices ginger (⅛ inch / 3 mm thick and 2 inches / 5 cm long)

6 cups (1.4 ml) chicken stock

⅓ cup (45 g) chopped preserved mustard stem (zhà cài, see page 285)

4 cups (280 g) sliced napa cabbage

2 tablespoons soy sauce

2 tablespoons toasted sesame oil

⅓ cup (20 g) julienned scallions

OPTIONAL ADDITIONS

Chili oil (homemade, page 274, or store-bought)

Mung bean vermicelli noodles, soaked for 20 minutes, or until softened

Steamed white rice, for serving

PLAIN CONGEE, AKA WHITE PORRIDGE

白粥
BÁI ZHŌU

Serves 4

PETER: For me, bái zhōu (white porridge) is as essential in the Chinese diet as steamed rice. It's often enjoyed as a light breakfast paired with affordable sides such as salted duck egg, pickled vegetables, salted peanuts, yóu tiáo (Chinese fried savory donuts, see page 290), or fermented bean curd (fǔ rǔ). The vast variety of possible toppings is what makes zhōu so enjoyable. It's also a very comforting, clean meal when you don't want to go too heavy on dinner, so you can enjoy a better night's rest (at my age, eating late at night is tough on the body). In the recipe below I start with raw rice to make a thick congee, but when I am pressed for time, I make pào fàn (see page 156), poaching cooked leftover rice in hot boiling water for 5 to 10 minutes, resulting in a more diluted, gruel-like consistency.

---

1 cup (185 g) jasmine rice

In a large pot, bring 10 cups (2.35 L) water to a boil over high heat. Add the rice, stir, and when the water returns to a boil, reduce the heat to low and cover with a lid. Simmer over the lowest heat for 40 minutes, occasionally stirring to prevent the rice from sticking on the bottom. Once the rice is soft and has the consistency of runny oatmeal, remove from the heat, let sit for 5 minutes, then serve.

CONGEE PARTY!: For tips on throwing a DIY Congee Party, see page 276.

PÀO FÀN

KATHY: Pào fàn, or poached rice, is my favorite way to refab leftover soup and cooked rice into a delicious, economical, easy five-minute meal. Take, for example, the curry chicken soup on page 135. The recipe makes quite a bit of broth, and after a few days, you may tire of sipping it as a soup.

The basic formula for pào fàn is simple: You'll need 1 part cooked white rice and 2 parts cooking liquid (or even 3 parts, if you want it even more liquidy). Combine the rice and liquid or broth in a medium pot. Bring to a boil and cook for 5 to 10 minutes, until it resembles congee or thin oatmeal. If you have some leftover stir-fried dish, chop it into smaller pieces and throw that into the pot in the last couple of minutes of cooking. If not, you could crack an egg into the pot, or add some minced greens.

If you want to up your pào fàn game, you can cook the rice in the pot without any liquid until the bottom of the rice toasts up into a crispy crust. Then add boiling water to the pot and boil the rice and liquid together for 2 minutes. Turn the heat off and let it sit, uncovered, for 5 minutes. This version of pào fàn is meant to be a palate/system cleanser after a big meal, almost like a tea made from regular steamed rice and toasted rice.

COUNTRY RICE CHOWDER WITH CORN, PEAS, AND PORK

玉米青豆猪肉咸泡饭
YÙ MǏ QĪNG DÒU ZHŪ RÒU XIÁN PÀO FÀN

Serves 1 to 2

KATHY: This country rice chowder was inspired by my Aunt Jean, who is famous in the Fang family for her xián pào fàn, or salt-poached rice. Salt-poached rice is rice simmered in water or broth with leftover vegetables and meats mixed in, resulting in a flavorful, porridge-like meal in less than five minutes. It was my aunt's favorite way to refab leftovers—and that's saying something, because Jean was the queen of leftovers. This is the aunt who had a lazy Susan on her dinner table and regularly prepared six to eight courses for all her dinners, even if they were for two people.

One look inside her fridge, and you'd realize your best move was to step away. She stored everything in ceramic or glass because she was paranoid about plastic giving you cancer (yet she covered all her dishes with plastic wrap . . .), and if you tried to bring her something, she'd scold you for trying to be helpful because every dish has its own place in this world of leftover-food Jenga. One bad move and all of her dishes from past and present would come tumbling out of the fridge, like the boulder chase scene from *Raiders of the Lost Ark*.

So, yes, this chowder is an ode to my aunt Jean, who showed me that leftover rice could become a delicious savory porridge. When I created this dish on the fly at House of Nanking, it was an off-menu item for a customer who just had her teeth extracted. She loved it so much, she asked if she could come back and order it again. This is how so many of our menu items are created—based on customer requests and feedback.

---

1 cup (160 g) leftover steamed white rice

1 cup (235 ml) chicken broth, plus more as needed

¼ cup (35 g) frozen corn

¼ cup (35 g) frozen peas

4 ounces (½ cup / 115 g) ground pork (or substitute ground turkey, ground chicken, ground beef, or even ground lamb)

1 teaspoon hoisin sauce

1 teaspoon Chinkiang vinegar

⅛ teaspoon ground white pepper

⅛ teaspoon cornstarch

1 tablespoon neutral oil

2 cloves garlic, thinly sliced

1 thin, coin-size slice of ginger, julienned

1 egg

½ teaspoon salt

1 tablespoon chili oil (homemade, page 274, or store-bought), for garnish

Mom's Gold Label XO Sauce (page 272), for garnish (optional)

1 scallion, chopped

In a small pot, combine the rice, broth, corn, and peas and bring to a boil over high heat. Reduce the heat to medium and let it simmer while you work on the pork.

In a small bowl, combine the pork, hoisin, vinegar, white pepper, and cornstarch. Heat the neutral oil in a small nonstick skillet over high heat. Add the garlic, ginger, and pork and stir-fry for 2 minutes, or until the pork is fully cooked, using your spatula to break up the meat. Remove from the heat and set aside.

Crack the egg directly into the pot with the rice mixture, stirring rapidly in a circular motion to beat the egg into the rice and broth until a thick, gruel-like consistency forms. Season with the salt and continue to stir for 30 seconds over medium heat. The consistency should resemble a slightly runnier version of risotto—if it's too thick, you can dilute it with ¼ cup (60 ml) water or chicken broth and stir again. Transfer to a shallow soup bowl, top with the cooked pork, drizzle with chili oil or XO sauce, if using, and garnish with scallions. Serve immediately.

CHICKEN AND SALTED PORK CONGEE

咸肉鸡粥
XIÁN RÒU JĪ ZHŌU

Serves 4

KATHY: Nothing goes to waste in a Chinese household, especially in our family. The poaching liquid from white cut chicken (page 213) has great chicken flavor, so we never throw it out. My a niáng always had Virginia ham in her fridge—it was her back pocket weapon, and just a few pieces of magic ham sprinkled into a soup, congee, or rice dish would result in an impossibly delicious meal. I typically don't have Virginia ham in my arsenal, so my replacement is pancetta, which I find in my fridge quite often.

¾ cup (140 g) medium- or long-grain white rice

7 cups (1.7 L) poaching liquid from Cold Poached Chicken (page 213) or chicken stock

½ cup (115 g) diced pancetta

Leftover Soy-Scallion Sauce from Cold Poached Chicken (page 213; optional), or substitute any of the sauces listed below

2 tablespoons julienned ginger

OPTIONAL TOPPINGS

Leftover shredded white cut chicken (page 213)

Crushed toasted peanuts

Chili crisp

Chinatown Chili Black Bean Sauce (page 275)

Chopped cilantro leaves

Chopped mint leaves

Julienned scallions

Julienned ginger

Soft-boiled egg

Rinse the rice under cold water until the water runs clear. Place the rice in a bowl and cover it with water, then allow to soak for 15 minutes. Drain the rice, then place it in a large pot along with the poaching liquid. Bring to a boil over high heat and boil for 2 minutes. Add the pancetta, reduce the heat to low, and simmer with the lid on but slightly ajar to let steam escape for 40 minutes. Divide into soup bowls, drizzle with soy-scallion sauce, if using, and garnish with julienned ginger and whatever toppings you desire.

LOTUS ROOT, RED BEAN, AND GLUTINOUS RICE CONGEE

莲藕红豆糯米粥
LIÁN ǑU HÓNG DÒU NUÒ MǏ ZHŌU

Serves 4

PETER: My family would never waste the liquid that is left over from boiling lotus root stuffed with glutinous rice (page 290). Instead, we use it to make one of my favorite types of congee. Served hot, it can be the starch component of a meal; consider serving it with pickles and cold dishes such as Marinated Chinese Celtuce Stem in Scallion Oil (page 59) or Spicy Garlic Cucumbers (page 61). Or, you can serve it hot or cold as a dessert: Encourage your guests to season the congee with sugar or honey to taste. Lotus root and red beans are known to increase iron and promote blood flow, so a bowl of this congee is very nutritious. It's a win-win: We don't waste anything and create a beautiful bowl of food from it that can feed the family.

NOTE: We would always use whatever leftover soaked rice we have from lotus root stuffed with glutinous rice. If it is less than ½ cup (100 g), it's fine to add unsoaked glutinous rice to make up the difference.

½ cup (100 g) dried red beans, aka adzuki beans, soaked in cold water for 6 hours

10 cups (2.4 L) cooking water from Glutinous Rice–Stuffed Lotus Root with Osmanthus Flower Syrup (page 72)

½ cup (100 g) glutinous rice, soaked in cold water for 2 hours (see Note)

In a large pot, combine the beans and cooking water from Glutinous Rice–Stuffed Lotus Root. (If you don't have 10 cups / 2.4 L] left over, top with tap water to reach 10 cups [2.4 L].) Bring to a boil over high heat, then reduce the heat to medium, give the beans a stir, cover with a lid, and simmer for 30 minutes, or until it reaches the consistency of porridge or oatmeal. Add the rice to the pot, increase the heat to high, and bring to a boil. Once boiling, reduce the heat to low, cover with a lid, and simmer for an additional 45 minutes, stirring every 10 to 15 minutes to prevent sticking. Remove from the heat and let it sit for 15 minutes before serving.

VEGET

KATHY: For some, San Francisco Chinatown's produce market is a sensory overload. The narrow aisles buzz with shoppers jockeying for space and vendors calling out prices in rapid-fire Cantonese. Vibrant greens, deep purples, and bright oranges greet you at every turn. Handwritten cardboard signs in bold Chinese characters hang above mounds of unfamiliar vegetables, accompanied only by hastily scrawled dollar signs. There's not a word of English in sight.

It can be an intimidating space for newcomers, but for me? This was my childhood playground. I grew up weaving through these crowded aisles, trailing behind my father and grandparents, sometimes visiting these markets two or three times a day. My father would confidently stride into the fray, skipping the line, shouting orders over the crowd to expertly select produce. He'd walk out with a casual "Put it on my tab!" thrown over his shoulder. This chaotic, colorful world of Chinese vegetables was my normal, and my connection to a culinary heritage as diverse as it is delicious.

China's vast geography, from subtropical regions to arid plateaus, has given rise to an incredible array of indigenous vegetables. Did you know that China cultivates more than three hundred varieties of vegetables? From familiars such as bok choy and Chinese broccoli to bitter melon and lotus root, each vegetable tells a story of its native region and the ingenuity of Chinese farmers and cooks.

Then there's tofu, a chameleon of the culinary world, which has been a staple of Chinese cuisine for more than two thousand years. Legend has it that tofu was accidentally discovered by a Chinese cook who curdled soy milk with nigari, the salt that is precipitated from seawater. Today, there are dozens of tofu products, from silken tofu soft as custard to tofu skin as thin as paper, each with its unique culinary applications.

We decided to group our vegetable and tofu dishes together into one chapter, since more and more people are moving toward plant-based diets. Although House of Nanking is not a vegetarian restaurant, we've become known for our exceptional vegetable dishes—and Chinese cuisine, with its long tradition of celebrating vegetables and tofu, offers a treasure trove of delicious, satisfying plant-based dishes. Whether you're a longtime lover of Chinese vegetables or a curious newcomer, I hope these recipes will inspire you to explore the vibrant, delicious world of Chinese produce and brave those markets.

#ABLES & TOFU

EXPLORING
CHINATOWN'S
GREEN
TREASURES

NANKING'S DRY-FRIED GREEN BEANS

干煸四季豆
GĀN BIĀN SÌ JÌ DÒU

Serves 2 to 4

NOTE: This version has been updated for the home kitchen, since you can't get the high heat of our restaurant on your home stove. Use haricots verts instead of blue lake beans, as they are more slender and easier to cook on a home stove.

PETER: When I first opened House of Nanking, many of our most popular dishes were exclusively vegetarian. You might read this and think, *Wow, the chef must really love vegetables.* The truth is, I don't like most vegetables. There are only a handful I enjoy, and most are things I grew up with in Shanghai that you can't find in the States. Gān biān sì jì dòu is an exception: I quite enjoy dry-fried green beans when done well. But there are two rules if you want to cook this dish successfully: (1) use the best-quality green beans you can find, and (2) time everything perfectly during the cooking process. If you don't get either of these two things right, the dish becomes below average, with stringy, lifeless beans.

When I discovered an heirloom variety called blue lake green beans at the market, they quickly became my favorite. I told my supplier to call me whenever these slender, tender beans—stiff, but with a little flexibility—were available. I'd comb through the entire box and send back any beans that had bruised skin, or were limp and didn't have a clean, easy snap.

Once I was sure of the beans' quality, the cooking would begin. I deep-fried the beans until they were 80 percent of the way cooked, then finished them in the wok with garlic and seasonings, which creates the powerful smell of garlic being caramelized in soy. Dry-frying (which we sometimes call "dry-braising") allows this fragrant sauce to penetrate the skin of the beans so they absorb flavor. My customers loved these beans so much, they would order them plus a bowl of rice and be set. That always made me so happy. At Nanking, even the simplest, most affordable side dish can become a major star.

- 1½ tablespoons soy sauce
- 1½ teaspoons dark soy sauce
- ½ teaspoon sugar
- ½ teaspoon MSG, plus more for finishing
- 1 teaspoon chili flakes
- 1 tablespoon minced garlic
- 1 cup (240 ml) neutral oil, for frying
- 12 ounces (340 g) trimmed haricots verts, cut in half and patted very dry
- Fine sea salt, for finishing
- Steamed white rice, for serving (optional)

In a small bowl, whisk together the soy sauce, dark soy sauce, sugar, MSG, chili flakes, minced garlic, and 1½ teaspoons water. Pour the neutral oil into a wok and heat over high heat until smoking. Add the haricots verts and set a timer for 2 minutes and 20 seconds. Fry the haricots verts, keeping them moving by using a spatula to scoop the beans from the bottom to the top to ensure they all get even exposure to the bottom of the wok. After 2 minutes and 20 seconds, the haricots verts should be tender but still have a bit of raw snap to them (call them 80 percent cooked). Turn off the heat and immediately use a spider to transfer the haricots verts to a bowl. Carefully pour all the oil out of the wok (if you'd like, you can store it in a glass bowl and use as cooking oil). Return the wok to high heat—there will be a bit of residual oil, which is okay. Once the wok begins to smoke, return the haricots verts to the wok and pour the sauce over them. Stir-fry for 2 minutes, continually bringing the beans from the bottom to the top so the beans touch the wok surface over and over, until the beans still have a little crunch but are also soft. In the last 30 seconds, season with sea salt.

Although many of my customers say they taste good cold, straight out of the takeout box from the fridge, I believe the best-tasting gān biān sì jì dòu must be enjoyed HOT, right out of the wok. If you let the beans sit and get to room temp, they shrivel a bit and lose moisture. So, serve hot as a side dish, or over a plate of steamed white rice for a simple meal.

NANKING'S SZECHUAN EGGPLANT

鱼香茄子
YÚ XIĀNG QIÉ ZI

Serves 4

NOTE: When sourcing eggplants, make sure to choose ones that are deep dark purple and firm to the touch. If you are a fan of our restaurant, you will notice that the cut and shape of the eggplant in this version is a little different. At the restaurant, we are able to cook over very high heat—much hotter than you can achieve at home. This means we can stir-fry larger pieces of eggplant and keep them juicy without becoming mushy. At home, you will have to cut the eggplant into thinner strips because your stove cannot get hot enough to cook through the larger cuts.

PETER: The alternate title for this recipe is "My Fortuitous Garlic Eggplant," because this is the dish that gave me my lucky break at the restaurant, the day I was visited by Peter Kaufman and Jiang Xiaozhen. Ms. Jiang is the daughter of Bai Yang, the most famous female movie star in China in the 1930s and '40s, and Peter is the son of famous film director and producer Philip Kaufman. I had no idea who they were when they walked in. When they sat down, Ms. Jiang told me her nose led them to me, and upon chatting, we found a connection. Both Ms. Jiang and I are from Shanghai, and anytime you find a fellow Shanghainese person, you feel this instant happiness, like you've found a long-lost friend. I was so excited to cook for them, especially for Ms. Jiang. I knew she missed the bold flavors from home, so I whipped up "fish-fragrant" yú xiāng eggplant. The dish does not have fish in it, but the name describes the savory, sweet, sour, and spicy flavors. At the restaurant we call it Szechuan or garlic eggplant to make it easier and less confusing for vegetarians. When she took a bite, Ms. Jiang said it brought her back to Shanghai. A week later, she and Peter brought Patricia Unterman, San Francisco's most famous food critic, to Nanking, who then wrote me an incredible review in the Sunday paper. The lines started that day and never stopped.

This is one of those dishes where the sheer power of the wok is what makes our eggplant so amazing. It is hard to re-create that type of extremely high-heat cooking at home (see page 44), so this recipe has been modified (see Note) for the home kitchen to achieve similar results.

- 2 Chinese eggplants (just under 2 pounds / 910 g; see Note)
- 1½ teaspoons salt
- 1 tablespoon Chinkiang vinegar
- 1 tablespoon dark soy sauce
- 2 teaspoons cane sugar
- 1 teaspoon soy sauce
- 1 teaspoon chili flakes
- 1 teaspoon MSG
- 1 teaspoon cornstarch
- 2 tablespoons neutral oil
- 5 cloves garlic, minced
- 2 scallions, chopped
- 5 dried whole red chilis
- Julienned scallions, for garnish (optional)
- Steamed white rice and Nanking's Veggie Wontons (page 92), for serving (optional)

Using a peeler, remove 75 percent of the eggplants' skin, leaving behind some purple streaks. Slice away and discard the top of the eggplants, then cut them into thin batons about 3½ inches (9 cm) in length and ¾ inch (2 cm) in width. Place the batons in a large bowl and season with the salt. Toss to incorporate and let it sit for 1 hour.

Meanwhile, prep the sauce. In a small bowl, whisk together the vinegar, dark soy sauce, sugar, soy sauce, chili flakes, MSG, cornstarch and 2 tablespoons water. Set aside.

Rinse the salt off the eggplant, then soak it in water for 1 minute. Pour out the water and repeat one more time. Drain the eggplant and pat dry with paper towels.

Heat a wok over high heat, add the neutral oil, and swirl the wok to coat. Once the oil is smoking, add the garlic and scallion, stir-fry for 2 seconds, then immediately add the eggplant. Cook, tossing the eggplant from bottom to top, until the eggplant begins to develop a light brown char on some of the edges and is soft enough to poke a chopstick through without difficulty, about 4 minutes. Pour the sauce and red chilis over the eggplant and wok toss the eggplant over and over until the sauce thickens and glazes the eggplant, about 1 minute. Garnish with scallions, if desired, and serve as a side or with white rice and veggie wontons, if desired, as a main.

NANKING'S GARLIC BABY PEA SHOOTS

蒜蓉小豆苗
SUÀN RÓNG XIǍO DÒU MIÁO (SYUN YÙHNG SÍU DAUH MÌUH)

Serves 2

NOTE: Jacobson black garlic salt adds umami to vegetables. My daughter, Kathy, turned me onto it and it has eliminated the need for me to reach for chicken bouillon or MSG for some simpler dishes.

PETER: In my memory, all the vegetables in Shanghai were exceptional—maybe because they were organic and only available seasonally. The pea shoots in Shanghai are particularly good. I always wanted to add pea shoots to the menu at Nanking, but the ones I found in the US were so tough compared to what I was used to in China. Lily would try to find tender ones at the market, but I would always tell her "No way, don't buy it . . . One bite of that and you will choke trying to swallow that tough plant down your throat."

Eventually I decided to use small dòu miáo, baby pea shoots that are the tender young tips of the pea plant. I first started making it the traditional Shanghainese way, where it comes out of the wok glistening in an oily garlic sheen. My customers found it to be too greasy and sweet; they said they couldn't taste the freshness of the pea shoots. So I dialed everything down and went much lighter on the oil. After that change, people loved it. They'd say, "These are the best baby pea shoots I've ever had; I can taste the vegetables and it feels so healthy!" At one point we sold so many pea shoots that our produce supplier allotted all their pea shoots just for us. We would get cases delivered to us a twice a day, every day, just to keep up with demand.

- 1½ teaspoons toasted sesame oil
- 1 teaspoon minced garlic
- ⅛ teaspoon chili flakes
- 4 ounces (115 g) baby pea shoots, rinsed, with excess water shaken off
- ⅛ teaspoon sugar
- ¼ teaspoon black garlic salt (see Note)
- ⅛ teaspoon ground white pepper

Bring a medium pot filled with water to a boil over high heat. While the water is heating up, in a small pan, heat the sesame oil over medium heat, then add the garlic and chili flakes and toast for 20 seconds, just to release the flavors, but be careful not to brown the garlic. After 20 seconds, turn the heat off but leave the garlic, chili, and oil in the pan.

Once the water is boiling, have a colander or spider skimmer ready. Toss the pea shoots into the boiling water and cook for no more than 10 seconds, using a chopstick to submerge and swish the pea shoots. As soon as the pea shoots are bright green, drain them using the colander or spider. Shake off excess water—don't skip this step!—and place the pea shoots into a bowl, spreading them out a bit so they're not all clumped together. Pat the pea shoots dry with paper towels and wipe away any water in the bowl. Pour the garlic-chili oil over the pea shoots, then add the sugar, black garlic salt, and white pepper and toss using chopsticks or tongs. If tossing is a little difficult, add a little more sesame oil to make it easier. Serve immediately.

FAVORITE PAIRINGS: Steamed rice, Crispy Tofu with Peanut Sauce (page 199), Steamed Chicken Wings in Black Bean–Garlic Sauce (page 210)

GARLIC YAM LEAF TIPS

番薯苗
FĀN SHŬ MIÁO
(FĀAN SYÚ MÌUH)

Serves 4

KATHY: Yam leaf is one of my favorite Asian leafy greens. Popeye had spinach; I have yam leaf. It's the most underappreciated vegetable, in my opinion. I eat yam leaf anytime I find it in the Chinese markets. It has more protein than spinach, double the amount of fiber than kale, and the same amount of vitamin K and A as those greens. I find the texture of the yam leaf to be the most palatable and tastiest: soft, tender leaves with a crunchy stem and no bitterness. It's super easy to cook and goes with anything. When yam leaf tips are in season, between March and October, I buy two pounds for the week and consume that with my family over a span of two days. That's how much I love this vegetable.

---

2 tablespoons toasted sesame oil, plus more to taste

1 tablespoon minced garlic

2 teaspoons salt, plus more to taste

1½ teaspoons sugar, plus more to taste

½ teaspoon ground white pepper

12 ounces (340 g) yam leaf tips

Bring a medium pot filled with 3 to 4 cups (710 to 945 ml) water about three-quarters of the way to a boil over high heat. Season the water with the sesame oil, garlic, salt, sugar, and white pepper. Stir to incorporate. Once the water reaches a boil, add the yam leaf tips and cook for just 1 minute, then remove them with a spider. Shake off excess water. Taste before serving: If you prefer a little more seasoning, give it a pinch of salt and sugar and drizzle on more sesame oil. Toss and serve!

SERVING TIP: Serve with a protein of your choice and some steamed white rice. One classic Cantonese pairing would be to serve it with Grandpa Fang's Perfect "Steamed" Whole Fish (page 256) and a side of steamed white rice. You can't get any more authentic in flavors and dinner spread than this.

SILK SQUASH WITH DRIED SHRIMP

丝瓜炒虾米
SĪ GUĀ CHǍO XIĀ MI

Serves 2 to 4

NOTE: If you can't find silk squash, zucchini will work beautifully as an alternative—cut it slightly smaller, into 1-inch pieces, since it won't shrink as much as the silk squash during cooking.

KATHY: Silk squash, also known as luffa squash, is a dark green squash that, when aged and dried, can be turned into an actual sponge—hence the name *luffa* (aka *loofah*). When raw, the flesh of the squash feels like foam, but when cooked, it has a soft and silky texture, which gives it its other name. Silk squash absorbs flavor and sauces well, but because of its mild flavor, it's best to use mild seasonings, to highlight and enhance the natural flavors of the vegetable. When cooked well, the squash will provide a juicy, silky, buttery mouthfeel. It's no surprise this vegetable was an instant hit when my a niáng prepared it for me. My a niáng loved using dried shrimp in her vegetable dishes and soups, which add a layer of umami (xiān wèi) .

- 2½ pounds (1.2 kg) silk squash (2 long pieces), see Note
- 2 tablespoons neutral oil
- 2 tablespoons minced ginger
- 1 tablespoon minced garlic
- 10 pieces small dried shrimp, soaked in cold water for 5 minutes then drained
- ¼ cup (60 ml) Shaoxing wine
- ¼ cup (60 ml) chicken stock or water
- 1 teaspoon sugar
- ½ teaspoon salt
- 2 tablespoons cornstarch whisked with 2 tablespoons water into a slurry
- 1 tablespoon toasted sesame oil

Cut both ends off the squash and slice in half crosswise, then use a vegetable peeler to peel it. (Because of its length, it's easier to peel after it's been cut in half.) Cut the squash on the diagonal (aka roll cut) into 2-inch (5 cm) pieces. Heat a wok over high heat, add the neutral oil, and swirl to coat the wok evenly. When the oil begins to smoke, add the ginger, garlic, and soaked shrimp and stir-fry for 1 minute, or until fragrant. Add the silk squash and stir-fry for 2 minutes to evenly coat the squash with ginger, garlic, and dried shrimp. In a small bowl, whisk to combine the Shaoxing wine, chicken stock, sugar, and salt. Pour it into the wok and stir-fry over high heat for 1 minute, to thoroughly coat the squash. Cover with a lid, reduce the heat to medium, and simmer for 2 minutes, or until the squash is soft, juicy, and easily pierced with a fork. Increase the heat to high and, stirring continuously, pour in half the cornstarch slurry in a circular motion to distribute it throughout the dish. Keep stirring until the sauce thickens, adding more slurry as needed. Finish with the sesame oil, then serve.

BABY NAPA CABBAGE WITH DRIED ANCHOVY, GINGER, AND CHILI

小鱼干炒娃娃菜
XIĂO YÚ GĀN CHĂO WÁ WA CÀI

Serves 2 to 4

KATHY: Baby napa cabbage (often called "wawa choy") is, as the name suggests, a smaller version of napa cabbage. The leaves are tighter and more crinkled, and the stems have a tender, delightful crisp when cooked right. Overall, it's a sweeter-tasting cabbage than its larger counterpart. It's great in stir-fries, where you can really appreciate its flavor and texture. (By contrast, I recommend the larger varietal when filling wontons or egg rolls or making a soup, as the taste difference will be negligible if it's minced up or cooked until soft.) Every home-cooked Chinese meal has a simple vegetable dish, and I created this one as a light, healthy way to highlight the natural flavors of the cabbage.

- 1 tablespoon neutral oil
- 6 dried anchovies
- 2 thin slices of ginger, julienned
- 1 red Thai bird chili, minced (optional)
- 2 small baby napa cabbage (wawa choy), quartered crosswise, stem ends removed
- ¼ cup (60 ml) aji-mirin
- ½ teaspoon dashi powder
- ½ teaspoon salt
- 1 tablespoon cornstarch whisked with 1 tablespoon water into a slurry

Heat a wok over high heat, add the neutral oil, and swirl to coat the wok. When the oil begins to smoke, add the anchovies, ginger, and chili, if using, and stir-fry for 30 seconds, or until fragrant. Add the cabbage and stir-fry for 1 minute. Add the aji-mirin and stir-fry for 1 minute, then reduce the heat to medium-low. Add the dashi powder and salt and continue to cook, stirring occasionally from bottom to top, for 4 minutes. Increase the heat to high and, stirring continuously to avoid clumping, drizzle in the slurry and cook until thickened. Serve immediately as a side.

STIR-FRIED TAIWANESE CABBAGE WITH MUNG BEAN GLASS NOODLES

粉丝炒高丽菜
FĚN SĪ CHǍO GĀO LÌ CÀI

Serves 2 to 4

PETER: Taiwanese cabbage are flatter and more oblong than the green cabbage you see in Western supermarkets, which tend to be completely round with very tight leaves wrapped around the core. The Taiwanese version is sweeter, crispier, and more tender, and I will always pick this version over the regular one. But, of course, for this recipe, you can use either cabbage. The other key ingredient in this dish is mung bean vermicelli noodles, fěn sī. These noodles cook within minutes and absorb sauces and flavors instantly. The combination of these two unlikely ingredients is such a fantastic pairing, and that is what I love about simple homestyle cooking, or what we call jiā cháng cài, which literally means "home frequent dishes."

1 tablespoon neutral oil

1 pound (455 g) Taiwanese cabbage, cut into 2-inch (5 cm) chunks

1 tablespoon peeled julienned ginger

1 tablespoon minced garlic

2 red Thai bird chilis, minced (optional, for a spicy kick)

¼ cup (60 ml) Shaoxing wine

1 teaspoon Chinkiang vinegar

1 teaspoon sugar

1 pinch of salt

1 bundle (2 ounces / 55 g) mung bean vermicelli noodles (such as Pagoda brand), soaked in cold water for 15 minutes, or until soft

2 tablespoons soy sauce

1 tablespoon toasted sesame oil

½ teaspoon dark soy sauce

1 pinch of ground white pepper

In a large wok, heat the neutral oil over high heat and swirl to coat evenly. Once the wok is smoking, add the cabbage, ginger, garlic, and chilis, if using. Stir-fry for 1 minute to evenly coat the cabbage with oil and aromatics. Add the Shaoxing wine, vinegar, sugar, and salt and stir-fry for 2 minutes. Add ¼ cup (60 ml) water to help cook down the cabbage. Once the liquid has mostly evaporated, about 3 minutes, add the noodles, soy sauce, sesame oil, dark soy sauce, and white pepper. Stir-fry to fully incorporate, about 2 minutes, then serve.

SERVING TIP: Serve this as a veggie side dish to accompany steamed rice and a protein, such as mapo tofu (page 224). To turn this into a main dish, add ground pork and la doubanjiang (page 287) before adding the cabbage—now you've got yourself a modified version of another traditional Chinese dish called ants on a tree (mǎ yǐ shàng shù). You can also add pre-soaked dried shrimp when you add the ginger, garlic, and chili to add a more pungent flavor to this simple dish.

SPICY PICKLED LONG BEANS WITH GROUND TURKEY

酸豆角炒火鸡肉末
SUĀN DÒU JIǍO CHǍO HUǑ JĪ RÒU MÒ

Serves 4 to 6

KATHY: My mom's dad, who I call Gōng Gong, is originally from Hunan. Hunan cuisine was quite popular when I was a kid in the late 1980s; people were drawn to the bolder flavors of spice and smoked meats, which were a big contrast to the more delicate flavors of Cantonese cuisine. But the Hunan cuisine that my mom and gōng gong cooked at home was nothing like the dishes at popular San Francisco Hunan restaurants. At home, everything was a lot spicier and a lot less saucy, loaded with dried chilis, fresh chilis, garlic, and scallions. Mom and Gōng Gong's flavor profiles were in the spicy, savory realm with occasional sour notes—a departure from the sweet and soy sauce–inflected Shanghainese cuisine my dad's side of the family cooked up. This dish is full of spicy, sour, salty, and umami flavors, and when I was pregnant with my first child, the sour notes hit my cravings big time, so I would keep a jar in the fridge at the restaurant and wrap the cold, spicy pickled long beans in a tortilla for a quick work snack.

The addition of goji berries is my mom's twist and not typical. The small pops of sweetness made the dish a little more manageable for me when I was younger. She would do the same with her chili chicken stir-fry, using Chinese jujubes to balance out the spice. This is how, bit by bit, my mom got me addicted to spice as a kid.

- 1 pound (455 g) ground turkey
- 2 teaspoons toasted sesame oil
- 2 teaspoons cornstarch
- 1 teaspoon Maggi sauce
- 1 teaspoon Shaoxing wine
- 1 teaspoon dark soy sauce
- ½ teaspoon salt
- ½ teaspoon sugar
- 2 tablespoons neutral oil
- 2 tablespoons minced garlic
- 1 teaspoon minced ginger
- 12 ounces (340 g) Chinese pickled long beans, homemade (page 266) or store-bought, drained and chopped
- 1 to 3 red Thai bird chilis, chopped
- ½ cup (30 g) chopped scallions
- ⅓ cup (40 g) dried goji berries, soaked in water for 1 minute before cooking
- ⅛ teaspoon ground white pepper
- 1 teaspoon Chinkiang vinegar
- Steamed white rice, Plain Congee (page 156), or Yáng Chūn Noodle Soup (page 142), for serving

In a medium bowl, combine the ground turkey, sesame oil, cornstarch, Maggi sauce, Shaoxing wine, dark soy sauce, salt, and sugar. Stir with chopsticks or a fork to integrate the seasonings and set aside.

Heat a wok over high heat until smoking, then add 1 tablespoon of the neutral oil and swirl the wok to evenly coat the cook surface. Once the wok begins to smoke again, add the garlic, ginger, and ground turkey. Stir-fry for about 2 minutes, breaking up the meat as it cooks, until the turkey is 80 percent done (it will still be slightly pink inside). Transfer the contents of the wok to a plate, then add the remaining 1 tablespoon neutral oil and wait for it to smoke again. Add the pickled long beans, chili, scallions, and goji berries. Stir-fry for 1 minute, or until fragrant. Add the turkey, garlic, and ginger back to the wok, then season with the white pepper and vinegar. Stir-fry for 2 minutes to develop deeper flavors. Serve with steamed white rice, congee, or yáng chūn miàn. Store any leftovers in the fridge for up to 5 days.

NOTE: If you can't find Chinese pickled long beans, use diced pepperoncini instead.

SAUTEED ASPARAGUS, LILY BULBS, AND GOJI BERRIES IN GARLIC SAUCE

蒜蓉炒芦笋百合枸杞子
SUÀN RÓNG CHǍO LÚ SǓN BǍI HÉ GǑU QǏ ZǏ

Serves 4

PETER: This is a very classic stir-fried vegetable dish in China, but it is not commonly found in the States. The star of the dish is the fresh lily bulbs, which I started finding vacuum-sealed in Chinatown markets only in the past decade or so. The first time I saw them, I knew I had to buy some for my wife, Lily, who eats more vegetables than any human I know. All the produce vendors in Chinatown know her and call her louh bāan ("boss lady"). They love her because she will buy even the most expensive vegetables. Me, on the other hand? I'm always looking for a deal before I'm inclined to try.

Dried lily bulbs have been available in the US for a while and can only be used for soups. Fresh lily bulbs, by contrast, can be stir-fried lightly to reveal a delicious sweet, crunchy, slightly starchy taste. They can even be used as a low-carb replacement for steamed rice. This recipe is the way my wife prepares lily bulbs: The goji berries bring out the natural sweetness of the lily bulbs and pair beautifully with tender asparagus. If you want a classic Chinese vegetable stir-fry that you can't find at most American Chinese restaurants, try this out!

- 2 ounces (55 g) fresh lily bulbs
- ¼ teaspoon dashi powder
- ¼ teaspoon salt
- ¼ teaspoon sugar
- ¼ teaspoon ground white pepper
- 12 ounces (340 g) asparagus
- 1 tablespoon neutral oil
- 1 tablespoon minced garlic
- 2 tablespoons dried goji berries, soaked in water for 5 minutes then drained
- 1 tablespoon Shaoxing wine
- 1 tablespoon cornstarch whisked with 1 tablespoon water to make a slurry, if needed
- 1 teaspoon toasted sesame oil

Peel the lily petals off the bulb. Wash the petals well so no dirt remains, then place them in a medium bowl and cover with water. Let soak for 10 minutes. Drain the lily petals and set aside.

In a small bowl, mix the dashi powder, salt, sugar, and white pepper. Set aside.

Trim the bottom 1 inch (2.5 cm) off the asparagus use a peeler to shave off any tough ends. Slice the asparagus, leaving the tip whole, into 1-inch (2.5 cm) bias-cut pieces.

Bring a large pot of water to a boil. Blanch the asparagus for 1½ minutes, or until it's bright green, then drain and rinse under cold water to cool. Set aside.

Heat a wok over high heat until smoking, then add the neutral oil and swirl to evenly coat the wok. Add the garlic and stir-fry for 5 seconds, then add the lily bulb and goji berries and stir-fry for 1 minute. Add the Shaoxing wine and stir-fry for another minute. Add the asparagus and dry seasonings and stir-fry for 1 minute to fully incorporate. If there is liquid in the bottom of the wok, add a touch of slurry to thicken the sauce. If there is no liquid, turn off the heat, drizzle in the sesame oil, and give it toss, then serve immediately.

SAUTEED ASPARAGUS WITH BLACK BEAN SAUCE

豆豉炒芦笋
DÒU CHǏ CHǍO LÚ SǓN

Serves 2

PETER: When I immigrated to the US, I was exposed to many vegetables that I had never tasted back in China. I remember hearing about asparagus in Shanghai, but it was expensive, hard to get, and mostly cultivated for Westerners. The first time I had asparagus, it reminded me of a type of bamboo shoot with a clean, sweet finish and crunch. I knew I had to use it at Nanking. Every year, I would wait until it came into season and pick out the ones that were firm to touch but snap easily and cleanly without the fibrous veins. I would do a simple stir-fry with black beans, fresh chilis, onion, and garlic. My customers loved it.

- 12 ounces (340 g) asparagus
- 1½ teaspoons hoisin sauce
- 1½ teaspoons oyster sauce
- 1 teaspoon Chinkiang vinegar
- ½ teaspoon sugar
- ½ teaspoon salt
- 1½ teaspoons neutral oil
- 2 garlic cloves, minced
- 2 tablespoons fermented dried black beans
- ¼ medium red onion, thinly sliced
- 1 tablespoon Shaoxing wine
- 1 teaspoon chili oil (homemade, page 274, or store-bought)

Snap off the tough bottom ends from the asparagus. Using a vegetable peeler, shave off the exterior of the remaining bottom 1 inch (2.5 cm) to expose the tender center. Cut the peeled asparagus on the bias into 2½-inch (6 cm) lengths.

In a small bowl, whisk together the hoisin sauce, oyster sauce, vinegar, sugar, salt, and ¼ cup (60 ml) water and set aside.

Heat a wok over high heat and add the neutral oil. When smoking, swirl to coat the wok. Add the garlic, black beans, and red onion, stir-fry for 5 seconds, then add the asparagus. Wok toss the ingredients and stir-fry for 1 minute, or until fragrant. Add the Shaoxing wine and continue to stir-fry for 1 minute. Add the reserved sauce and stir-fry for 4 minutes, or until the sauce begins to evaporate and coat the asparagus. Drizzle the chili oil over the asparagus, give it one last toss in the wok, then transfer to a serving plate.

SERVING TIP: To turn this into a main dish, add 4 ounces (115 g) of ground Italian sausage when you add the garlic and black beans and serve over rice.

MASHED FAVA BEANS WITH PRESERVED MUSTARD GREENS

咸菜蚕豆
XIÁN CÀI CÁN DÒU

Serves 4

NOTE: Grandma Fang used frozen skinned broad beans (aka fava beans) for this dish, because she'd consider it a waste to mash up fresh young fava beans. If you do want to use fresh, deshelled fava beans, I recommend stir-frying them rather than boiling them. Grandma Fang would say don't mash them, in that case.

KATHY: The first time Grandma Fang placed a plate of mashed fava beans on the dinner table (which, incidentally, was right in front of a TV blasting Chinese soap operas—the TV was always on at Grandma Fang's house), I remember thinking to myself, *Wow, how did she make these mashed potatoes green?!*

In my world as a kid, the mashed potatoes from KFC—you know, the ones served in a Styrofoam cup with a plastic lid—were the ultimate treat, something we'd get once or twice a year and always made me feel so American. The mashed potatoes were even better to me than the corn on the cob, biscuits, and fried chicken, because texturally, they were so unusual. There's really no mashed or pureed equivalent in the Chinese meals I grew up eating.

That is until I tried Grandma Fang's fava beans with a glistening drizzle of sesame oil on top, which made me think of melted butter sitting on top of potatoes. I dug in and I couldn't believe it. My grandma had channeled the texture of mashed potatoes but delivered it in a Shanghainese form, with more complex flavors including umami, a slight sweetness, salt, and richness from the sesame oil. What's even cooler about this dish is that it's just as tasty eaten cold, directly out of the fridge. It almost tastes like a chunky hummus with bold Asian flavors. It's a two-for-one deal!

---

1 pound (455 g) frozen fava beans (aka broad beans; see Note)

4 ounces (115 g) xián cài (salted mustard greens or cabbage leaf)

2 tablespoons toasted sesame oil, plus more for drizzling on top

1 tablespoon chili oil (homemade, page 274, or store-bought)

⅛ teaspoon ground white pepper

1 pinch of salt

1 pinch of MSG

In a large nonstick or saute pan, bring 1¼ cups (300 ml) water to a boil over high heat. Add the frozen fava beans and boil for 3 minutes, or until the favas are softened and mashable. Drain the favas, then use the flat part of a wooden spoon to mash them to a chunky consistency. Add the xián cài, sesame oil, chili oil, white pepper, salt, and MSG, return to high heat, and stir. Cook for an additional 3 minutes, stirring to fully incorporate the flavors and the greens. If the mixture looks too chalky and dry, add up to ¼ cup (60 ml) water as needed to achieve a slightly chunky mashed potato texture. Transfer to a shallow bowl and serve with toasted sesame oil on top.

SERVING IDEAS

1. *For an East meets West spin, serve this as a replacement for mashed potatoes alongside roasted chicken or steak.*
2. *For a more traditional pairing, serve as a side dish with plain white congee (page 156).*
3. *Make crispy egg and fava toast with leftovers: First, drizzle extra-virgin olive oil over a piece of toast, then spread with a generous portion of cold mashed fava beans, and top with a sunny side-up fried egg. Drizzle with chili oil or top with chili crisp.*

FLOWERING CAULIFLOWER WITH CURED CHINESE PORK BELLY

腊肉松菜花
LÀ RÒU SŌNG HUĀ CÀI

Serves 2 to 4

KATHY: My dad and I love to find quiet, under-the-radar spots in Chinatown where the food is good, fresh, and affordable—and when you walk in, you feel like you're in some hole-in-the-wall restaurant in Hong Kong. New Louey Goey, located on the basement floor of a building on Jackson Street, is exactly that. It's the type of place where you never look at the menu; you just peruse the items handwritten on the wall to see if there are any specials, and subtly check to see if there have been any price changes. We've been going to New Louey Goey for twenty years, and we always get the same thing: salt and pepper sole rice plate with garlic pea shoots and salt and pepper frog with peanuts and green beans. We are creatures of habit, so you can imagine my shock when one day, Dad asked them to make our usual salt and pepper sole rice plate with sùhng choi fāa (Cantonese for "loose flower," aka flowering cauliflower) instead of pea sprouts. Going off the script? My dad gave me a nod and smile—the kind that indicates you are in for a treat.

As always, he was right. Instead of the dense, watery cauliflower I'm used to, sùhng choi fāa reminded me of Broccolini. The stems are skinny, crisp, a little sweet, but light. The florets are sparse, leaving ample gaps for sauce, garlic, chilis, and all sorts of goodies to nestle into it. This version is an ode to that first encounter with sùhng choi fāa. The flavorful florets mixed with the salty, smoky aroma of the wok hei and Chinese pork belly (laahp yuhk in Cantonese) is so good, I usually eat half of the dish out of the wok before it even makes it to the table.

---

1 tablespoon neutral oil

12 ounces (340 g) baby cauliflower or flowering cauliflower florets (see page 282), sliced in half lengthwise

¼ cup (30 g) sliced (cut crosswise into ¼-inch / 6 mm pieces) là ròu/laahp yuhk (Chinese cured bacon or pork belly, see page 281)

2 garlic cloves, minced

1 teaspoon Shaoxing wine

1 teaspoon duò jiāo (Chinese salted chopped chilis, see page 285) or sambal oelek

½ teaspoon sugar

2 pinches of salt

Heat a wok over high heat until smoking, then add the neutral oil and swirl the wok to coat. Add the cauliflower and stir-fry for 1 minute. Add the cured pork belly and garlic and stir-fry for 1 minute. Add the Shaoxing wine and cook for 1 minute. Add the duò jiāo, sugar, salt, and ¼ cup (60 ml) water and stir to incorporate. Stir-fry until the water evaporates and the wok is dry, then serve immediately.

VEGGIE ABC WITH EGGPLANT, MUSHROOMS, AND TOFU

茄子蘑菇炒豆腐

QIÉ ZI MÓ GU CHĂO DÒU FU

Serves 2

PETER: When I look back at the names for some of the dishes I created, I'm surprised they all worked. Growing up in Shanghai, I learned very minimal English, and when I moved to the US, I felt like I didn't know the language at all. I would have liked to take English classes, but there was no time for school. I had to just listen and figure it out.

When it came to naming dishes, I looked to Kathy's schoolbooks for inspiration, and to her for advice on menu descriptions. I figured, *She's going to school for English, she must know more than I do in this category—even if she's eight.* That's how dishes like "Veggie ABC" appeared on our Nanking menu, despite the fact that none of the main ingredients start with A, B, or C. My customers loved my famous eggplant (see page 168) but often asked if they could add tofu or sweet potato to make it more substantial. What I love about this dish is that all three ingredients play a star role. The mushrooms are perfectly cooked, juicy and still crisp, not soft, the tofu with the crispy exterior absorbs all the seasonings, while still having a soft interior bite, and the eggplant itself is juicy, soft, and full of flavor. For our signature eggplant dish we use Chinese eggplant because of the way it's sliced and cooked. But for this dish, I recommend Japanese eggplant because it's meatier, more flesh-to-skin ratio, and thus has a different mouthfeel.

---

3 cups cubed (1 inch / 2.5 cm) Japanese eggplant (from 1 pound / 455 g eggplant)

2 teaspoons salt

SAUCE

1 tablespoon minced garlic

1 tablespoon hoisin sauce

1 tablespoon duò jiāo (Chinese salted chopped chilis; see page 285) or sambal oelek (optional)

1 tablespoon soy sauce

1 tablespoon Chinkiang vinegar

1½ teaspoons dark soy sauce

1 teaspoon MSG

¼ teaspoon salt

¼ teaspoon cumin powder

1 teaspoon cornstarch whisked with 1 teaspoon water into a slurry (optional)

1 cup (240 ml) neutral oil

7 ounces (200 g) medium-firm tofu, cut into 1-inch (2.5 cm) cubes and patted dry

5 large or medium button mushrooms, quartered

3 thin, medallion-size slices of ginger, julienned

Steamed white rice, for serving

Place the eggplant in a large bowl and season with the salt, tossing to coat the eggplant well. Cover with water and let soak for 30 minutes to 1 hour.

In a small bowl, whisk together all the sauce ingredients except the slurry. Set aside.

In a wok, heat the neutral oil over high heat. Once it registers 350°F (175°C) on a deep-fry thermometer, add the tofu and fry for 5 minutes, or until golden brown. Use a spider or slotted spoon to transfer the tofu to a shallow, paper towel–lined bowl to drain.

Allow the oil to return to 350°F (175°C). Remove the eggplant from the water and pat very dry.

Working in batches so you don't crowd the wok, fry the eggplant for 3 minutes, or until easily pierced with a chopstick. Transfer to the bowl with the tofu.

Fry the mushrooms for 1 minute, then transfer to the bowl with the tofu and eggplant.

Carefully pour the hot oil into a bowl. Keep the wok over high heat, and once it begins to smoke again, add the ginger and stir-fry for 10 seconds, or until fragrant. Add the sauce to the wok and heat for 5 seconds, then return the tofu, eggplant, and mushrooms to the wok and wok toss to fully coat the ingredients and get some caramelization, about 20 seconds. If there is sauce pooling on the bottom of the wok, add the slurry to thicken. If there is no liquid left over, turn off the heat and serve with rice!

TOMATO STIR-FRIED EGG WITH EGG TOFU

番茄玉子豆腐炒蛋
FĀN QIÉ YÙ ZǏ DÒU FU CHǍO DÀN

Serves 4

PETER: Tomato stir-fried egg is a quintessential staple that almost every Chinese household will know how to make, but from what I know, the dish first began appearing in restaurants in my hometown, Shanghai, back in the early 1900s. Shanghai is very cosmopolitan, and tomato egg is certainly influenced by the West. Despite the simple ingredients, the flavor profiles are not basic by any means: You've got savory, sweet, sour, and umami notes all in one bite. And just like many home-cooked staples, there are many variations from region to region and even from family to family. Some like it sweeter, and I've found the southern version tends to be saucier (which is my preference as well), where the tomatoes are cooked down until they resemble a tomato sauce with small pieces of tomato. The eggs are scrambled till light and fluffy before being added to the sauce to simmer and absorb all flavors. As you move farther north in China, the dish becomes drier. The sliced tomatoes are stir-fried to extract flavor, but not so long as to lose their shape. There won't be much of a sauce, and you will be able to pick up a piece of tomato and eat it whole. The tomatoes are wok-tossed with scallions, seasonings, and scrambled eggs.

Both versions are delicious in their own way. In the last few years, I've cut down my rice intake and replaced it with healthy lean proteins to keep me full so I can work all day every day. I now add egg tofu into my tomato stir-fried egg to substantiate the dish.

- 2 teaspoons neutral oil
- 1 (8-ounce / 225 g) tube egg tofu (see page 281), cut into 10 slices
- 3 eggs, whisked
- 3 medium vine-ripened tomatoes, cut into wedges
- 3 bias-cut slices ginger (⅛ inch / 3 mm thick and 2 inches / 5 cm long)
- 1 tablespoon sugar
- 1 tablespoon Shaoxing wine
- 1 tablespoon tomato paste
- 1 tablespoon ketchup
- 2 teaspoons dashi powder
- 1 teaspoon salt
- 1 teaspoon soy sauce
- 2 teaspoon cornstarch whisked with 2 teaspoons water into a slurry
- ¼ cup (15 g) chopped scallions
- 2 tablespoons toasted sesame oil
- Steamed white rice, for serving

Heat a large nonstick skillet over high heat and add the neutral oil. When the pan is hot, add the egg tofu slices and pan-fry for 1 minute per side, or until a light golden color develops. Reduce the heat to medium, then pour in the whisked eggs. Tilt the skillet to allow the eggs to run and fill the empty pockets of the surface, around the pieces of egg tofu. Let cook until lightly set or scrambled, using a spatula to break the egg into chunks. Add the tomatoes and incorporate carefully, without breaking the egg tofu. In a small bowl, combine the ginger, sugar, Shaoxing wine, tomato paste, ketchup, dashi, salt, and soy sauce along with 1 cup (240 ml) water. Whisk until smooth, then pour into the pan, give it a toss, and bring to high heat. Cover with a lid and cook for 5 minutes. Remove the lid, add the cornstarch slurry to the pan while stirring with a spatula or wooden spoon, and cook until the sauce is thickened and fully incorporated, 10 to 20 seconds. Add the scallions and sesame oil, toss again to fully incorporate, and serve with steamed rice.

THE LANGUAGE OF FAMILY IN OUR KITCHEN

KATHY: If you've ever dined at House of Nanking or Fang, I'm sure you've noticed it: Our kitchen is loud. Like, really loud. There have been complaints about it over the years, and I used to feel embarrassed. But now? I realize it's just who we are.

Our kitchen language is mostly Cantonese, and if you know anything about Cantonese, you know it's not exactly a quiet language, with all of its tones and expressions. Sometimes it sounds like we're really freakin' angry, even when we're just asking to pass the salt. Throw in the typical noise from any restaurant kitchen, and yeah, it can get pretty intense.

The thing is, this "noise" is actually just the sound of our restaurant family. (At least in my experience, whenever one big family shares one small space together, things get pretty loud.) And even if it sounds like we're yelling, we're actually communicating in a way that shows the respect and care we have for one another. At our restaurants, we use terms like "a jé" (阿姐) for older female staff, which is like saying "big sis." They call me "a néui" (阿女), which basically means "daughter" and is most often used to familiarly refer to someone else's daughter. It's a way of saying "You're close enough to me that you may as well be my daughter." After fifteen years of running a grueling business, it feels good to walk into my workplace and feel like I am home.

We never sat down and planned our "company culture"; it just happened naturally, based on how my dad runs things. My dad never read any business or management books. He just works and operates the way he wants to live his life as a person. He's always taught me to hold true to a core set of values, values that are common in Chinese culture and personally significant to him, but are also pretty universal. This restaurant is his baby, and since it's a family affair with my mom and me, he runs it like he's raising a child. He's always there to groom, shape, guide, and help, switching between being tough and supportive as needed.

When the staff sees all three of us living these values and demonstrating that family unity, it rubs off on them. Back in the day, our restaurant was basically our wider family's living room, with aunts, uncles, and grandparents all dropping by to hang out. Our staff saw this, and pretty soon, their families became part of our big, noisy restaurant family, too. Maybe that's why most of the people who work here have been with us for decades, watching me grow up from a teenager to an adult (who's now running the place thirty-plus years later!).

So yeah, we're loud. But that noise? It's the sound of people who care about each other, working hard to make great food. It's the sound of family. And in my book, that's something to be proud of.

NEW-STYLE MUSHU TOFU

木须豆腐
MÙ XŪ DÒU FU

Serves 4

NOTE: At stores specializing in Chinese ingredients, you will find packets of mushu wrappers labeled "Moo-Shoo Shells." I'm not sure why they call them "shells," but this is the product you're after. Our favorite brand is Wei-Chuan.

KATHY: Mushu (or moo-shoo) pork is a quintessential dish you find at all the old-school Chinese restaurants. And what is there not to like about it? A greasy plate of pork stir-fried with cabbage, eggs, soy sauce, sugar, MSG, and onions, with pancakes to sop up all the delicious juices. It's such a popular dish, every restaurant came up with mushu chicken, shrimp, tofu, beef, all done the same way.

My dad, being the person he is, wanted to change things up. So, he took traditional mushu pork off the menu entirely and created his own mushu tofu. He fried up tofu until it was crispy and wrapped it up with raw tomatoes, scallions, lettuce, crispy peanuts, and hoisin sauce. He wanted fresh vegetables inside, rather than the greasy wilted cabbage, and he wanted a crunch factor, hence the peanuts. His inspiration for the tomatoes and lettuce came from the burrito, because mushu is essentially a Chinese burrito, minus the rice and beans. This dish really made an impact on me—texturally, it is just so good. When he created it, I was in middle school and was starting to understand a lot more about food. I was also cooking for myself and made my own breakfast, lunch, and dinner. This dish was so good, I would replicate it at home for myself. So, here's the at-home version to make for your family! (See photo on pages 200–201.)

---

2 cups (360 g) diced Roma tomatoes (from 4 or 5)

1½ tablespoons soy sauce

1 tablespoon toasted sesame oil

½ cup (75 g) honey-roasted peanuts or chen pei peanuts

Neutral oil, for deep-frying

1 (16-ounce / 455 g) pack medium-firm or firm tofu, drained, cut into 1-inch cubes, and patted dry

2 pinches of salt

2 pinches of sugar

1 pack (10 pieces) moo-shoo shells (see Note), defrosted if frozen

2 cups (110 g) shredded iceberg lettuce

½ cup (30 g) julienned scallions (green parts)

½ cup (120 ml) hoisin sauce

¼ cup (60 ml) chili oil (homemade, page 274, or store-bought)

In a medium bowl, toss the diced tomatoes with the soy sauce and sesame oil. Set aside.

Place the peanuts in a paper or ziplock bag and, using a rolling pin or mallet, crush the peanuts until they're coarsely ground. Set aside.

Fill a Dutch oven with 2 to 3 inches (5 to 7.5 cm) of oil and heat over high heat until it registers 365°F (185°C) on a deep-fry thermometer. Working in batches so you don't crowd the pan, fry the tofu, stirring occasionally to prevent the tofu from sticking together, until crispy and golden brown, about 5 minutes.

Use a spider or slotted spoon to transfer the tofu to a plate and immediately season with a pinch of salt and a pinch of sugar. Repeat with the remaining tofu.

Separate a few of the moo-shoo shells (they will likely be stuck together), just so it's easier to separate the layers after they're steamed. In a bamboo steamer over medium heat, gently steam the moo-shoo shells for 8 minutes, or until warm and softened. Wrap the shells in a damp paper towel and microwave them for 10 to 20 seconds, until warm and pliable.

To serve, set out small bowls with the marinated tomatoes, peanuts, lettuce, scallions, hoisin sauce, and chili oil. Encourage your guests to take a moo-shoo shell and spread about 1 heaping teaspoon of hoisin in the center. Top with tofu, tomatoes, lettuce, and peanuts, and drizzle with chili oil for a little kick of heat. Wrap up like a burrito and enjoy!

CRISPY TOFU WITH PEANUT SAUCE

炸豆腐配花生酱
ZHÁ DÒU FU PÈI HUĀ SHĒNG JIÀNG

Serves 2 to 4

PETER: Many of my most successful dishes work because of the sauces I create. My famous peanut sauce was originally designed to accompany fried potstickers, but I soon realized it was wonderful with pan-fried buns, onion cakes, and shrimp cakes. I knew it would work with proteins, too. Take salt and pepper tofu, a classic dish you can find at almost every Chinese restaurant. It's good, but dry, no sauce. Try eating that with steamed white rice, which is also dry. Dry on dry is not great. I had trouble watching people eat this, which is how I came up with crispy tofu drizzled with our sweet, tangy, slightly spicy peanut sauce. People loved it. Even my staff loved it. I would catch my servers as they started their shifts with a white to-go box with hot, crispy, juicy tofu in peanut sauce. They would say, "Good snack, boss!"

- 1 (14-ounce / 400 g) pack medium-firm tofu
- 1½ teaspoons salt
- 1½ teaspoons ground black pepper
- 1 teaspoon sugar
- 1 teaspoon paprika
- Neutral oil, for frying
- Nanking's Famous Peanut Sauce (page 270)
- Steamed white rice, for serving

Drain the tofu and gently pat it dry with paper towels. Slice it in half horizontally (crosswise), cutting through the equator. Then slice each rectangular piece in half in both directions, to create 8 squares of tofu, total. Cut each of these 8 pieces in half on the diagonal to create triangles.

Lay the tofu on a sheet pan. In a small bowl, mix together the salt, black pepper, sugar, and paprika with a fork to fully incorporate. Season both sides of the tofu with the mixture and let it sit for 15 minutes to marinate.

Fill a cast-iron skillet or deep pan halfway with oil and heat over high heat until the temperature reads 365°F (185°C) on a deep-fry thermometer. Working in batches so you don't crowd the pan, carefully drop in the tofu. Fry until golden brown, about 3 minutes per side, and flip halfway to ensure even cooking. Transfer to plates and serve drizzled with peanut sauce. To complete the meal the Nanking way, serve with a side of white rice and drizzle some peanut sauce on the rice, too.

PAIRING IDEA: Try this with our garlic spicy marinated cucumbers (page 61).

SOUTHEAST ASIAN TOFU BOWL

东南亚豆腐饭
DŌNG NÁN YÀ DÒU FU FÀN

Serves 2 to 4

NOTE: You can use freshly minced garlic, lightly heated up in some oil, instead of jarred minced garlic. My restaurant grandma used minced garlic in the jar, and that smell and taste just goes together for me when it comes to fried "stinky" tofu, which is why I used it in this recipe.

KATHY: Although you'd never guess it based on the name, the origins of this dish come from a Ningbo specialty called stinky tofu. My restaurant grandma served Ningbonese and Shanghainese cuisine at her restaurant, Star Lunch (Shànghǎi Xiǎo Chī), on Jackson Street, just a couple steps away from House of Nanking. Up front, she had the oldest cash register I'd ever seen—it looked like a triple-decker typewriter—and next to that, there was always a large bucket of moldy stinky tofu, fermenting under layers of bok choy leaves that had turned a dark, slimy green. This specialty, which she only served on weekends, had the color palette of a murky swamp. To anyone unfamiliar with the dish, the smell can be . . . off-putting. But I love it, and think it smells delicious fried. Restaurant Grandma would fish out the tofu with her hands, wipe off the mold, cut it into four smaller squares, and deep-fry it until crisp and golden brown. It was served stacked nicely on a plastic plate with a side of minced garlic, hoisin sauce, and fresh chili sauce. I was that kid in a bowl cut, sitting on a red stool enjoying my piping hot stinky tofu, a snack I would pick over Doritos any day.

What really made this dish pop was the dipping sauce. I couldn't believe how three simple ingredients could make fried stinky tofu taste so good. Thirty years later, when I set out to create an affordable grab-and-go lunch option for our restaurant Fang, I channeled this very sauce. However, I used fresh tofu instead of stinky, and topped it off with pickled carrots and radish to give it a bright, crunchy pop. As for the name, well, I figured "Southeast Asian Tofu Bowl" sounded more catchy than "Stinky Tofu Minus the Stink."

- 1 pound (455 g) medium-firm tofu, drained
- Salt
- 2 cups (480 ml) neutral oil
- ¼ cup (60 ml) hoisin sauce
- 1 tablespoon duò jiāo (Chinese salted chopped chilis; see page 285) or sambal oelek
- 1 tablespoon chili oil (homemade, page 274, or store-bought)
- 1 tablespoon toasted sesame oil
- 1 tablespoon minced garlic (see Note)
- Steamed white rice, for serving
- ½ cup (50 g) Pickled Daikon and Carrots (page 265) or Spicy Garlic Cucumbers (page 61)
- ¼ cup (10 g) chopped cilantro, scallions, or a combination, for garnish
- Chinatown Chili Black Bean Sauce (page 275; optional)

Drain the tofu and gently pat it dry with paper towels. Slice it in half horizontally (crosswise), cutting through the equator. Then slice each rectangular piece in half in both directions, to create eight squares of tofu, total. Cut each of these eight pieces in half on the diagonal to create triangles. Season generously with salt.

In a large, deep skillet or Dutch oven, heat the neutral oil over medium-high heat until it reaches 375°F (190°C) on a deep-fry thermometer. Working in batches to prevent sticking and clumping, fry the tofu until golden brown and crispy, 3 to 4 minutes. Use a spider to transfer the tofu to a medium stainless-steel bowl.

In a separate small bowl, whisk together the hoisin sauce, duò jiāo, chili oil, sesame oil, and garlic, then drizzle over the tofu. Using a large spoon, gently toss the tofu to coat with sauce. Serve over bowls of steamed rice, topped with pickled carrots and radish or spicy garlic cucumbers. Garnish generously with cilantro or scallions, and add chili black bean sauce for another layer of spicy, umami kick. Enjoy while the tofu is hot!

EGGS, PO & ME

THE HEART OF
HOME COOKING

蛋禽肉 #5 肉类

KATHY: The dishes in this chapter share a few things in common: They're all affordable, accessible, and, most importantly, delicious. What you'll find here isn't fancy or pretentious, whether it's a common folk dish such as steamed pork hash with eggs (page 228), or a House of Nanking classic that our customers have been raving about for thirty-five-plus years, such as the sesame chicken with sweet potatoes (page 218) or velvety chicken in Tsingtao beer sauce (page 217). The beauty of these recipes is their simplicity: They're easy to make yet pack a real flavor punch.

The philosophy of creating unfussy, deeply satisfying dishes that make the most of each ingredient has been the cornerstone of our cooking at House of Nanking and Fang from the start, even if we didn't always realize it. Our financial constraints in the early days taught us to work magic with what we had, especially with precious (and expensive!) proteins. We worked hard to achieve tenderness, juiciness, and flavor, universally pleasing qualities we strive for in every dish.

Over the years, we've perfected our approach to cooking chicken, beef, pork, and other proteins. But as you explore these recipes, remember that Chinese cooking doesn't have to be all about fancy techniques. It's about understanding your ingredients, respecting their flavors, and coaxing out their best qualities with a few tips and tricks. Whether you're stir-frying, braising, poaching, or steaming, these dishes will teach you to approach proteins with confidence and creativity.

ULTRY

AT

POACHED EGGS IN HONEY MILK

蜂蜜牛奶煮蛋
FĒNG MÌ NIÚ NĂI ZHŬ DÀN

Serves 1 to 2

PETER: Everything I look at now is sugar free, no sugar this, no sugar that . . . it's crazy. When I was young, sugar and honey were considered luxury items and didn't have the negative associations that exist now. In fact, anytime one of us kids felt slightly under the weather or low on energy, my mother would feed us a bowl of poached eggs in honey milk. It was considered a special treat, and not something we would have regularly. My mom would say, "Eggs and milk will make you strong, give you the energy you need to do your homework." I didn't care if it was true or not; to me this was more than just a bowl of nourishment. It was a culinary revelation. Who would think a runny yolk would taste so good in sweet milk?

1½ cups (360 ml) whole milk
1½ tablespoons honey, or to taste
2 eggs

In a small pot, bring the milk to a boil over high heat. Once it reaches a boil, reduce the heat to medium, add the honey, stir, and taste. Adjust the sweetness to your preference (see Tip). Adjust the heat level to maintain a steady simmer, then crack the eggs into a bowl. Gently slide the eggs into the simmering pot of milk and stir gently in a circular motion to ensure the eggs don't stick to the bottom of the pot. Cook until the whites are set, 2 to 3 minutes. Once the whites are set, turn off the heat and carefully ladle the eggs and milk into a bowl. Serve.

TIP: Traditionally, the milk is supposed to be rather sweet, but you can adjust the sweetness to your liking. The best way to enjoy it is to take a bite of the egg with a spoonful of the milk. Let the remaining yolk run into the milk, stir, and enjoy.

EATING EGGS WITH A STRAW

KATHY: The restaurant business meant my dad came home from work way past midnight most days, then had to face a brutal morning after only five hours of sleep. When you work thirteen to fourteen hours a day on your feet, mornings become a blur. Dad made our routine short and sweet—ten minutes or less. As long as I had clothes on and breakfast in hand, we were out the door. Brushed teeth or combed hair didn't matter; those were details Dad couldn't fuss over. He did, however, create a system for breakfast on-the-go that I'm pretty certain no one has replicated since. He perfectly cooked soft-boiled eggs every morning, making sure they were just runny enough for me to suck out using a straw.

Yes, you heard right. Dad would punch a hole in the top of the egg, insert a pre-cut straw, and hand it to me as we dashed out. Just in time to catch the N Judah from Inner Sunset to Chinatown, where Dad would catch another twenty minutes of shut-eye while I, sporting an uneven bowl cut (Dad's money-saving haircuts), sat quietly sucking my egg breakfast through a straw.

I never complained that the egg was sometimes part warm, part cold, or that it wasn't exactly gourmet fare. When you're young and witness your parents' relentless hard work, it leaves a deep impression. You don't want to burden them with complaints. And to Dad's credit, an egg for breakfast is one of the healthiest ways to start the day. High-quality protein, essential vitamins, and minerals to support growth and health. Maybe Dad does always know best.

SILKY EGGS WITH CHINESE BBQ PORK OVER RICE

滑蛋叉烧饭
HUÁ DÀN CHĀ SHĀO FÀN

Serves 2

KATHY: All throughout middle and high school, my dad would pick me up after school and take me out to lunch. Well, it would be lunch for my dad, and second lunch for me. Back then I had the appetite of a football player—my dad would joke that I had another stomach hiding somewhere. New Lun Ting Cafe on Jackson Street in Chinatown, which serves Cantonese-influenced Western dishes, was always on our rotating list. We always went for the same three dishes: pork chop onion over rice and cabbage, roasted pork with gravy on rice with corn, and braised oxtail over rice. Until one day I branched out. My dad's eyebrow raised: "No pork chop onion over rice today?" I explained that I always see other tables get waht daan (the name of this dish in Cantonese is "waht daan chā siu faahn"), and I wanted to try it for myself. Lucky for me, the dish tasted as good as it looked—the eggs were cooked 80 percent of the way, with the tops still wet, resulting in deliciously soft, silky eggs with flecks of pork. I was so taken with the dish, it became part of my repertoire at home.

- 4 eggs, whisked with a splash of water until air bubbles form
- 1 tablespoon toasted sesame oil
- 2 dashes of Maggi sauce
- 1 pinch of ground white pepper
- 1 pinch of sugar
- 1 pinch of salt
- 1½ tablespoons neutral oil
- ¾ cup (80 g) sliced chā shāo/chā siu (Chinese BBQ pork, aka char siu) or diced ham
- ¼ cup (35 g) frozen green peas, defrosted
- Steamed white rice, for serving
- Mom's Gold Label XO Sauce (page 272), Chinatown Chili Black Bean Sauce (page 275), or store-bought chili sauce, for serving (optional)

In a medium bowl, whisk together the eggs, sesame oil, Maggi sauce, white pepper, sugar, and salt until fully incorporated. Heat a wok over high heat, add ½ tablespoon of the neutral oil, and swirl the pan in a circular motion to evenly coat. Add the BBQ pork and peas to the pan and saute for 30 seconds, or just until the peas are warmed through. Allow to cool slightly, then whisk into the bowl with the eggs. Using a paper towel, wipe down the wok to remove any bits of food—oil is fine, though. Add the remaining 1 tablespoon neutral oil to the wok, still over high heat, and pour in the eggs. Once the eggs begin to puff up, after about 10 seconds or so, remove the wok from the heat. Using a flat spatula, lift some of the cooked egg and flip it toward the center of the pan—this will result in some of the uncooked eggs running to come into contact with the wok. Return the wok to the heat and let the eggs cook for 10 seconds more. Again, remove the wok from the heat, use your spatula to lift and flip a portion of the cooked egg toward the center, allow the uncooked eggs to make contact with the wok, and return to the heat. Continue this process until all the eggs have been cooked but each layer still has a soft, slightly wet top. Serve over a plate of steamed white rice. For a kick of spice, add XO sauce or chili sauce.

CHINESE CHIVE AND EGG SCRAMBLE

韭菜煎蛋
JIǓ CÀI JIĀN DÀN

Serves 4

KATHY: Chinese chives are divisive: The smell is so distinctive and garlicky that some find it a little off-putting. I, however, don't belong in that camp; I love the flavor and slight crunch. Chinese chives are used in some of my favorite dim sum offerings, such as chive pancakes and pan-fried shrimp and chive dumplings. But these dishes take some work to prepare. So when I see really fresh Chinese chives at the Chinatown market and don't want to go to the effort of DIYing dumplings, I like to scramble them with eggs. The end result is moist, fluffy eggs that are full of flavor from the seasonings and garlicky bite of the chives.

You could simply serve this over a bowl of rice and your favorite chili sauce, or as an accompaniment to a main dish. Store extra scramble in the fridge and enjoy it cold with a bowl of hot white porridge (page 156) or add a few pieces as a topping to your yáng chūn miàn (page 142). My dad would stuff the cold chive egg scramble and a spoonful of his soy-marinated jalapeños (page 265) in between a sliced toasted croissant to make a mean breakfast sandwich.

NOTE: Traditionally, we go heavy on the Chinese flat-leaf chives. But if this is a new ingredient to you, you might want to start with less (say, two bunches instead of three), as they are quite pungent and assertive to those who are trying them for the first time!

- 5 eggs
- 1 teaspoon Maggi sauce
- 1 teaspoon chili oil (homemade, page 274, or store-bought)
- ½ teaspoon toasted sesame oil
- ½ teaspoon salt
- ½ teaspoon dashi powder
- ¼ teaspoon sugar
- ⅛ teaspoon ground white pepper
- 2 cups (90 g) chopped Chinese chives (from about 3 bunches, see Note)
- 2 tablespoons neutral oil
- Steamed white rice, for serving
- Chili crisp, Mom's Gold Label XO Sauce (page 272), or sriracha, for serving

In a medium bowl, whisk together the eggs, Maggi sauce, chili oil, sesame oil, salt, dashi powder, sugar, white pepper, and 3 tablespoons water until frothy. Add the chopped chives and whisk again to fully incorporate.

Heat a wok over high heat and add the neutral oil. Once the oil begins to smoke, pour in the egg mixture and let it bubble on the sides. Reduce the heat to medium and use a spatula to start pushing the cooked eggs into the center of the wok, tilting the wok down to allow the raw egg to run to the edges and make contact with the wok. Now use the spatula to flip the cooked bottom layer over the top and keep layering until the eggs are gently scrambled and slightly golden, about 2 minutes.

Serve in a shallow bowl with a dollop of your favorite hot sauce.

STEAMED CHICKEN WINGS IN BLACK BEAN–GARLIC SAUCE

蒜蓉豆豉蒸鸡翅
SUÀN RÓNG DÒU CHǏ ZHĒNG JĪ CHÌ

Serves 2 as a main or 4 as a snack

NOTE: Party wings are wings that have been split into the wingette and drumette, with the wing tip discarded.

KATHY: If you are ever in a Chinese household with immigrant parents, grandparents, or other relatives, it is not unusual to see the adults hovering over a child, using kitchen scissors to remove meat from the bone and transferring the meat straight into the kid's rice bowl. This is how I grew up: My grandparents and aunts would always give me the prized meat pieces, saving me from having to perform mouth gymnastics on a piece of bony, fatty, or cartilaginous meat.

This job was particularly daunting when it came to steamed spareribs with black bean–garlic sauce. If you've ever had this dish at a dim sum restaurant, then you know there's really not a ton of meat on the bone. Sometimes it's straight cartilage, sometimes there's a chunk of fat, and every now and then you score a nice piece of flavorful meat. Yet it's one of the most-ordered dishes at dim sum restaurants, on par with the popularity of a har gow (hā gáau) or shumai (sīu máai). So why can you find this dish on almost every single table? Is it really THAT good? In my opinion, it's the sauce that is addictive. My pó po made a version at home knowing the kids really enjoyed it—but I don't have the time or patience my pó po had to meticulously cut pieces of meat off a bone for my kids. This is why I swapped the pork spareribs for party wings, but kept my pó po's sauce recipe as-is. My kids can eat wings on their own, and I don't have to hover with a pair of kitchen scissors and chopsticks until my hand cramps up.

---

1 pound (455 g) party wings (see Note)

3 cloves garlic, finely minced

2 slices ginger, julienned

2 tablespoons fermented dried black beans, rinsed to remove debris

1 tablespoon Shaoxing wine

2 teaspoons oyster sauce

½ teaspoon sugar

½ teaspoon salt

¼ cup (30 g) cornstarch

1 tablespoon soy sauce

1 tablespoon sesame oil

2 red Thai bird chilis, thinly sliced (optional, if you like it spicy)

Place the wings in a large bowl and top with the garlic, ginger, fermented dried black beans, Shaoxing wine, oyster sauce, sugar, and salt. Use your hands to massage the seasoning to fully incorporate and coat each wing, then add the cornstarch and massage it into the wings. Cover with plastic wrap and place in the fridge to marinate for 1 hour.

Remove the chicken wings from the fridge and bring to room temperature for 30 minutes. Set up a steamer by placing a metal steaming rack inside a large pot. Pour cold water into the pot until the water level is slightly above the halfway mark of the metal steaming rack.

Find a shallow, round or flat-bottomed heatproof bowl (porcelain or stainless steel) that fits inside the pot with the lid closed tightly. But don't put the bowl in the pot yet—first, heat the pot over high heat to bring the water to a boil. Place the wings and their marinade inside the bowl and drizzle the soy sauce and sesame oil on top of the wings. Sprinkle the chilis on top of the wings, if using. Once the water is boiling, using an oven mitt, carefully lower the bowl with the wings on top of the steaming rack. (To be extra cautious, you can also turn the heat down when placing the bowl inside the pot. Turn the heat back on to high after the bowl is secured inside the pot on top of the rack.) Steam over high heat, with the lid on, for 20 to 30 minutes, until the juices run clear.

When the wings are done, turn off the heat, use oven mitts to carefully remove the bowl with the wings from the pot, and transfer the wings and any accumulated cooking liquids to a shallow serving bowl.

PAIRING IDEAS: For a full traditional meal, serve with steamed white rice and a side of garlic Chinese vegetables.

WHITE CUT CHICKEN (AKA COLD POACHED CHICKEN) WITH SOY-SCALLION OIL

白切鸡
BÁI QIĒ JĪ (BAAHK CHIT GĀI)

Serves 2

KATHY: White cut chicken is most commonly known as a dish from Southern China, mainly Hong Kong and Guangdong. "White cut" refers to the fact that the whole chicken is cooked in a poaching liquid then cut up into pieces with the bone in and skin on, resulting in a dish that is all white in color when served. In Southern China, the chicken is paired with gēung yùhng, a classic dipping sauce made from ginger, scallion, garlic, and hot oil.

Growing up in San Francisco, where the majority of Chinese immigrants are originally from Southern China, I had my fair share of this version of baahk chit gāi, which we purchased at a sīu laahp pōu, aka Chinese barbecue meat shop. The shops we frequented were always incredibly loud and boisterous, and we'd line up to yell out our order to a butcher wearing a plastic apron and galoshes, standing in front of a greasy splash guard covered in barbecue meat juices and guts. There would be a round butcher block about one foot thick, which the butcher pounded with a giant cleaver every few seconds, dishing out plastic containers filled with roasted duck, roasted pork, goose wings, and white cut chicken.

Although it's generally associated with Southern China, white cut chicken is popular among Chinese families from other parts of China, too, who often use the same poaching method but might use different sauce ingredients or types of chicken. When my a niáng immigrated to San Francisco, she brought over her own recipe for making bái qiē jī the Shanghainese way. The sauce is completely different, in that it has soy sauce and is heavy on the sugar. Her chicken preference was for yellow feather chicken (huáng máo jī), a more flavorful chicken with less fat and tighter muscles, and thus not as tender as the Southern counterpart.

My first experience with yellow feather chicken was less than ideal. All Chinese adults will give the kid the largest piece of meat in any dish, usually the white meat, so I took a huge bite, expecting the tenderness I was used to from white cut chicken from the BBQ shop up the street. I struggled to chew through it and swallow it. A Niáng was staring right at me, looking for a nod of approval, so I forced the chicken down my throat and smiled with slight tears in my eyes. That's when I learned the trick: Dip the chicken in sauce to coat it well, and take a small bite.

For this recipe, I've swapped out yellow feather chicken for a much more tender and petite substitute, Cornish game hen, which is easy to prepare and the perfect size for two people. Be sure to save the sauce if you don't finish it. It keeps for three days and gets even better as it sits in the fridge. Drizzle it over fried or hard-boiled eggs, mix it over rice and grilled salmon, or serve it with congee (page 156). It's absolutely delicious, more versatile and less greasy than gēung yùhng, in my opinion.

NOTE: If you want to save the poaching liquid, remove and discard the ginger and scallion, then use the liquid to make Chicken and Salted Pork Congee (page 161).

continued

Place the hen in a medium or large pot and add enough water to cover the hen by 1 inch (2.5 cm). Remove the hen from the water and set the hen aside. Add the scallions, ginger, and salt to the water and bring to a rolling boil over high heat. Slowly lower the hen in by its legs, stretching them to open up the body and ensure that water can touch the whole surface of the hen. Be sure the hen is fully submerged in the boiling water. Cover with a lid and continue cooking over high heat for 5 minutes. Reduce the heat to achieve a low simmer and cook for 15 minutes, skimming any impurities that rise to the surface. Turn off the heat, keep the pot covered, and let the residual heat cook the chicken for an additional 5 minutes. To check for doneness, insert a thermometer into the thickest part of the thigh—it should register as 165°F (75°C). (Alternatively, poke the hen with a chopstick to see if water runs clear of blood.) If the hen is undercooked, turn the heat back on to achieve a low simmer and continue cooking until the internal temp reaches 165°F (75°C).

While the hen is cooking, in a bowl large enough to hold the hen, prepare an ice water bath. Once the hen is done, submerge it in the ice water bath.

Remove the hen from the ice water bath and dry with paper towels. Remove the meat from the bone and use your hands to shred it into a bowl. To serve, in a serving bowl, toss the shredded hen with the sliced cucumbers and ¼ cup (60 ml) of the scallion-oil soy sauce, then garnish with the sprigs of cilantro. Serve over steamed white rice or with a side of mei fun for a refreshing salad, with more scallion-oil soy sauce on the side.

1 Cornish game hen (about 1¼ pounds / 565 g), brought to room temperature for 30 minutes

2 scallions

4 bias-cut slices ginger (⅛ inch / 3 mm thick and 2 inches / 5 cm long)

1 teaspoon salt

4 Persian cucumbers, unpeeled and thinly sliced

Scallion-Oil Soy Sauce with Ginger (page 275)

4 cilantro sprigs

Steamed white rice or dried rice stick noodles (mei fun), soaked in water until soft (see page 286), for serving

THE CAR THAT TSINGTAO BOUGHT

PETER: For more than fifteen years, I carried only one beer at Nanking—the most recognizable Chinese beer, Tsingtao. I made this decision because our fridge was small, and because we were so busy that we didn't have time to allow customers to waver about what type of beer they wanted. All you had to do was ask for a beer, and the iconic green bottle would show up. On an average day, we would sell up to twelve cases—that's 288 bottles. During the summer, holidays, and the Lunar New Year parade, it was more like 24 cases or 576 beers sold per day. We often ran out of places to stack the beer boxes, and on many occasions, when we ran out of chairs, customers would sit on beer boxes.

You would think the customers would complain, but they didn't. Turns out, they loved it. These were some of my favorite moments inside the restaurant; if only I had a camera and the time to take photos, I'd have snapshots of people drinking their Tsingtao beers, sitting on a Tsingtao beer box with the biggest smile on their face, like they won the lottery. The energy in our dining room has always been very electrifying. It's loud, people packed inside like sardines, strangers sitting next to each other, people are laughing, talking, some yelling, rubbing shoulders, sharing food, making friends and memories. When I think about what kind of restaurant I want to eat at, it's Nanking. I want all of that.

For several years, we were the number-one Tsingtao customer in the Bay Area, and I believe, the West Coast. The beer rep would give us these plaques and swag every few months. And when their head of distribution came to check out our place, he couldn't believe his eyes. "This is the place that sells the most Tsingtao beers on the West Coast? It's tiny."

You won't be surprised to learn that we had a lot of beer bottles at the end of every shift. So many, in fact, it was enough to help a family buy a new car.

For more than a decade, I had two dishwashers: a husband-and-wife duo who would split shifts with each other. Within the first few nights of working for me, they asked if they could take all the beer bottles and soda cans home. I of course said yes; it was a win-win for me, as I saved on recycling fees and helped others make some extra dollars on the side. And let me tell you, this system was far more reliable than the inconsistent Recology service we were getting at the time. The couple never missed a day. At the end of each shift, their two kids would show up with empty polypropylene rice bags and would stuff them with crushed cans and empty Tsingtao beer bottles. They did this for more than a decade, and I watched the kids grow taller and taller, as they moved from elementary school through high school.

One night, the kids drove a brand-new van to Nanking and grabbed my hand to show me proudly what they had purchased. I'll never forget it: It was a gray minivan with an automatic door that would slide open. "We bought this with all the money we saved from the recycled cans and beers you gave to us every night!" I couldn't believe it. I was deeply moved and impressed by their frugality and perseverance.

CHICKEN IN TSINGTAO BEER SAUCE

啤酒鸡
PÍ JIǓ JĪ

Serves 2 to 4

KATHY: When I was in middle school, I worked weekends at Nanking, bussing tables, getting drinks for customers, seating guests, and grabbing checks. When the line got ridiculously long, that was my cue to start selling Tsingtaos to people eagerly waiting to get seated. It was good business: nine times out of ten, people would buy one (or even two or three) to help make waiting in line more enjoyable, and I got some generous cash tips. The forty or fifty people outside, laughing, hanging out, and drinking their green beers, were like a living advertisement for Tsingtao beer. Tsingtao boxes also became my go-to storage vessel, like those clear bins you get at the Container Store. I used them to haul groceries, store paper receipts (yes, back then we didn't have a fancy POS), and store my old homework and clothing.

So . . . of course we had to have a dish or two featuring our favorite beer. My dad created Chicken in Tsingtao Beer Sauce as an ode to a famous Shanghainese fish dish my family loves. The light flavor of alcohol is commonly used in Shanghainese cooking in dressings and marinades. This dish with chicken and zucchini channels those old-school flavors—tender meat coated in this white, almost translucent, sweet sauce with a fragrant aroma of booze—but subbing beer for Shaoxing wine in a twist that Americans can enjoy. This dish is so good, you could just drink the sauce.

CHICKEN

1 pound (455 g) chicken breast tenders, cut on the bias into thin slices

2 tablespoons toasted sesame oil

1½ teaspoons cornstarch

2 teaspoons aji-mirin

½ teaspoon sugar

½ teaspoon salt

1 pinch of ground white pepper

1 large zucchini, sliced in half lengthwise, then sliced horizontally into 1-inch (2.5 cm)-thick half-moons

BEER SAUCE

2 tablespoons neutral oil

2 garlic cloves, smashed and minced

¾ cup (180 ml) Tsingtao beer

2 tablespoons sugar

1 tablespoon toasted sesame oil

1 teaspoon powdered chicken bouillon

½ teaspoon salt

1 pinch of ground white pepper

1½ tablespoons cornstarch whisked with 1½ tablespoons water into a slurry

Steamed white rice, to serve

Chili oil (homemade, page 274, or store-bought), to serve (optional)

Marinate the chicken: In a medium bowl, combine the chicken, sesame oil, cornstarch, aji-mirin, sugar, salt, and white pepper and stir with a fork or chopsticks until well-integrated. Let marinate for 15 minutes at room temperature.

Precook the zucchini and chicken: Bring a medium pot of water to boil and cook the zucchini for 3 minutes, or until medium-soft (call it 70 percent cooked). Use a spider or slotted spoon to transfer the zucchini to a colander to drain excess water.

Boil the chicken in the same water for 1 minute, or until 80 percent of the way done; it should be slightly pink in the middle. Use the spider or slotted spoon to transfer to the same colander as the zucchini.

Make the sauce and finish the dish: Heat a wok over high heat, add the neutral oil, and swirl to coat the wok. Once the oil is smoking, add the garlic and stir-fry for 3 seconds, then add the beer. Let the alcohol burn off, about 20 seconds, then add the sugar, sesame oil, chicken bouillon, salt, and white pepper. Allow to cook on high for 45 seconds, or until slightly reduced. While whisking, slowly pour the slurry into the sauce in a circular motion to create an even, glossy, thick sauce that isn't clumpy. Once the sauce has thickened, add the chicken and zucchini to the wok. Wok toss to glaze the ingredients, about 10 seconds. Serve immediately with rice and a drizzle of chili oil, if using. Make sure to ladle the sauce over the chicken and rice!

NANKING'S SESAME CHICKEN

南京芝麻鸡
NÁN JĪNG ZHĪ MA JĪ

Serves 4

PETER: This sesame chicken is probably the most famous dish at our restaurant. I've already covered the origin story on page 17—one day, a customer asked me to make them something that tasted like Thanksgiving. I couldn't give them turkey . . . but moist, succulent chicken thigh meat is better than turkey, anyway. I thinly sliced sweet potatoes and fried them, another nod to American Thanksgiving. I guess you could say people like it, because now we go through more than one hundred pounds of sweet potatoes every day, just for this dish.

NOTE: If you'd rather bake the sweet potato instead of frying it, arrange the slices on a baking sheet, drizzle them with extra-virgin olive oil, and roast them for 10 minutes in a 400°F (205°C) oven.

- 1½ pounds (680 g / about 4 pieces) boneless, skinless chicken thighs, cut into 1-inch (2.5 cm) pieces
- ¾ cup (95 g) cornstarch
- 1½ tablespoons aji-mirin
- 1 tablespoon sugar
- 1 tablespoon garlic powder
- 1 teaspoon salt
- 1 teaspoon smoked paprika
- 1 teaspoon MSG
- ½ teaspoon ground white pepper
- 2 cups (480 ml) neutral oil, for frying
- 1 medium sweet potato, sliced down the middle lengthwise, then thinly sliced ¼ inch crosswise
- Nanking Sauce (page 270)
- Toasted sesame seeds, for garnish
- Julienned scallions, for garnish (optional)
- Steamed white rice, to serve

In a medium bowl, combine the chicken, cornstarch, aji-mirin, sugar, garlic powder, salt, smoked paprika, MSG, white pepper, and ⅓ cup (80 ml) of water. Use your hands to massage the marinade into the chicken to create an even coating. The consistency of the marinade should be like Elmer's glue; if it's too chalky or dry, add a splash more water. Cover and marinate in the fridge for at least 2 hours and ideally overnight.

Remove the chicken from the fridge and allow it to temper for 30 minutes.

In a wok (or Dutch oven, if preferred), heat the neutral oil over high heat. The oil level should be slightly below the middle line of the wok. When the oil registers 350°F (175°C) on a deep-fry thermometer, fry the chicken in two or three batches to avoid overcrowding. Using a wok spatula, stir the chicken to prevent it from clumping or sticking to the bottom of the wok. Once the chicken is frying in individual pieces, leave it alone. Fry the chicken until cooked through, 3 to 4 minutes. It should be incredibly juicy with a light crisp on the exterior. Transfer the chicken to a serving bowl, make sure the oil returns to 350°F (175°C), and repeat with the remaining batches.

Working in two batches, fry the sweet potato slices for 2 minutes, or until you can easily pierce through a sweet potato without it falling apart. (Alternatively, you can bake the sweet potato—see Note.) It should have a stiff, crisp texture and not be too soft. Transfer the sweet potatoes to the bowl with the chicken, then repeat with the remaining potatoes.

While frying the second batch of sweet potatoes, in a small pot, reheat the Nanking sauce over medium heat until warm.

Transfer the remaining sweet potatoes to the serving bowl, then drizzle the warmed sauce on top and toss to evenly coat. Garnish with sesame seeds and scallions, if using, and serve immediately with rice.

PAIRING IDEA: Complete the meal with a side of Chinese vegetables or cold marinated celtuce (page 283).

CHICKEN AND SNOW PEAS WITH GARLIC SAUCE

蒜蓉荷兰豆炒鸡肉
SUÀN RÓNG HÉ LÁN DÒU CHǍO JĪ RÒU

Serves 2 to 4

PETER: Every so often, a customer would come in and say, "I only eat white meat chicken. Not fried, please, and not too much sauce. Can you boil the chicken?" My first thought was always, *Why come to a restaurant when you can make that at home?* But then I realized I had to honor my customers' wishes while also offering something better than they can make themselves. This is how I came up with chicken and snow peas in a light, translucent garlic sauce.

This dish utilizes two common Chinese cooking techniques to ensure the meat is tender, moist, and flavorful while using less oil. The first method is velveting, where you marinate a protein with seasonings, cornstarch, baking soda, and occasionally egg whites. The seasonings flavor the protein, and the cornstarch creates a jacket that prevents the juices from escaping during cooking. I knew that baking soda and egg whites would be overkill for a protein as delicate and mild as chicken breast, which is why I use only cornstarch. The second technique is called "passing through water," which means the protein is cooked 80 percent of the way by swishing it in boiling water, then immediately removed from the pot using a spider. This technique is also great for cooking vegetables, as it maintains the vegetables' bright colors and crunchy texture.

The customer may have asked for boiled chicken and veggies, but when they take their first bite of this dish, their eyes widen, a smile forms on their lips, and they nod with happy approval. That's how I know I've done my job as a chef.

- 1 pound (455 g) chicken tenders, thinly sliced on the bias
- 2 tablespoons toasted sesame oil
- 1½ teaspoons cornstarch
- 1½ teaspoons aji-mirin
- 1 teaspoon sugar
- 1½ teaspoons salt
- 1 pinch of ground white pepper
- ¼ cup (60 ml) Shaoxing wine
- 1 teaspoon MSG
- 1 pinch of chili flakes
- 10 ounces (280 g) snow peas, tips and strings removed
- 1½ teaspoons neutral oil
- 3 cloves garlic, minced
- 3 thin bias-cut slices of ginger, julienned
- 1½ teaspoons cornstarch whisked with 1½ teaspoons water into a slurry
- Steamed white rice, for serving

In a medium bowl, combine the chicken, 1 tablespoon of the sesame oil, the cornstarch, aji-mirin, ½ teaspoon of the sugar, ½ teaspoon of the salt, and the white pepper and stir with a fork or chopsticks until well-integrated. Let marinate for 15 minutes at room temp.

Meanwhile, in a small bowl, whisk together the Shaoxing wine, remaining 1 tablespoon of sesame oil, remaining ½ teaspoon sugar, remaining 1 teaspoon salt, the MSG, and chili flakes. Set aside.

Bring a medium pot of water to boil. Cook the snow peas for 50 seconds, or until they're about 80 percent cooked. Remove the snow peas with a spider and set aside in a bowl. To the same pot of boiling water, add the chicken and stir immediately to prevent sticking and ensure even cooking. Cook the chicken for 1 minute, or until 80 percent done (it should be slightly pink in the middle). Remove with a spider and transfer to the same bowl as the snow peas.

Heat a wok over high heat, add the neutral oil, and swirl to coat the wok. Once the wok is smoking, add the garlic and ginger, stir-fry for 3 seconds, then add the reserved sauce. Cook for 10 seconds, then add the chicken and snow peas back the wok. Stir-fry until the chicken and snow peas are evenly coated with the sauce, about 40 seconds. While stirring, drizzle in the cornstarch slurry in a circular motion to prevent clumping. Wok toss for 10 seconds, then turn off the heat and serve with a bowl of steamed rice.

BASTARD EGGS WITH SPICY GROUND PORK AND GINGER-SCALLION SAUCE

香辣肉末盖黄包蛋
XIĀNG LÀ RÒU MÒ GÀI HUÁNG BĀO DÀN

Serves 2

KATHY: When I was growing up, my relatives all took turns taking care of me in our home. Every year or so, they'd alternate who lived with us, so I wouldn't be home alone while my parents worked. My mom's older sister stayed with us for a few years and I found her to be a bit short-tempered and not the best cook. Her meals always felt hasty, like they were just tossed together last minute with whatever she found in the house: think salami intended for sandwiches thrown in a pan and served over rice with a side of bok choy. Now that I have two kids, I have more sympathy for my aunt. She had both me and her daughter to deal with.

One night she fried up some eggs, dressed them up with spicy ground pork and scallion sauce, and served it with rice. I was shocked by how good it was. I asked her what this dish was called, thinking it was something she had re-created from China. She called it fried sunny-side egg. She wasn't big on creativity. In Chinese, it's huáng bāo dàn. I had trouble pronouncing the second word and called it huáng bā dàn, which means "bastard." (In my defense, I made only one slight change in intonation, but one that completely changed the word.) She and her daughter burst out laughing till tears rolled down their cheeks. And ever since then, she called this dish "the Bastard." I would ask, "What's for dinner tonight?" and she would say, "Bastard." I would get so excited.

- 8 ounces (225 g) ground pork
- 1 tablespoon toasted sesame oil
- 2 teaspoons Shaoxing wine
- 1 teaspoon soy sauce
- 1 tablespoon minced ginger
- 1 tablespoon minced garlic
- 1 teaspoon cornstarch
- 1 pinch of ground white pepper
- 2 tablespoons neutral oil
- 4 eggs
- 1 to 2 jalapeños, seeded and thinly sliced (or substitute green bell pepper if you don't want heat)
- 1 teaspoon sugar
- 1 tablespoon hoisin sauce
- 1½ teaspoons Tabasco sauce
- 1 tablespoon fermented bean paste
- ½ cup (30 g) chopped scallions
- Steamed white rice, for serving
- Chili crisp or chili sauce (such as Chinatown Chili Black Bean Sauce, page 275; optional)

In a medium bowl, season the pork with the sesame oil, Shaoxing wine, soy sauce, garlic, ginger, cornstarch, and white pepper. Mix everything together with chopsticks or your hands to fully incorporate it and set aside for 5 minutes.

Heat a large nonstick skillet over medium heat and drizzle in 1 tablespoon of the neutral oil. Cook the eggs sunny-side up, then transfer them to a plate and set aside.

In the same pan you used to cook the eggs, increase the heat to high and add the remaining 1 tablespoon of neutral oil. Add the ground pork and saute for 2 minutes, or until about halfway cooked, breaking it up with a spatula or wooden spoon as it cooks. Add the jalapeño, sugar, hoisin sauce, Tabasco sauce, and fermented bean paste and stir to incorporate. Add ½ cup (120 ml) of water and allow the sauce to simmer for 3 minutes, or until the water reduces by three-quarters (if your pan is smaller than 12 inches / 30 cm, this might take longer). You are looking for a saucy dish—not watery, but not dry either. Add the scallions and cook, stirring, for 30 seconds.

To serve, place steamed white rice in each of 2 shallow bowls, top each with 2 of the eggs, then ladle the sauteed pork and sauce over the eggs. Break the yolks into the rice and mix with the ground pork. Add chili crisp or chili sauce if you'd like to pump up the heat even further!

MAPO TOFU WITH HOT ITALIAN SAUSAGE

麻婆豆腐炒意大利香肠
MÁ PÓ DÒU FU CHǎO YÌ DÀ LǏ XIĀNG CHÁNG

Serves 2 to 4

KATHY: I love the delicious, rich blend of flavors in mapo tofu, but feel it often leans too heavily on the má là aspect of the dish—má là being the spicy, numbing sensation that comes from Sichuan peppercorn and chili—ending in a slight bitter note. When we decided to put mapo tofu on the menu at Fang, I wanted to balance out the má là and with savory, umami notes. So instead of just using ground pork, we use our own house-made sausage with five-spice, sweet mei can, ginger, and scallions. When customers try the mapo tofu at Fang restaurant, they always mention how good it is and how it's different from any other mapo tofu they've had, and they ask, "How do I replicate this at home?" Instead of sharing all our secrets, I tell them to use hot Italian sausage rather than attempting to make their own sausage with Chinese flavors. This is actually how I make it at home; it's a really neat Italian and Chinese blend of flavors in a classic Sichuan dish.

---

2 tablespoons fermented bean sauce

1 teaspoon chili flakes

½ teaspoon powdered chicken bouillon

½ teaspoon sugar

½ teaspoon Sichuan pepper oil (see page 289)

1 pinch of smoked paprika

1 pinch of salt

1 tablespoon neutral oil

2 hot Italian sausage links (about 8 ounces/225 g total), casing removed

1 tablespoon minced garlic

6 ounces (170 g) silken or medium-firm tofu, drained, patted dry, and cut into 1-inch (2.5 cm) cubes

2 tablespoons cornstarch whisked with 2 tablespoons water into a slurry

Steamed white rice, to serve

¼ cup (10 g) chopped cilantro or scallions, for garnish

Chili oil (homemade, page 274, or store-bought), for garnish

In a medium bowl, whisk the fermented bean sauce, chili flakes, chicken bouillon, sugar, Sichuan pepper oil, paprika, salt, and 1 cup (235 ml) water. Set aside.

Heat the neutral oil in a 12-inch (30 cm) nonstick skillet over high heat. Add the sausage and cook, using a wooden spoon to break apart the sausage into smaller chunks, until the sausage is about 80 percent cooked, about 3 minutes. Add the garlic and stir-fry for 30 seconds, or until fragrant. Pour the reserved fermented bean sauce mixture and the tofu into the pan simmer for 2 minutes, or until the tofu has absorbed the flavors and the sausage is fully cooked. While stirring constantly, pour the cornstarch slurry into the pan in a circular motion to prevent clumping. The sauce should thicken, and the dish should have a thick, stew-like consistency. Serve in a shallow bowl with white rice, garnished with chopped cilantro or scallions. Drizzle chili oil over the top.

PORK TENDERLOIN STIR-FRIED WITH CHIVE BLOSSOMS AND TOMATO

蒜苗炒肉丝
SUÀN MIÁO CHǍO ROÙ SĪ

Serves 1 or 2

NOTE: If you're a spice lover, mince up the chilis rather than leaving them cut in half. But beware, the seeds will make the dish much hotter!

PETER: I always thought it was interesting that Kathy would say I was the better chef at Nanking, but at home, Lily took the title. I never understood how I could be good in one place and not the other. It wasn't until Kathy was much older that I understood her rationale. By the time Kathy hit middle school, she was self-sufficient enough to take care of all her own meals, which meant there were many long and lonely nights when she would cook and eat by herself while Lily and I worked. She never complained about it, but I felt so guilty. So I started sending my wife home early on certain nights, so she could cook a proper meal for Kathy. The next day at school pickup, Kathy would always talk to me about what mom had prepared and what she loved about it. This pork tenderloin stir-fried with chive blossoms (aka garlic chives) and tomato was a particular favorite. Kathy would explain to me in great detail how she loved the combination of tomato with soy sauce, how the umami in tomato makes Chinese stir-fries particularly tasty, and the combination of tender sweet chive blossoms made her finish two bowls of rice. It became clear to me that those occasional mom-cooked meals meant everything to her.

- 5 ounces (140 g) pork tenderloin
- 2 teaspoons soy sauce
- 1 teaspoon Shaoxing wine
- 1 teaspoon toasted sesame oil
- 1 teaspoon cornstarch
- 1 pinch of sugar
- Salt
- 4 ounces (115 g) chive blossoms (aka garlic chives)
- 2 tablespoons neutral oil
- 3 thin bias-cut slices ginger, julienned
- 2 cloves garlic, minced
- 2 small vine-ripened tomatoes, diced
- 1 tablespoon aji-mirin
- 2 red Thai bird chilis, cut in half (see Note)
- 1 tablespoon soy sauce
- Steamed white rice, to serve
- 2 teaspoons chili oil (homemade, page 274, or store-bought)

Slice the pork into thin (¼-inch / 6 mm) slices with the grain. Cut those slices into thin threads, resulting in 2-inch (5 cm)-long, ¼-inch (6 mm)-wide matchsticks. Transfer the pork to a small bowl and add the soy sauce, Shaoxing wine, sesame oil, cornstarch, sugar, and a pinch of salt. Stir to combine and allow to marinate for 5 minutes.

Meanwhile, cut off and discard the bottom 1 inch of the chive blossoms, then cut the remaining portion into 2-inch (5 cm) lengths.

Heat a wok over high heat, add 1 tablespoon of the neutral oil, and swirl to coat the wok evenly. When the oil begins to smoke, add the ginger and garlic. Cook for 10 seconds, or until aromatic, then add the pork and stir-fry for 45 seconds, or until about 90 percent cooked through (with a tiny bit of pink in the middle). Remove the pork from the wok and set aside. Leave the heat on high, add the remaining 1 tablespoon neutral oil, then add the tomatoes. Stir-fry for 30 seconds, then season with a pinch of salt and the aji-mirin. Stir-fry for another 30 seconds, or until the tomatoes begin to soften. Add the chive blossoms, chilis, and soy sauce. Stir-fry for 1 minute, then add pork back to the wok. Wok toss the ingredients for 20 seconds, or until the pork is cooked through, to fully incorporate. Serve immediately over steamed white rice and drizzled with chili oil.

SERVING TIP: Spoon over a plate of steamed white rice, then mix everything together so the tomato sauce coats the rice and seasons it. Pair with a bowl of watercress pork soup (page 131) or papaya soup (page 128) to complete the meal.

HOMESTYLE STEAMED PORK HASH WITH EGGS

家常肉饼蒸蛋
JIĀ CHÁNG RÒU BǏNG ZHĒNG DÀN

Serves 4

KATHY: Steamed pork hash with eggs is a staple in most Chinese households, and something I would call the Chinese version of American meatloaf. But instead of the minced or ground meat getting baked in a pan with various seasonings and a softening agent, in this dish, pork is formed into a round patty then steamed. There is no glaze or sauce served over it, which might make American readers raise an eyebrow. I'll admit that at first glance, American meatloaf not only sounds more appetizing but also looks better. Steamed pork hash comes out looking pale and plain. But once you mix it with rice and dig your chopsticks in, you'll understand why this dish is a classic for most families, especially among the kids. My daughter asks for it regularly, especially if she feels under the weather. The meat is soft, tender, moist, and flavorful—but light. The juices from the hash get spooned over the rice as the "sauce" and you mix it all up with the steamed eggs, creating a very satisfying bite that always hits home. If you want to dress it up, you can add salted duck eggs on top or a few slices of dried salted fish. But as I grow older, I appreciate dishes like this more and more. Food doesn't need to be big and bold for it to be delicious.

---

4 (⅛-inch / 3 mm) coins of ginger, julienned

2 scallions, sliced or julienned

1 pound (455 g) ground pork

2 teaspoons soy sauce

1 teaspoon Shaoxing wine

1 teaspoon oyster sauce

1 teaspoon cornstarch

½ teaspoon salt

1 pinch of sugar

3 eggs

Steamed white rice, for serving

Place the ginger and scallions in a bowl and cover them with ½ cup (120 ml) water. Using your hands, squeeze the ginger and scallions to extract their juices into the water. Let steep for 15 to 20 minutes.

Meanwhile, bring a large steamer to a boil over high heat.

In a large bowl, combine the pork, soy sauce, Shaoxing wine, oyster sauce, cornstarch, salt, and sugar. Strain out the solids from the ginger-scallion water, but do not discard them. Add the water to the bowl with the pork. (The water will lighten the hash and help tenderize it.) Mixing thoroughly, spread the mixture into a shallow, 9-inch (22.5 cm) round stainless steel pan or pie tin. Smooth it out and create three indentations. Crack the eggs into each indentation and scatter the reserved ginger and scallions over the surface of the mixture. When water begins to boil, add the pan to the rack. Steam for 10 minutes, or until the eggs are set and the pork is cooked through, then serve immediately with steamed white rice.

SERVING TIPS: For adult diners, drizzle with Soy-Marinated Jalapeños (page 265) or chili crisp to give it a spicy kick. Pair with a nice plate of Chinese vegetables, such as gailan with the Fermented Bean Curd Sauce on page 268, or Silk Squash with Dried Shrimp (page 175).

李錦記
KUM KEE
辣椒油
CHILI OIL
NET 7 fl oz (207 ml)

FRIED PORK "CHOP" OVER RICE WITH POOR MAN'S AU JUS

炸排骨饭
ZHÁ PÁI GǓ FÀN

Serves 4

KATHY: My restaurant grandma's restaurant was so authentically Ningbonese, it became almost a kind of novelty spot. Very few people spoke the Ningbonese dialect or even knew about this area of China and its food, but her super niche dishes drew a handful of loyal customers. She was famous for two things: the weekend stinky tofu (see page 200) and pork chop over rice, which became her number-one seller.

Restaurant Grandma had a special relationship with her butcher, who would slice the chops extra-thin for her, which allowed for a shorter marinating time, a faster cook time, and a great deal, since she included two pieces rather than one. Restaurant Grandma would scoop steamed rice onto a white, plastic oval plate, press it down, add blanched spinach, ladle a healthy pour of warm au jus from her bain-marie over the vegetables and rice, and top it with two slices of perfectly fried and seasoned pork chop.

---

8 boneless pork tenderloin chops, pounded until ¼ inch (6 mm) thick
3 tablespoons cornstarch
1 tablespoon soy sauce
1 tablespoon dark soy sauce
1 tablespoon oyster sauce
1 tablespoon Shaoxing wine
2 teaspoons sugar
1 teaspoon ground white pepper
1 teaspoon garlic powder
1 teaspoon MSG
½ teaspoon baking soda
½ teaspoon salt
¼ teaspoon cumin powder
¼ teaspoon cinnamon powder

AU JUS
1 cup (240 ml) beef broth
1 tablespoon oyster sauce
2 teaspoons soy sauce
5 cloves
1 cinnamon stick
3 star anise
Pinch of salt
¼ teaspoon sugar
2 teaspoons MSG

8 ounces (225 g) baby spinach
1 cup (240 ml) neutral oil
Steamed white rice, to serve
Chinatown Chili Black Bean Sauce (page 275) or Worcestershire sauce, to serve (optional)

In a shallow pan or medium bowl, combine the pork chops, cornstarch, soy sauce, dark soy sauce, oyster sauce, Shaoxing wine, sugar, white pepper, garlic powder, MSG, baking soda, salt, cumin, and cinnamon. Use your hands or chopsticks to toss to coat, then cover the bowl with plastic wrap. Marinate for at least 2 hours or, ideally, overnight.

Prepare the au jus: In a small pot, combine all the ingredients and 1½ cups (355 ml) water and cook over high heat for 1 minute. Reduce the heat to low and simmer for 8 minutes. Remove from the heat and set aside.

Bring a medium pot of water to a boil. Boil the spinach for 10 seconds, then drain and set aside.

In a large skillet, heat the neutral oil over high heat until it registers 350°F (175°C) on a deep-fry thermometer. Working in batches so you don't overcrowd the pan, fry the pork chops, 1 minute per side, or until golden.

To assemble your rice plates, scoop about 1 cup (200 g) of steamed rice onto each of 4 plates and slightly press it down. Place the spinach over the rice and ladle a few tablespoons of au jus over the top. Top each plate with 2 pieces of fried pork chop. Add Chinatown Chili Black Bean Sauce or Worcestershire sauce, if using, and serve immediately.

PORK-STUFFED GLUTEN PUFF

油面筋酿肉
YÓU MIÀN JĪN NIÀO RÒU

Serves 2

PETER: Gluten puff is one of my favorite things to eat. The puff is made of water and wheat gluten that's fried into balls that are both crunchy and airy—the best of both worlds. You can buy gluten puffs at most Chinese markets, where they are sold in sealed bags and might be labeled "Fried Round Gluten." When they are cooked in sauces, they soften into a slightly chewy and smooth bite that absorbs a lot of flavor, like a sponge. A classic Shanghainese way to enjoy this is to stuff it with ground pork, braise it in a sauce, and serve with rice.

PUFFS

10 ounces (280 g) ground pork

1 egg

¼ cup (15 g) minced scallions

1½ teaspoons cornstarch

1 teaspoon soy sauce

1 teaspoon oyster sauce

1 teaspoon Shaoxing wine

1 teaspoon toasted sesame oil

1 teaspoon grated fresh ginger

½ teaspoon sugar

½ teaspoon dashi powder

12 gluten puffs

SAUCE

2½ cups (600 ml) water or chicken broth

1 tablespoon Shaoxing wine

1½ teaspoons dark soy sauce

1 teaspoon dashi powder

1 teaspoon toasted sesame oil

½ teaspoon ground white pepper

1 pinch of sugar

1 pinch of salt

1 tablespoon neutral oil

3 coin-sized slices of ginger

1 teaspoon cornstarch whisked with 1 teaspoon water into a slurry (optional)

¼ cup (15 g) minced scallions

Steamed white rice, for serving

Make the puffs: In a medium bowl, combine the pork, egg, scallions, cornstarch, soy sauce, oyster sauce, Shaoxing wine, sesame oil, ginger, sugar, and dashi powder and mix with chopsticks or your hands to fully incorporate.

Using a chopstick, poke a hole in the center of each gluten puff and carve out a pocket, taking care not to pierce through the entire puff. Use the chopstick to push the filling down to make room for more, about 4 teaspoons of filling per puff. There should be no space left inside. Repeat with the remaining puffs.

Make the sauce: In a small bowl, whisk together the water or broth, Shaoxing wine, dark soy sauce, dashi powder, sesame oil, white pepper, sugar, and salt.

Cook the puffs: Heat a large nonstick skillet over high heat and add the neutral oil. Add the stuffed gluten puffs, pork-side down, and the ginger and sear until golden brown, about 1 minute. Add the sauce to the pan and, using a spatula, give the puffs a good toss so they are coated. Cover the skillet and braise the puffs for 6 to 8 minutes, until the sauce thickens and the puffs soften and shrink around the pork meatball. If there is still a fair amount of sauce, drizzle in the slurry in a circular motion while stirring constantly to thicken the sauce and glaze the puffs. If the sauce has reduced nicely, no need to add the slurry. Add the scallions and give it a good toss before serving over a bowl of rice.

IDEAL PAIRING: Serve this with rice and a side of wawa choy with dried sardines, ginger, and chili (page 176) and you've got yourself a comforting, healthy, and balanced Chinese meal.

FILET MIGNON WITH HONG KONG–STYLE BLACK PEPPER SAUCE

港式黑胡椒牛排
GǍNG SHÌ HĒI HÚ JIĀO NIÚ PÁI

Serves 4

My mom used to work at Pacific Café in Chinatown, which served Western food with a Cantonese twist. Every meal started with a choice of creamed corn or borscht, garlic bread, and a salad with Thousand Island dressing. In my mind, Pacific Café was incredibly fancy. The red booth seating reminded me of a Johnny Rockets diner, which to me was the epitome of chic.

Every so often, Restaurant Grandma would take me to dinner at Pacific Café after she'd closed her own place. My favorite entrée was the Hong Kong–Style Black Pepper Chicken Steak: flattened, deboned chicken thigh with the skin on, served on a hot skillet. They would pour the sauce over the steak in front of you and it would sizzle, the smell of black pepper and onions wafting to every table.

When I hit fifth grade, I was diagnosed with anemia, and our pediatrician recommended I consume as much iron as possible. So my mother decided to personally cook me a steak for lunch every other day and hand-deliver it, still hot, to me at school. I will never forget my mom standing outside the fence, rain or shine, waiting for us to get out for lunch. She'd hand me a Tupperware container filled with a piece of filet mignon smothered in my favorite black pepper sauce, alongside rice and vegetables. For my parents, filet mignon was the gold-standard cut of all red meats—so this lunch was the highest level of love my parents could have shown me. Digging into my steak, watching the kids around me eat sandwiches from a brown paper bag, I felt like the luckiest kid alive.

STEAK

4 center-cut filets mignons (2 inches / 5 cm thick, about 7 ounces / 200 g each), dried thoroughly with paper towels

Coarse sea salt

Freshly cracked black pepper

HONG KONG–STYLE BLACK PEPPER SAUCE

1 tablespoon neutral oil

½ medium yellow onion, minced

4 cloves garlic, minced

2 tablespoons ground black pepper

2 tablespoons Maggi sauce

1 tablespoon soy sauce

1 tablespoon dark soy sauce

1 tablespoon ketchup

1 tablespoon sugar

1 tablespoon Worcestershire sauce

1 tablespoon cornstarch whisked with 1 tablespoon water into a slurry

1 tablespoon unsalted butter

TO FINISH

2 tablespoons neutral oil

Steamed white rice or cooked spaghetti

Season the steak: Generously season both sides of each steak with sea salt and pepper and allow to rest at room temperature for 45 minutes.

Arrange a rack in the center of the oven and preheat to 350°F (175°C).

Make the black pepper sauce: Heat a medium saucepan over high heat. Add the neutral oil and swirl it in the pan to coat. When the oil is hot, add the onion, garlic, and black pepper. Reduce the heat to medium and cook for 5 minutes, or until the onions soften. Add the Maggi sauce, soy sauce, dark soy sauce, ketchup, sugar, and Worcestershire sauce and cook for 3 minutes to allow the flavors to absorb into the onions. Add 1 cup (240 ml) water, reduce the heat to medium-low, and cook for 5 minutes at a low simmer.

Increase the heat under the saucepan with the onion-soy mixture to achieve a steady simmer, then add the slurry, whisking immediately and constantly until the sauce thickens. To finish, whisk in the butter. Remove from the heat and set aside for later.

Cook the steak: Heat a large cast-iron skillet over high heat until it's close to smoking. Add the neutral oil, making sure to coat the entire skillet. Sear the steaks for 2 minutes on each side, or until a golden-brown crust forms. Transfer the skillet into the oven and cook for 8 to 12 minutes (timing will vary depending on the thickness of your filet). Use a thermometer to measure the internal temperature in the thickest part of the steak—pull it at 120 to 125°F (49 to 52°C) for medium-rare (keeping in mind that there will be about 10 degrees Fahrenheit of carryover cooking while the filets rest).

Let the filets rest for 5 minutes. Reheat the sauce over high heat, stirring to prevent sticking. Serve the steak over white rice or plain spaghetti with the sauce drizzled over the top. Serve any extra sauce on the side.

BEEF STIR-FRY WITH JALAPEÑO

LÀ JIĀO SĪ CHǍO NIÚ RÒU
辣椒丝炒牛肉

Serves 2

NOTE: Shaved beef is pretty widely available—I've seen it sold in plastic-wrapped packages at Trader Joe's. Or you can ask your butcher to shave meat for you on the slicer (sirloin, rib eye, and top round all work well here). If you want to shave the beef at home, freeze your steak for an hour (this will make it easier to cut), then use a knife to cut it as thinly as possible against the grain.

KATHY: If there was anyone in the Fang family who knew how to be frugal (dare I say, stingy?), it was my dad's younger sister, Little Aunt Shao Yang Yang. It was a well-known fact that if you were invited to her home for dinner, nine times out of ten, you would only be served one dish. And for the duration of that dinner, you would be frequently reminded of how resourceful of a cook she is. She'd tell you how she stretched a quarter pound of meat to feed four, how she hates leftovers (a sign of a good meal is to not have any leftovers!), and she'd open her fridge to show off how empty it was (she would only buy produce that she could use right away, never more than she needed). I remember one year she decided dish soap was frivolous and proceeded to wash all her dishes under a very slow hot stream of water, claiming it was the ultimate disinfectant.

When my little aunt immigrated to the US from China, she moved in with me, my mom, and my dad. I'll never forget the first night I spent at our home with her, sitting at our black granite kitchen counter as she looked through our fridge. "You've never had Shao Yang Yang's cooking before, have you? Do you eat spicy?"

She then proceeded to cook me the most delicious bowl of noodle soup, with spicy jalapeños and fragrant ginger-garlic beef. She explained that cutting meat into small pieces allowed the flavors to penetrate the meat faster, and how a little goes a long way as long as you make it taste good. Nowadays, I love to cook up the beef and jalapeño topping and serve it over rice, which makes for the easiest weeknight stir-fry. Or you can follow Little Aunt's lead and serve it over yáng chūn miàn (see Variation). If frugal always tasted like this, we would all be rich.

- 1 cup (6 ounces / 170 g) shaved beef (see Note), sliced into thin strips
- 1 cup (55 g) chopped scallions
- 2 teaspoons Shaoxing wine
- 2 teaspoons toasted sesame oil
- 2 teaspoons cornstarch
- 1 teaspoon oyster sauce
- 1 teaspoon salt
- 1 pinch of MSG
- 1 pinch of ground white pepper
- 1 pinch of sugar
- 2 tablespoons neutral oil
- 6 thin, coin-size slices of ginger, julienned
- 4 cloves garlic, minced
- 4 jalapeños, seeded and julienned
- Steamed white rice, to serve
- Chili oil (homemade, page 274, or store-bought) and black pepper, to serve (optional)

In a medium bowl, combine the beef, scallions, Shaoxing wine, sesame oil, cornstarch, oyster sauce, salt, MSG, white pepper, and sugar and use chopsticks or a fork to integrate the seasonings. Set aside to marinate for 15 minutes while you preheat your wok.

Heat your wok over high heat until smoking. Add 1 tablespoon of the neutral oil, swirling to coat the cooking surface. Stir-fry the ginger for 5 seconds. Add the beef and stir-fry for 40 seconds, or until 80 percent done. Transfer the contents of the wok to a large bowl, then add the remaining 1 tablespoon neutral oil to the wok. Stir-fry the garlic and jalapeños for 1 minute, then add the beef and ginger back in, tossing continuously, and cook until the beef has no pink in it at all, 30 to 40 seconds more. Serve over rice, drizzle with chili oil, top with black pepper, if using, and enjoy right away!

VARIATION (My Frugal Bowl of Jalapeño Beef Noodle Soup): Instead of white rice, you can divide the stir-fry and serve it over two bowls of yáng chūn miàn (page 142).

PÓ PO'S STEAMED BEEF PATTY

婆婆的清蒸牛肉饼
PÓ PO DE QĪNG ZHĒNG NIÚ RÒU BǏNG

Serves 2 to 4

KATHY: On many weekends, my cousins and I would get sent to stay with my maternal grandmother, Pó po. My aunt would do the shopping in Chinatown and then we would have a big family meal at my grandma's house. My mom and dad's families were culturally quite different. My dad's side had rosewood dining tables with glass covers and a lazy Susan. Meals would be eight to ten courses with matching ornate servingware, smooth melamine chopsticks, and porcelain spoons and holders. My pó po's dining table was large but always covered in a plastic checkered tablecloth that she taped to the table. She would wipe it down and reuse it until it tore, then layer another one on top and tape that down. Her servingware never matched, and she used old wooden chopsticks that had dull ends to them and were always wet because she'd wash them right before we used them.

But don't let the street food–style dining environment fool you. The food my pó po served was incredibly good and very technically refined, comparable to restaurant quality in Hong Kong. Her preferred methods of cooking were steaming and braising (typical of Cantonese cuisine), going light on the soy, sugar, and MSG, and leaning more on natural flavor profiles from the ingredients themselves. Her minced beef is the perfect example.

To make perfect steamed minced beef, you can't cut corners and use ground beef—the texture would come out completely different. You have to hand mince flank steak with a cleaver over and over, until all the filaments and protein are transformed into something that resembles super ground beef. Then you put the meat into a large bowl, start forming it into a ball, and slam it into the bowl. Beat the meat over and over. This helps aerate the minced meat and loosens the muscle, thereby producing a smooth bite when steamed. The meat should be tender, smooth, and springy, and have absolutely no iron or gamey flavor to it. Seasoning is minimal: salt, white pepper, a touch of light soy sauce, and the most important part, ginger scallion juice. Ginger scallion juice helps bring out the natural flavors of the flank, as opposed to garlic, which masks and fights with the natural flavors. (This is also why you would make beef bone broth with ginger and not garlic.) The juice that comes from the beef should taste like pure beef consommé, and the meat itself should taste like it's been cooked in that consommé. Pó po tops the minced beef with finely slivered ginger, and it's perfection. When that dish hits the table, all of us are ready with our wet chopsticks and rice bowl.

continued

Using a cleaver or chef's knife, mince the flank steak into what resembles ground beef. To do this, alternate chopping with the sharp edge of your cleaver and pounding with the flat end until it's fully ground, which should take 5 to 8 minutes. The goal is to break down the fibrous part of the steak. Feel the meat with your hands and fish out any long white fibrous pieces. Transfer the meat to a large bowl (stainless-steel is preferable because it's light and easy to mix in) and add the water chestnuts, egg white, soy sauce, sesame oil, cornstarch, Shaoxing wine, oyster sauce, salt, sugar, and white pepper. Use your hands to fully mix and incorporate.

Form the minced flank into a large ball and slam the ball into the bowl with force. Repeat this process over and over for 10 minutes. (If the ball feels too large to form in your hands, you can form two smaller balls and do the same thing.) The goal is to aerate the minced flank by forcing oxygen into the meat. If you repeat this process for a good 10 minutes, you will see the minced meat come together and become sticky to the touch. You'll know it's done when it no longer feels loose, becomes harder to form into a ball, and develops a slight sheen.

Combine the scallions and ginger matchsticks in a small bowl. Add just enough water to barely cover the aromatics, about ½ cup (120 ml). Using your hands, squeeze the scallions and ginger until the juices come out. The water should start to turn green from the scallions. Let the aromatics steep in the water for 10 minutes, then strain out and discard the solids. Spread the minced meat into a shallow stainless-steel or ceramic bowl or plate. Be sure the meat is not any thicker than ½ inch (1.25 cm). If it's thicker than ½ inch (1.25 cm), you need to use a larger bowl or plate, or work in batches. Pour ½ cup (120 ml) of the ginger-scallion water over the meat, then cover it with plastic wrap and let the meat absorb the ginger-scallion water at room temperature for 30 minutes.

Prepare a steamer with a rack that is large enough to comfortably fit the bowl with the beef inside. Add enough water to come halfway to the steaming rack. Bring the water to a boil. Place the bowl with the minced meat on the steamer rack, then sprinkle the julienned ginger garnish over the meat. Cover the steamer with a lid and steam for about 6 minutes, until the juices run clear. Check at the 6-minute mark by poking the middle of a patty. If the juices run clear, the patty is done. If there's still a bit of blood, continue to steam. Turn off the heat and keep the lid on while you set up your bowls of rice.

Serve the minced patty directly from the shallow bowl. Encourage your guests to spoon meat onto their rice, then spoon some broth over the rice and mix.

SERVING SUGGESTIONS: Enjoy with a side of garlic Chinese vegetables (such as Garlic Yam Leaf Tips, page 172) to make it a complete clean and comforting meal. For those who like a little heat, add chili crisp or sriracha for a spicy pop. Pairing it with sweet pickled vegetables such as pickled daikon (page 265) makes for a nice contrast of flavors and texture as well.

12 ounces (340 g) flank steak

3 water chestnuts, finely minced

1 egg white, whisked

2 tablespoons soy sauce

1½ tablespoons toasted sesame oil

1½ tablespoons cornstarch

1 tablespoon Shaoxing wine

1 tablespoon oyster sauce

½ teaspoon salt

½ teaspoon sugar

1 pinch of ground white pepper

2 scallions (white and green parts), julienned

4 (⅛-inch / 3 mm) coins of ginger, cut into matchsticks

4 paper-thin slices of ginger, julienned, for garnish

Cooked white rice, for serving

SEA
FOO

TREASURES FROM THE WATER

PETER: The texture, sweetness, and natural umami of seafood have captivated my taste buds ever since I was a child in Shanghai. I can still remember the first time I tasted perfectly steamed Mandarin fish (guì huā yú), its delicate flesh melting in my mouth, or the sweet pop of freshly caught river shrimp (hé xiā) from the Yangtze. These were flavors that made my eyes light up with joy. The local yellow croaker (huáng yú), whether braised or in soup, was a treat I always looked forward to. But perhaps most memorable was the pungent stir-fry of melt-in-your-mouth black eel (hēi shàn) with ginger and white pepper. The aroma would hit your nose before you even saw the dish, a scent so powerful and enticing that it still haunts me in the most delicious way.

In China, coastal regions have long relied on the bounty of the sea, while inland areas prized fish from rivers and lakes. When we immigrated to America, the waters off San Francisco offered different treasures than those we knew in Shanghai. Where we once enjoyed freshwater fish like carp and bream, we now had access to an abundance of Pacific seafood: bass, shrimp, and varieties of sole we had never seen before.

In this chapter, we're excited to share some of House of Nanking's standout seafood dishes, including Honey Apple Shrimp (page 249), a dish that perfectly balances sweetness and savory flavors, and Crispy Sole with Pea Shoot Salad (page 261), which showcases the delicate nature of the fish while adding a satisfying crunch. No Chinese seafood repertoire would be complete without a classic steamed whole fish, a dish that embodies the Chinese philosophy of preserving the natural flavors of ingredients, so we offer our family's version on page 277.

These recipes reflect both our Shanghainese roots and our San Francisco influences. They honor traditional Chinese cooking techniques while incorporating the seafood available in our adopted home.

PRAWNS IN TSINGTAO BEER SAUCE

啤酒大虾
PÍ JIǓ DÀ XIĀ

Serves 1

PETER: If you ask me where the best seafood I've ever tasted comes from, I'll tell you without a doubt, it's Shanghai. Our city sits right where the Yangtze River meets the East China Sea, and the waters are like nature's own seafood buffet. As a boy, I was lucky to taste many of Shanghai's specialties, and one of my favorites was stir-fried river shrimp (qīng chǎo hé xiā). The "qīng chǎo" cooking method refers to a light stir-fry that aims to maintain the original taste and texture of the main ingredient—in this case, delicate river shrimp that are tender with a slight, delightful bounce. In Shanghai, this dish is prized for its simplicity and prepared with minimal seasoning—often just a bit of salt, white pepper, MSG, a generous splash of Shaoxing wine, and a pinch of sugar. My love for this dish is what inspired my prawns in Tsingtao beer sauce, in which I swap out Shaoxing wine for beer. My customers were curious how a dish would taste with their favorite beer in it . . . and they loved it! And I was thrilled to share flavors of Shanghai I dearly missed, but with shrimp pulled out of the Pacific Ocean instead of the Yangtze River.

- 10 large prawns, shelled but with the tails on
- 1 pinch of ground black pepper
- 1 pinch of sugar
- 1 pinch of salt
- 1 tablespoon plus 1 teaspoon cornstarch
- 2 tablespoons neutral oil
- 1 teaspoon minced garlic
- 1 teaspoon minced ginger
- ½ cup (120 ml) Tsingtao beer
- 2 teaspoons sugar, plus more to season the prawns
- 2 teaspoons toasted sesame oil
- ½ teaspoon MSG
- ¼ teaspoon ground white pepper
- ½ cup (75 g) petite green peas
- Steamed white rice, for serving

Place the prawns in a medium bowl, then add the black pepper, sugar, salt, and 1 tablespoon of the cornstarch. Mix by hand and set aside to marinate for 5 minutes while you heat your wok.

In a saute pan over high heat, heat the neutral oil. Swirl the pan to coat it evenly. Add the prawns to the pan and stir-fry until they are cooked 75 percent of the way, which should take no more than 2 minutes—they will be translucent, which means there's still some rawness. Transfer the prawns to the bowl you used to marinate them. Add the garlic and ginger to the same pan you used to cook the prawns and stir-fry for 5 seconds, then add the beer. Bring the beer to a boil and add the remaining 2 teaspoons sugar, the sesame oil, MSG, and white pepper. Continue cooking, stirring, for 2 to 3 minutes, until the alcohol flavor has mostly been cooked off. Meanwhile, combine the remaining 1 teaspoon cornstarch with 1 teaspoon water and whisk to make a slurry.

Return the prawns to the pan, add the peas, stir for 30 seconds, then drizzle the slurry into the pan in a circular motion. Stir to coat the prawns in the sauce for another 30 seconds to 1 minute. The sauce will thicken up and coat the prawns to create a glossy glaze.

Serve with white rice. To make Prawns in Twin Happiness Sauce, arrange the prawns in beer sauce on one side of the serving plate and Nanking's Sesame Prawns (page 247) on the other side.

NANKING'S SESAME PRAWNS

芝麻大虾
ZHĪ MÁ DÀ XIĀ

Serves 1

PETER: Whenever I reminisce about the early House of Nanking days with our original fans, they always talk about a dish we called "Prawns in Twin Happiness Sauce." It was one of our most popular offerings and was basically a two-for-one deal: these sesame prawns, plus prawns in beer sauce (see page 246). Back then, a lot of the quick dine-in Chinese restaurants in Chinatown had combo plates. You could pick two entrees to add to your rice plate and it felt like such a great deal, even to me. So I took this idea, but instead of a lunch plate, I turned it into an entrée—one dish with two times the happiness. One prawn was crispy, sweet, sour, and spicy, red in color. The other was in a delicate white sauce made of Tsingtao beer, with a touch of savory umami flavors. The contrast of colors, textures, and flavors made this a big hit!

- 3 tablespoons ketchup
- 2 tablespoons white vinegar
- 2 tablespoons sugar, plus more to season the shrimp
- 1 tablespoon soy sauce (or tamari for a gluten-free dish)
- 1 teaspoon neutral oil
- ¼ teaspoon ground white pepper
- ¼ teaspoon chili flakes
- 10 large prawns, shelled but with the tails on
- 1 pinch of ground black pepper
- 1 pinch of salt
- 4 tablespoons (30 g) plus ½ teaspoon cornstarch
- Neutral oil, for deep-frying
- Steamed white rice, for serving

In a small bowl, whisk together the ketchup, vinegar, sugar, soy sauce, neutral oil, white pepper, chili flakes, and 1 teaspoon water. Set aside.

Place the prawns in a medium bowl, then add the black pepper, salt, 1 tablespoon of the cornstarch, and a pinch of sugar. Mix by hand and set aside to marinate.

In a separate medium bowl, make a batter by combining 3 tablespoons of the cornstarch with 2 tablespoons water and stir with a fork or your finger until the mixture has a thick, Elmer's glue–like consistency. (If it's too thick, add a touch more water.)

Fill a 12-inch (30 cm) cast-iron skillet halfway with oil, then heat over medium-high heat until it reaches 365°F (185°C) on a deep-fry thermometer. Submerge the prawns in the batter, allowing any excess batter to drip off, then gently drop them into the oil. (Our move is to dip a prawn in the batter, add it to the oil, then dip another prawn, until they're all battered and fried. But if you can't move quickly, you should pre-batter the prawns and return them to the bowl you marinated them in, then transfer all the battered shrimp to the oil at once.) Test-fry one prawn to make sure the oil is hot enough: It should become light golden brown after 2 minutes. If it takes longer than 2 minutes, your oil needs to be hotter. Working in batches as necessary to not crowd the pan, fry the remaining prawns for 2 minutes, or until they're light golden brown.

Transfer the prawns to a rack to drain. In a separate saute pan over medium-high heat, add the reserved sweet and sour sauce. Bring to a boil. Meanwhile, combine the remaining ½ teaspoon cornstarch with ½ teaspoon water and whisk to make a slurry. Once the sauce is boiling, add the slurry and stir immediately with a spatula so the slurry doesn't clump up. The sauce should thicken up within seconds. Keep stirring and add the prawns to the pan. Stir to coat evenly in the sauce.

Serve with white rice. To make Prawns in Twin Happiness Sauce, arrange the sesame prawns on one side of the serving plate and prawns in Tsingtao beer sauce (page 246) on the other side.

HONEY APPLE SHRIMP

蜂蜜苹果虾
FĒNG MÌ PÍNG GUǑ XIĀ

Serves 1

KATHY: When I was growing up in Chinatown in the 1980s and '90s, there was only one way to celebrate birthdays, weddings, baby showers, and other milestones, and that was a big, elaborate banquet. If you've sat through more than one Chinese restaurant banquet, you'll know they are all the same. Every single restaurant served the same copycat menu. Honestly, I didn't mind it—you know what you get, no surprises. My memories of most of these dishes has faded, but there is one I'll always remember and still love: honey walnut shrimp. The crispy, tender shrimp coated in a creamy sweet sauce with crunchy candied walnuts were such a welcome reprieve from jellyfish salad and roasted squab, and I think it was every kid's favorite.

Honey walnut shrimp is a classic Cantonese dish that originated from Hong Kong and became wildly popular in California in the early 1980s. I first made it for a custom banquet menu at Fang. My dad was a little surprised—"Honey walnut shrimp? Isn't that kind of old? You think Americans still want to eat this dish?" To which I said, hell yes we do. But as you've probably figured out by now, whenever we put something old-school on our menu, we always find a way to make it a little new-school. So out went the walnuts (sorry purists) and in came diced Fuji apples, which added a fruity, light, juicy aspect that complemented the shrimp. It's now one of our most popular dishes at Fang and Nanking; people call it "the shrimp and apples dish."

- 8 medium shrimp, shell removed but tail on
- 1 egg, whisked
- ½ cup (65 g) cornstarch
- ½ cup (120 ml) Kewpie mayonnaise
- 1 tablespoon condensed milk
- 1 tablespoon honey
- 1 teaspoon lemon juice
- ½ teaspoon chili oil (homemade, page 274, or store-bought)
- Neutral oil, for deep-frying
- 1 small Fuji apple, peeled, cored, and cut into 1-inch cubes

In a medium bowl, combine the shrimp and whisked egg. Place the cornstarch in a separate bowl and toss in the shrimp to coat (there will be extra cornstarch in the bowl). Set aside.

In a small bowl, whisk together the mayonnaise, condensed milk, honey, lemon juice, and chili oil. Set aside.

Fill a medium pot halfway with neutral oil. Heat the oil over high heat until it reaches 375°F (190°C) on a deep-fry thermometer. Drop the shrimp into the oil one by one so they don't stick together when they fry. Fry the shrimp, using a spider to move the shrimp around to prevent sticking, for 1 minute and 20 seconds, or until the shrimp is just cooked and slightly golden brown. Use the spider to transfer the shrimp to a wire rack.

Add the cubed apple to the bowl of cornstarch and toss to coat the apple in the remaining cornstarch. Once the oil has returned to 375°F (190°C), add the apples to the pot and fry for 1 minute and 20 seconds, or until slightly golden brown, using a spider to move the apple cubes around to prevent sticking. Use a spider to transfer the apples to the rack with the shrimp and turn the heat off.

Add 2 tablespoons of the honey-mayo sauce to a large bowl, then add the shrimp and apples and toss to coat. Add more sauce as desired. (Any remaining sauce can keep in the fridge for up to 5 days and used as a dipping sauce for fries, fried wontons, fried chicken, or even a spread for sandwiches.) Transfer the shrimp and apples to a serving platter and serve immediately.

FIVE-MINUTE STEAMED PRAWNS IN CHILI BLACK BEAN SAUCE AND GARLIC OIL

辣豆豉蒸大虾
LÀ DÒU CHǏ ZHĒNG DÀ XIĀ

Serves 1

KATHY: After leaving corporate America, I moved into my parents' place and worked with them at Nanking seven days a week for about year. During this year, I ate lunch with my dad between the busy lunch and dinner shifts every single day. Ninety percent of those meals were in Chinatown, and half of those were at New Woey Loy Goey, an old-school underground Guangdong restaurant located on Jackson and Grant that's been around for a century.

Whenever New Woey Loy Goey had fresh geoduck on the menu, our order was easy—two a piece, perfectly steamed with chili black beans, fried garlic, garlic oil, a touch of soy, and scallions, then served over glass noodles, which soaked up all the flavors.

I love this style of steaming seafood, and you can swap out the geoduck for fish, clams, lobster, crab, oysters, or prawns—even defrosted frozen. At home, I swap out glass noodles for shirataki noodles to cut down the carbs and add a little more texture. Shirataki noodles are made from a root vegetable called konjac; the texture is crunchier than noodles but still soft. You can substitute glass noodles if you can't find them; either way, you'll end up with an affordable, healthy, gourmet meal in five minutes!

- 8 ounces (225 g) shirataki knots (my preference) or mung bean vermicelli noodles, rinsed and drained
- 8 medium prawns, peeled but with the tail on
- 1 tablespoon minced garlic
- 1 tablespoon neutral oil
- 1 tablespoon Chinatown Chili Black Bean Sauce (page 275)
- 2 tablespoons chopped scallions
- 1 tablespoon soy sauce

Bring a large steamer to a boil over high heat. Make sure the water level is at least 1 inch below the rack.

In a round, shallow tray (you can even use a 9-inch pie tin) that will fit in your steamer setup, arrange the shirataki knots in an even layer. Arrange the prawns over the shirataki knots. Set aside.

In a small nonstick skillet, combine the garlic and oil and cook over medium heat just until the garlic is softened and lightly golden, about 1 minute. Pour the garlic and oil evenly over the prawns, then spread the chili black bean sauce evenly over the top.

Once the water is boiling, place the tray with the shrimp on the steamer rack. Cover with the lid and steam for 2 minutes. Open the lid and scatter the scallions on top, drizzle with soy sauce, re-cover, and steam for 1 to 2 minutes more, until the prawns are fully cooked.

Serve directly from the tray. Dinner couldn't be any easier or faster!

TSINGTAO

GINGER SCALLION PRAWNS WITH SOY BUTTER SAUCE

黄油葱姜大虾
HUÁNG YÓU CŌNG JIĀNG DÀ XIĀ

Serves 2

KATHY: My father and I share a passion for a Cantonese dish called sih yàuh wòhng ha, or "prawns in supreme soy," a delicacy of large, shell-on prawns with their tails and heads intact (the juicy heads are considered the best part). The dish earns its "supreme" title from the use of aged or high-quality soy sauce, which forms the base of its flavor.

The magic happens as sugar, soy sauce, scallions, and ginger caramelize in the pan with the prawns, creating a mouthwatering sauce that elevates peel-and-eat shrimp to new heights. In my home version, I've introduced a small twist: butter, inspired my daughter's love for prawns sauteed in butter, garlic, and olive oil. It's a beautiful fusion dish that's become one of our favorites, and best yet, it takes five minutes to cook!

- 1 tablespoon neutral oil
- 4 scallions, quartered
- 4 thin, bias-cut slices of ginger
- 12 large, head-on prawns
- 2 tablespoons aji-mirin
- 2 tablespoons butter
- 1 tablespoon dark soy sauce or premium aged soy sauce
- 1 tablespoon soy sauce
- 1 tablespoon ketchup
- 1 teaspoon sugar
- 1 teaspoon ground white pepper
- 1½ teaspoons cornstarch whisked with 1½ teaspoons water into a slurry
- 1 tablespoon olive oil
- Steamed white rice, for serving

Heat a large nonstick skillet over medium heat. Add the neutral oil and, once hot, add the scallions and ginger. Saute for 30 seconds, then add the prawns. Increase the heat to high, add the aji-mirin, and saute for 30 seconds more. Add the butter, dark and regular soy sauces, ketchup, sugar, and white pepper and saute for 1 minute, or until the prawns are almost cooked through. Add ¼ cup (60 ml) water and cook until the prawns are completely cooked. Working in a circular motion to prevent clumping, drizzle in the slurry and stir until well-integrated and the sauce is thickened. Finish with the olive oil, toss the prawns to evenly coat, and transfer to a serving platter. Serve with white rice.

HOW TO EAT HEAD-ON PRAWNS LIKE A PRO: Begin by savoring some of the sauce-coated shell. Then, twist to separate the head from the body, making sure to indulge in the flavorful juices within the head, which will have mingled with the sauce. Finally, peel the shrimp and bite into the tender, sweet meat. Enjoy spoonfuls of steamed white rice mixed with the savory sauce and fragrant scallions.

CRISPY BASS WITH CHINKIANG VINEGAR DIPPING SAUCE

炸鱼沾香醋
ZHÀ YÚ ZHĀN XIĀNG CÙ

Serves 2 to 3

PETER: One of my favorite things to eat in the world is from Shanghai, and I still can't get it in the US: Shanghai hairy crab, dà zhá xiè. It's a medium-sized freshwater crab that has fur on its claws, and it's considered a delicacy in Shanghai. The ones from Yangcheng Lake are the most prized. The crab meat is incredibly sweet and melt-in-your-mouth tender, and the roe, which is often used to elevate dishes such as noodles, tofu, and soup dumplings, has a rich flavor that reminds me of uni. But if you ask me, the best way to enjoy the crab is steamed, with a ginger-heavy sauce made of Chinkiang vinegar.

It's still impossible to find dà zhá xiè in the US, which has forced me to look for substitutes. Here in San Francisco, Dungeness crabs are most widely available, but their meat is firmer. If you live on the East Coast, blue crabs are sweeter and closer to dà zhá xiè. But at House of Nanking, I skip crab completely and offer this crispy sea bass, which guests dip in the ginger vinegar sauce I crave from Shanghai. The sweetness of the sea bass summons the spirit of the original dish.

CHINKIANG VINEGAR DIPPING SAUCE

- ¼ cup (60 ml) Chinkiang vinegar
- ¼ cup (50 g) cane sugar
- 2 tablespoons minced ginger

CRISPY SEA BASS

- 1 pound (455 g) sea bass fillet, skin and any large bones removed
- 1 tablespoon aji-mirin
- 1 teaspoon fish sauce
- 1 teaspoon ground black pepper, plus more for seasoning
- 1 pinch of ground white pepper
- ¼ cup (30 g) plus 1 teaspoon cornstarch, plus more as needed
- 1 egg, whisked
- Neutral oil, for frying
- 1 teaspoon chili oil (homemade, page 274, or store-bought)
- 1 pinch of sea salt
- 1 pinch of sugar
- 1 scallion, julienned

Make the dipping sauce: In a small saucepan, combine the vinegar, sugar, and ginger and bring to a boil over high heat, whisking frequently. Once the sugar has melted, turn off the heat and allow the sauce to cool to room temperature. Transfer to a small serving bowl and store at room temperature or in the refrigerator—it tastes even better after it sits overnight.

Make the crispy sea bass: Cut the sea bass into small pieces, about 1½ inches (3.75 cm) long and ½ inch (1.25 cm) thick. Place in a medium bowl with the aji-mirin, fish sauce, black pepper, white pepper, and 1 teaspoon of the cornstarch and let marinate for 15 minutes.

Pour the whisked egg into the bowl with the sea bass, then use your hands to thoroughly mix and coat the fish with egg. Add the remaining ¼ cup (30 g) cornstarch to the fish and mix with your hands to thoroughly coat. Add more cornstarch as needed to ensure each fillet has a light coating.

Fill a Dutch oven halfway with neutral oil and heat over high heat until it registers 350°F (175°C) on a deep-fry thermometer. Working in two batches, quickly but carefully add the battered fish pieces to the oil, stirring occasionally to prevent sticking and clumping. Cook for 3 to 4 minutes, until the fish floats to the top and is golden brown. Transfer the fish to a stainless-steel bowl and season with the chili oil, sea salt, sugar, and a pinch of black pepper. Toss to coat evenly and transfer to a shallow bowl. Garnish with the scallion and serve with dipping sauce on the side.

GRANDPA FANG'S PERFECTLY "STEAMED" WHOLE FISH WITH GINGER AND SOY FISH SAUCE

方爷爷的专属蒸鱼
FĀNG YÉ YE DE ZHUĀN SHǓ ZHĒNG YÚ

Serves 4 to 6

NOTE: You can substitute a whole branzino for the tilapia. A smaller branzino will need 6 to 7 minutes in the microwave; a larger one will take 8 to 9 minutes.

PETER: There is a saying in China that Shanghai men make the best husbands. In Shanghainese, "ma da dao" means "shop, wash, cook." We Shanghai men not only accompany our wives to shop, but also carry all their bags, help clean, and cook, oftentimes better than the wife. From what I noticed during my years in Shanghai, this stereotype is more accurate than false. Some say this is a result of societal changes at the end of the first Opium War, in the late 1800s. At this time, Shanghai became an open international port: The British, French, and Americans came in and carved out concessions where they could work, live, and eat and drink. With that came rapid growth in the service industry, and women were preferred for these jobs over men. This created a role reversal of where Shanghai women became breadwinners and men took over many of the household chores.

Well, my father somehow missed the ma da dao gene. He couldn't stand grease or oil on his hands, which made washing dishes a very uncomfortable experience. I will never forget my mother complaining about having to cook and clean, only to find my father attempting to wash a rice bowl by holding it down against the bottom of the sink with a pair of chopsticks while scrubbing with a sponge so he would not have to touch the bowl with his fingers. Whereas everyone else in my family loved food—studied it and learned how to cook—my father had no interest in it and only knows how to cook three things: egg fried rice, glass soup, and "steamed" fish, which is actually microwaved. The first two dishes are ones he would make only for himself. The last dish turned out to be so good that he'd make it for the whole family, to give my mother a break in the kitchen.

- 1 (2-pound / 910 g) whole tilapia (see Note)
- 6 thin slices ginger, plus 1 tablespoon julienned ginger
- 1 scallion, cut into thirds, plus ¼ cup (15 g) julienned scallions
- 1½ tablespoons Shaoxing wine
- 1½ tablespoons fish sauce
- 3 tablespoons seasoned soy sauce for seafood
- A few leaves of cilantro (optional)
- ¼ cup (60 ml) neutral oil
- Steamed white rice, for serving

Clean the tilapia by rinsing it under cold water, making sure to get the underside gill area. Pat the fish dry and place it in a large, shallow microwave-safe (preferably porcelain or ceramic) bowl that can fit the entire fish, from head to tail. On the side of the fish that faces up, make 3 shallow vertical slits along the body of the fish. Place the ginger slices over the body and tuck 2 below the gill area. Scatter the scallion thirds on top of the fish. Drizzle the Shaoxing wine over the fish. Cover with microwave-safe plastic wrap and form a tight seal around the bowl so steam does not escape. Microwave for 8 minutes. Allow the fish to remain sealed in plastic in the microwave for 2 minutes—the residual heat will cook the fish further—before taking out the plate. Remove the plastic wrap and, using an oven mitt or hand towel, grab the end of the bowl and tilt it over the sink to pour out and discard the steaming liquid.

In a small bowl, mix the fish sauce and seasoned soy sauce and then pour it over the fish. Scatter the cilantro (if using), julienned ginger, and scallions over the top. In a small pot over high heat, heat the neutral oil until it smokes. Pour the hot oil directly over the scallions and ginger, from tail to head. The scallions and ginger will sizzle, creating a fragrant aroma. To serve, using a spoon, scoop the sauce that is sitting below the fish and baste the meat with it. Serve with steamed rice and enjoy with the scallions and ginger in the sauce. Pair it with a Chinese vegetable for a complete meal.

TIP: Chinese people enjoy the texture of fish skin, even when it's steamed. But some people do not enjoy the slippery and fatty mouthfeel and are more accustomed to crispy fish skin. In this case, you can easily remove the skin from the flesh to reveal the tender, moist meat.

PAN-FRIED BRANZINO FILLET WITH BUTTER AND PICKLED MUSTARD GREEN SAUCE

黄油酸菜煎鱼
HUÁNG YÓU SUĀN CÀI JIĀN YÚ

Serves 2

KATHY: You know what always gets people? When I tell them Italian is my favorite cuisine to cook at home. But in San Francisco, North Beach (home of the city's old-school Italian American community) and Chinatown sit right next to each other like old friends. Italian food was always my childhood favorite, and it turned out to be the perfect "gateway" to Western food for my parents, too.

The more you look at these cuisines, the more beautiful parallels you see: noodles and pasta, jasmine and Arborio rice, dumplings and ravioli, all dancing to the same melody. Those analogies might seem obvious, but here's the wild one that really blows people's minds: pickled mustard greens (xián cài) and capers, which both bring a briny, acidic punch with just the right amount of salt and texture to any dish they grace.

This is what inspired me to put my own spin on sole piccàta, one of my all-time favorite Italian dishes. In the traditional version, I love the gorgeous butter-caper sauce, which has a rich, luxurious base and bright, salty pops of flavor. It reminds me so much of suān cài yú piàn, an amazing Chinese dish with fish slices in a hot-and-sour broth with fermented mustard greens.

So, I thought, why not bring these worlds together? Swap out the capers for pickled mustard greens, keeping that tender white fish as the star. It works whether you go with sole or branzino, and is a perfect marriage of the two culinary traditions.

- 4 branzino or sole fillets (about 8 ounces / 225 g)
- Salt and freshly ground black pepper
- ¼ cup (30 g) all-purpose flour
- ¼ cup (30 g) chopped pickled sour mustard greens (suān cài, page 284)
- ½ teaspoon sugar
- ½ teaspoon ground white pepper
- ¼ cup (60 ml) neutral oil
- 2 tablespoons unsalted butter
- 1 tablespoon brine from pickled sour mustard greens (suān cài, page 284)
- ¼ cup (60 ml) sake
- Roasted potatoes or crusty bread, for serving

Season the fish fillets on both sides with salt and black pepper, then sprinkle the flour on both sides and press to make sure the fillets are really coated. Set aside.

In a small bowl, mix the chopped pickled mustard greens, sugar, and white pepper. Set aside.

In a large cast-iron skillet, heat the oil over medium heat. Working in batches as needed so you don't crowd the pan, sear the fillets for 2 minutes per side, or until the flesh is cooked through and firm to the touch. Transfer the fillets to a plate and set aside.

Reduce the heat to medium-low and add the butter, pickled mustard greens, mustard green brine, and sake to the skillet. Cook, stirring, for 30 seconds, or until the butter has melted. Return the fish to the skillet, spoon the sauce over the top, and serve immediately with roasted potatoes or crusty bread.

CRISPY SOLE WITH PEA SHOOT SALAD

龙利配豆苗沙拉
LÓNG LǏ PÈI DÒU MIÁO SHĀ LĀ

Serves 1

KATHY: I'll never forget the day I decided this dish—crispy, flaky, tender sole topped with a bright refreshing salad of crunchy greens, with hot, cold, crunchy, soft, and moist all in one bite—must be in our cookbook. I was at the Ferry Building farmers' market, picking up produce in my House of Nanking hoodie. When I stopped at the fresh-pressed juice stand, the owner looked at my shirt and said, "Nanking! OMG, I love that place. I used to go there once a week when I lived in the city. I'll never forget your crispy sole with Chinese greens."

Truthfully, my dad and I hadn't thought about that dish in decades. He's created so many recipes over the span of thirty-five years; it's hard for us to remember them all. Sometimes it takes a loyal HoNK lifer to remind us. When your food has left that lasting an impact on someone's life, that's how you know you are doing something right. For reminding us of a favorite from twenty years ago, I wanted to thank this man. This recipe is for you! I'll be coming to your juice stand soon.

- 1 (6- to 8-ounce / 170 to 225 g) fillet of sole
- Juice of ½ lemon
- 1 teaspoon fish sauce
- 1 pinch of ground black pepper
- 1 pinch of sugar
- Cornstarch
- 1 cup (240 ml) neutral oil
- Sea salt, to taste
- Three-Tiered Baby Pea Shoot Salad (page 69), minus the sweet potato garnish
- Chili oil (homemade, page 274, or store-bought), to finish
- Nanking Sauce (page 270), to finish (optional)

Place the fish in a shallow bowl and add the lemon juice, fish sauce, black pepper, and sugar. Allow to marinate in the fridge for 30 minutes. Transfer the sole to a flat plate and sprinkle cornstarch on both sides, pressing down to ensure every inch of the fish is coated with cornstarch. You should not see any flesh of the fish. Set aside.

In a heavy-bottomed skillet large enough to fit the whole fish, heat the neutral oil over high heat until it reaches 350°F (175°C) on a deep-fry thermometer. (Alternatively, if you only have a smaller skillet, you can cut the fish on a 45-degree bias into 4 equal pieces.) Right before you drop the fillet in, check for any bald spots and add more cornstarch as needed. Shake off excess and shallow-fry the fish for 1 to 2 minutes per side, until golden brown and cooked through. The fish is rather thin and should fry in less than 3 minutes.

Transfer to a serving plate and immediately season with sea salt. Spoon the pea shoot salad over the fish. (Or, if you cut it into pieces, mound the pea shoot salad on the serving plate and arrange the fish on top.) Drizzle chili oil over the fish and pea shoots. For an extra pop of flavor, drizzle some Nanking Sauce, too. Serve!

PICKLES, PR

腌菜

調味品

CONDIM

THE SECRET WEAPONS OF CHINESE CUISINE

KATHY: In Chinese cooking, the difference between a good dish and an unforgettable one often lies in the supporting cast—the condiments, sauces, and pickles that add depth and complexity to every bite. From the delicate but fiery kick of Soy-Marinated Jalapeños (page 265) to the crisp, tangy crunch of Pickled Daikon and Carrots (page 265), each condiment and pickle in this chapter plays a crucial role in the House of Nanking flavor palette . . . but can also be a versatile addition to your own home repertoire.

Some of these recipes, like Nanking's Famous Peanut Sauce (page 270) and the cryptically named Nanking Sauce (page 270), have become synonymous with our restaurant's identity. Others, like the versatile Scallion-Oil Soy Sauce with Ginger (page 275) and the potent Chili Oil (page 274), are staples in Chinese kitchens across the world.

Think of these condiments, sauces, and pickles as more than just accompaniments; they're transformative ingredients that can elevate the simplest of dishes. A spoonful of là jiàng transforms a plain bowl of noodles into a quick, satisfying five-minute meal, while a dash of our Sweet Chili Sauce will make even the humblest stir-fried vegetable sing. Experiment, mix and match, and discover how these recipes can become staples in your home cooking.

ESERVES,

ENTS

SAUCES

CLOCKWISE FROM TOP: Sesame Sauce (page 271), Soy-Marinated Jalapeños (page 265), Nanking's Famous Peanut Sauce (page 270), Sweet Chili Sauce (page 271), Chinatown Chili Black Bean Sauce (page 275)

SOY-MARINATED JALAPEÑOS

酱油腌青辣椒
JIÀNG YÓU YĀN QĪNG LÀ JIAO

Makes about 1 cup (240 ml)

PETER: I've always loved spice, and back in the day, I would consume all sorts of hot sauces. But now I find that my seventy-four-year-old body can't handle chili pastes and sauces the way I used to. That's why I have this soy and fresh jalapeño condiment in my fridge at all times. It's a great way to add a little heat to dishes—I find it's milder than chili paste but still has a nice pop of flavor and crunchy texture. It's great as a dipping sauce for boiled dumplings (place one piece of jalapeño on the dumpling, spoon a little of the soy marinade over the top, and eat dumpling and pepper together), on mild seafood like steamed fish or shrimp, and on top of noodle soups, fried rice, or fried over-easy eggs.

NOTE: Remove the seeds from the jalapeños if you'd like to keep things milder. But make sure to wear food-safe gloves to do it—you don't want jalapeño oils on your fingers!

- 5 tablespoons (75 ml) hot water
- 3 tablespoons soy sauce
- 2 tablespoons toasted sesame oil
- 1 tablespoon Shaoxing wine
- 1 tablespoon fish sauce
- 1 tablespoon sugar
- ½ teaspoon white vinegar
- ½ teaspoon MSG
- 3 large jalapeños, sliced crosswise ½ inch thick (see Note)
- 2 red Thai bird chilis, thinly sliced crosswise
- 2 cloves garlic, thinly sliced

Combine all the ingredients in a pint-size glass jar, seal tightly, and shake to disperse everything evenly. Refrigerate overnight to let the flavors meld, then enjoy the next day. Store refrigerated for up to 1 week—but this usually doesn't last that long for me. I make a fresh batch every few days.

PICKLED DAIKON AND CARROTS

甜酸红白萝卜
TIÁN SUĀN HÓNG BÁI LUÓ BO

Makes about 3 cups (300 g) to serve 2 to 4

KATHY: This is a versatile quick pickle that we use at Fang in our Southeast Asian Tofu Bowl (page 200); to give our famous bao an acidic, crunchy pop; and also serve dressed in sesame oil and fried shallots as a cold dish appetizer. In Chinese culture, eating something sour prior to a meal is said to wake up one's appetite. So, this would be a great precursor to a larger meal, or you can use it as a sweet and sour condiment on any dish that needs brightening up.

- ¾ cup (150 g) sugar
- ½ cup (120 ml) rice vinegar
- 1 teaspoon salt
- 1 cup (125 g) julienned daikon
- 1 cup (140 g) julienned carrots

In a small pot, combine the sugar, rice vinegar, salt, and 1½ cups (360 ml) water and heat over medium-high heat until the sugar and salt dissolve. Remove from the heat and allow to cool to room temp.

Place the daikon and carrots in a quart-size mason jar, then pour the pickling liquid over the top. Press down to make sure they're submerged (add a bit of water, if not). Cover and place in the fridge to pickle for 2 to 3 days before using. Store in the fridge for up to 1 week.

FERMENTED CHINESE LONG BEANS, AKA PICKLED LONG BEANS

酸豆角
SUĀN DÒU JIAO

Makes ½ gallon (2 L)

PETER: My wife has a beautiful blue and white ceramic fermentation jar that she has kept with our family for the last forty-five years. It looks like a large vase with a narrow neck that also has a moat around it for you to pour water in. The round lid that covers the opening on the neck fits right into the moat, creating a natural seal that prevents oxygen from entering. This is how Chinese people fermented, pickled, and preserved ingredients back in the days before proper refrigeration.

Traditionally you would just add whatever spices you had to the jar, but the most prominent two flavors are usually sour and salty. The sour element is created via fermentation, not a vinegar brine. Store the beans in the salted, spiced brine for 10 to 12 days in a cold dark place, and they will naturally develop a pungent sour taste, while still maintaining a nice crunch.

- 1 pound (455 g) Chinese long beans, blossom ends trimmed
- 1 tablespoon salt
- 3 red Thai bird chilis, chopped
- 3 star anise
- 1 teaspoon Sichuan peppercorns (optional)

Make sure your beans are washed and dried completely before starting.

Fill your fermentation vessel, such as a 64-ounce (½-gallon / 2 L) jar or traditional Chinese fermentation jar, so it's a little less than three-quarters filled with water. Now pour this water into a large pot. Add the salt, chilis, star anise, and Sichuan peppercorns, if using, and bring to a boil. Boil for 2 to 3 minutes, until you can begin to taste the spice. Adjust the salt if needed; it should taste like very lightly salted water. Allow the brine to cool completely to room temperature. Stuff the long beans into the jar and press down.

If you are using a traditional Chinese fermentation jar, pour the brine into the jar until it reaches the bottom of where the neck opening begins. Add the weights and cover with the lid. If you are using a Mason-style canning jar, make sure the brine covers the beans completely. Add weights to keep the beans submerged before sealing the lid. Place the jar in a cool, dark place for 10 to 12 days.

If not using immediately, dice the long beans and store them submerged in the brine in the refrigerator for up to 2 weeks.

LÀ JIÀNG

辣酱

Makes 30 ounces (890 ml)

KATHY: In my household, a jar of là jiàng in the fridge means you can throw together a million different dishes in less than five minutes. We use it as a topping, a condiment, a sauce, or a side. And just like hot sauce, you can enjoy it cold, straight out of the jar. You don't even need to reheat it; simply add it to hot noodles, rice, congee, or toast and it will melt in.

- 1 cup (240 ml) neutral oil
- 14 ounces (400 g) pork tenderloin, cut into small dice (1¼ cups)
- 1¼ cups (90 g) raw peanuts
- 9 ounces (255 g) savory baked tofu or marinated firm tofu, cut into small dice
- ¼ cup (20 g) dried shrimp, rinsed then soaked in cold water for 30 minutes
- 6 tablespoons (90 ml) hoisin sauce
- ¼ cup (60 ml) la doubanjiang (chili broad bean sauce)
- 1 tablespoon sambal oelek
- 1 teaspoon MSG

In a wok, heat the neutral oil over high heat. When it begins to smoke, swirl to coat the wok, then add the pork and stir with a wok spatula to keep the ingredients moving and prevent sticking. Fry for 5 minutes; your goal is to pull out as much moisture as you can, which prevents spoilage and extends the shelf life. Using a spider, transfer the pork to a bowl and set aside.

Reduce the heat to low and add the peanuts. Fry, stirring to ensure even cooking, for 4 minutes, or until a very light golden hue. Use a spider to transfer to the bowl with the pork.

Increase the heat to high, add the marinated tofu, and fry, stirring, for 2 minutes. The tofu should develop a light golden hue. Use a spider to transfer to the bowl with the pork.

Drain the shrimp and dry with a paper towel. Reduce the heat to low and fry the shrimp, stirring, for 4 minutes, or until the shrimp begin to puff up and turn golden. Add the pork, peanuts, and tofu back to the wok with the shrimp. Increase the heat to high and add the hoisin sauce, la doubanjiang, sambal oelek, and MSG. Stir-fry for 2 minutes to fully incorporate and season the ingredients. Add ½ cup (120 ml) water and reduce for 5 minutes, or until the water evaporates and only oil is left.

Remove from the heat and store in glass jars with the lid off. Once completely cooled, close the lid and store in the fridge for up to 1 month.

FERMENTED BEAN CURD SAUCE

腐乳酱
FŬ RŬ JIÀNG

Makes about ¼ cup (60 ml)

KATHY: Every first-gen Asian kid has probably had their stinky lunch moment at some point in their life. For me it was not a moment; it was more like a five-year, drawn-out experience that went from full embarrassment to me just growing a hard shell and not being bothered by it. It didn't help that I had the ugliest lunch bag ever. All the other kids had either cool themed lunch boxes or paper bags. I had a Chinatown plastic grocery bag, ostensibly because it's reusable and durable, but really because it's free. I looked like a Chinese grandma carrying her groceries to the schoolyard during lunchtime. But after a few weeks, I got over it and accepted my fate. The one lunch moment that I could not accept, however, was the day my dad replaced my ranch dressing with fermented bean curd sauce as a dip for carrot sticks. Without asking, my friend leaned over, grabbed a stick, dipped it into the sauce, and popped it in her mouth. She then spit it out and screamed, "It stinks! Get it out of my mouth!"

Now that I'm an adult, I have a lot of sympathy for my dad. Yes, this sauce does have a distinctive smell; it's FERMENTED, for god's sake. But it's also a complex dip with flavors reminiscent of white miso and La Tur Italian cheese, whipped together with toasted sesame oil. This is something you would pair with farmers' market greens and charge $26 for in San Francisco in 2024. I never had it again at school after that traumatic day, but now it's a delightful dip for my crudité platter.

- 6 cubes white fermented bean curd (see page 281)
- 1 tablespoon toasted sesame oil
- 1 tablespoon agave nectar
- 2 teaspoons chili oil, homemade (page 274) or store-bought
- Raw vegetables, such as Persian cucumbers, baby radishes, sugar snap peas, and little gem lettuce, cleaned and trimmed, for serving

In a small bowl, whisk together the bean curd, sesame oil, agave, and chili oil until you achieve a smooth, creamy consistency. Chill in the fridge for 30 minutes, then serve with the raw vegetables. Store in an airtight container in the fridge for up to 4 days.

NANKING'S FAMOUS PEANUT SAUCE

花生酱
HUĀ SHĒNG JIÀNG

Makes 1 cup (240 ml)

PETER: I'll never forget the day Kathy led me down the aisles of the grocery store, explaining she wanted to make something she'd seen her classmates eating: a peanut butter and jelly sandwich. Back home, before heading to Nanking for dinner shift, we made sandwiches together. As always, I tasted the ingredients first—it's a habit of mine before cooking anything. When I tried the peanut butter, I was blown away. Back in Shanghai, we have sesame paste, which is delicious. But this peanut butter was like an amped-up version, whipped into a sweet, creamy, nutty dream. I examined the jar: blue lid, "Skippy" in bold red. I thought to myself, *This stuff is even better than sesame paste. I have to make a sauce with it.* It was an instant hit, and my customers wanted it on everything: fried onion cakes, shrimp cakes, fried tofu, and even plain rice.

- ½ cup (120 ml) creamy peanut butter (we use Skippy brand)
- ¼ cup (60 ml) toasted sesame oil
- ¼ cup (60 ml) light agave nectar
- 2 tablespoons soy sauce
- 2 tablespoons Chinkiang vinegar
- 1 tablespoon white distilled vinegar
- 2 teaspoons sambal oelek
- 1 teaspoon chili flakes
- ½ teaspoon finely minced garlic

In a medium bowl, whisk together the peanut butter and sesame oil until fully emulsified. Add the remaining ingredients and stir to incorporate. Let the sauce sit for 10 minutes before serving. The viscosity should resemble a thick BBQ sauce. If the sauce is too thick, dilute with hot water, 1 teaspoon at a time. The sauce can be stored refrigerated in an airtight container for up to 3 days.

NANKING SAUCE

南京酱
NÁN JĪNG JIÀNG

Makes about 1½ cups (360 ml)

KATHY: When my dad hears the word "marketing," he usually runs the other way—which is why I was so surprised when one day he decided to take a stab at "marketing" one of our most popular sauces. Our Nanking Sauce is essentially sweet and sour sauce, minus the food coloring, artificial flavor, and ultra-thick goopiness, plus a pop of acid, subtle sweetness, and a kick of spice. It's good on everything—shrimp, scallops, mushrooms, pork, you name it—and our customers were obsessed. So Dad decided to take my second-grade class photo, blow it up, and tape it to a sheet of paper with my chicken scratch writing: "My favorite thing to eat is Hamburger with Nanking Sauce." He framed it and hung it on the back wall of our restaurant. There you have it, our one and only stab at marketing.

- ½ cup (120 ml) soy sauce
- ¼ cup (60 ml) white distilled vinegar
- ¼ cup (60 ml) honey
- 2 tablespoons sugar
- 1 teaspoon chili powder or flakes (optional)
- 2 tablespoons cornstarch whisked with 2 tablespoons water into a slurry

In a small pot, combine the soy sauce, white vinegar, honey, sugar, chili powder, and 1 cup (240 ml) water and bring to a boil over high heat. Reduce the heat to achieve a simmer, then cook, whisking, for 1 minute. Increase the heat to high again and, while whisking, slowly drizzle the slurry into the sauce in a circular motion to prevent clumping. You may not need all the slurry—stop when the sauce has thickened to a thick honey-like consistency. Store in an airtight container in the fridge for up to 3 days.

SERVING TIP: Extra sauce is great on grilled or roasted chicken, or as a dipping sauce.

SESAME SAUCE

芝麻酱
ZHĪ MA JIÀNG

Makes 1½ cups (360 ml)

PETER: This is one of Nanking's signature sauces, which we use on our Sesame Noodles (page 114). It also works as a dressing for salad, dip for crudité, or sauce for fried vegetables and dumplings.

Chinese sesame paste has a different flavor profile and consistency than tahini. Tahini uses untoasted sesame seeds, whereas Chinese sesame paste starts with toasted sesame seeds, resulting in a thicker, darker, more aromatic paste. For Chinese recipes, use Chinese sesame paste if possible. But for this recipe, tahini works fine, because when I first developed it at Nanking, I used tahini. Back then, Chinese sesame paste was very expensive and hard to find in bulk. Tahini, by contrast, was available in bulk at the grocery store at 22nd Avenue and Irving Street in the Inner Sunset, which I used to pass on my way to the restaurant in the mornings.

- ½ cup (120 ml) tahini or sesame paste
- 1 tablespoon minced garlic
- 2 tablespoons toasted sesame oil
- 2 tablespoons soy sauce
- 1½ teaspoons dark soy sauce
- 2 tablespoons Chinkiang vinegar
- 1 tablespoon white distilled vinegar
- 3 tablespoons agave nectar
- Pinch of MSG or dashi powder (optional)

In a small bowl, combine the tahini and minced garlic. Working one ingredient at a time, and waiting until the previous ingredient is fully incorporated before adding the next, whisk in the sesame oil followed by soy sauce, dark soy sauce, Chinkiang vinegar, white vinegar, and agave nectar. The MSG or dashi powder goes in last, if using. The consistency should be like Caesar dressing; if the sauce is too thick, add water, a tablespoon at a time, to thin it out.

Store the sauce in an airtight container in the fridge for up to 1 week.

SWEET CHILI SAUCE

甜辣酱
TIÁN LÀ JIÀNG

Makes 1¼ cups (300 ml)

KATHY: This is a fabulous dipping sauce for anything fried—even your kids' chicken nuggets. Or use it to glaze grilled chicken.

- 2 tablespoons sugar
- 2 tablespoons white distilled vinegar
- 1½ tablespoons soy sauce
- 1 tablespoon strawberry jelly
- 1 tablespoon ketchup
- 1 teaspoon toasted sesame oil
- 1 teaspoon duò jiāo (Chinese salted chopped chilis, see page 285) or sambal oelek, or more if you like it spicy
- 1 pinch of white pepper
- 1 pinch of salt
- 1 pinch of chili flakes
- 1 tablespoon cornstarch whisked with1 tablespoon water into a slurry

In a medium saucepan, combine the sugar, vinegar, soy sauce, jelly, ketchup, sesame oil, duò jiāo, white pepper, salt, and chili flakes with 1 cup (240 ml) water. Whisk until smooth, then heat over medium heat until the sauce simmers. Simmer for 2 minutes, then, while whisking vigorously, drizzle in the slurry in a circular motion to prevent clumping. Allow the sauce to thicken for 30 seconds, then turn the heat off. The sauce can be stored refrigerated in an airtight container for up to 3 days.

MAMA'S GOLD LABEL XO SAUCE

妈妈的金牌XO 酱
MĀ MA DE JĪN PÁI XO JIÀNG

Makes 4½ cups (36 ounces / 1 kg)

NOTE: It may seem like this recipe calls for a lot of oil, but you need all of it to help extend the shelf life of XO. The scallop and shrimp mixture should always have oil above it, otherwise it might spoil. When you take some XO sauce out of the jar to use, use a clean, dry chopstick rather than a spoon—this allows you to get the XO without scooping out a lot of oil. Regardless, you should always use a clean, dry utensil when you dig into the jar, to prevent moisture from entering.

KATHY: My mom's father is originally from Hunan, where spice plays a big part in the regional cuisine. Her mom, who was originally from Shanghai, moved to Hong Kong when she was in her thirties and identifies more as Cantonese than Shanghainese. So it's no surprise that my mom, combining her Hunan and Cantonese background, makes literally the best XO sauce in the world. The quality of her ingredients plays a huge part in why it's so good: She only uses the best of the best, and a bottle can cost around $100 to make. This is one of those recipes that is for serious foodies and chefs who want to make a hardcore XO sauce (and are willing to shell out some cash for it). But between the level of spice and the umami flavors that come from all the dried ingredients, it's quite possibly the best hot sauce you'll ever taste. Use it as a dipping sauce for dumplings, on egg fried rice, in a simple bowl of noodles, or on scrambled eggs. A small spoonful goes a long way, and we savor every bit.

Drain the soaked scallops. Place a layer of paper towels on a cutting board, then arrange the scallops on top and cover them with another layer of paper towels. Further dry the scallops by massaging them through the paper towels, pushing down to squeeze out excess moisture from the scallops. Remove and discard the paper towels, then blot the scallops dry with fresh paper towels. Once the scallops are dry, working one handful at a time, place them on a clean, dry cutting board and use the flat part of your cleaver or chef's knife to scrape and press the scallops, thereby shredding them into thin, separate pieces. Once one handful is nicely shredded, repeat the process until all the scallops are shredded.

Drain the soaked shrimp, wrap them in a layer of paper towels, and use your hands to wring them dry. Set aside.

In a large saute pan, heat the neutral oil over medium heat. Add the dried scallops and dried shrimp to the oil and stir frequently to ensure even cooking and that nothing burns or sticks to the bottom of the pan. Fry the scallops and shrimp for 8 minutes, or until all the remaining moisture has evaporated. To test if the scallops are ready, try a piece. It should be almost crisp, like the consistency of dried squid, and close to golden brown in color.

Add the Thai bird chilis, red chili powder, dehydrated garlic, and dehydrated shallots and reduce the heat to low. Continue to cook, stirring frequently, for another 10 to 15 minutes, until the scallops and shrimp turn a dark shade of golden. Adjust the heat to ensure the seasoning is bubbling gently in the oil to extract flavor. Add the baijiu and cook for 2 to 3 minutes, until the alcohol taste has mellowed. Add the oyster sauce, la doubanjiang, sugar, and soy sauce and stir to combine.

When you're happy with the taste, turn off the heat and immediately use a ladle to transfer the XO sauce to airtight glass jars (it's important to do this while the sauce is hot, not cooled). Make sure there is at least 1½ to 2 inches (4 to 5 cm) of oil above the scallop and shrimp mixture, which will help preserve the sauce. Seal the sauce and allow the jars to cool at room temperature, then store in the refrigerator for up to 6 months.

5¼ ounces (150 g) dried scallops, soaked overnight (or until soft)

3¼ ounces (90 g) dried baby shrimp (xiā mǐ, see page 289), soaked for 1 hour (or until soft)

3½ cups (840 ml) neutral oil (see Notes)

2 to 5 red Thai bird chilis (depending on how spicy you like it), thinly sliced

½ cup (65 g) red chili powder

¼ cup (25 g) dehydrated chopped garlic

¼ cup (15 g) dehydrated shallots

1½ tablespoons baijiu (Chinese liquor) or 3 tablespoons Shaoxing wine

2 tablespoons oyster sauce

2 tablespoons la doubanjiang (chili broad bean sauce)

1 tablespoon sugar

1 teaspoon soy sauce

IDEAS FOR ENJOYING YOUR XO SAUCE

- Use as a dipping sauce for dim sum, or add a tiny dollop on your dumplings.
- Add a small spoonful into your egg fried rice.
- Add a small spoonful into a simple bowl of noodles.
- Scramble eggs, add a dollop after your eggs are cooked, and stir to mix.

CHILI OIL

辣油
LÀ YÓU

Makes 1¼ cups (300 ml)

KATHY: At both House of Nanking and Fang, we make all our hot sauces and chili oils from scratch. Our Chinatown Chili Black Bean Sauce (page 275) is the mildest of the bunch and has a pronounced savory and salty flavor profile, making it one of our customers' favorites. This chili oil is more of a finisher than a condiment; it's our kitchen workhorse, and you'll see a huge bowl of it by our serving station. It gets used to finish our dumplings, soups, noodles, buns, mapo tofu, and five-spice whitefish.

The oil packs a medium amount of heat, which makes it approachable, and has bits of toasted chili flakes that add nuttiness and texture that helps the sauce grab onto the food better than just straight oil. When you spoon straight chili oil over, say, a wonton sitting on a spoon, the oil slides off. If you spoon chili oil that has chili flakes in it, it will grab onto the wonton. Maybe I'm weird, but it gives me joy to see that on my food.

TIP: If you prefer more oil and less chili flakes, reduce the flakes to ¼ cup (30 g). Or, if you want to give this a floral má là note, add 1 tablespoon Sichuan peppercorns.

- 1½ cups (360 ml) neutral oil
- 1 teaspoon cloves
- 5 star anise
- 2 bay leaves
- ½ cup (60 g) chili flakes
- 2½ tablespoons chili powder
- 2 teaspoons salt, or to taste

In a small pot over medium heat, combine the neutral oil, cloves, star anise, and bay leaves. Once bubbles start to form, immediately reduce the heat to low. Use a deep-fry thermometer to maintain a steady oil temperature of 225°F (105°C). If the temp climbs above that level, remove from the heat and wait until it drops back down to 200°F (95°C) before heating again. Make sure you keep an eye on the spices, which can burn rather quickly. If that happens, dump everything and start over. Simmer over low heat for 20 to 30 minutes; the spices should gradually turn a darker brown.

In a separate bowl, combine the chili flakes, chili powder, and salt.

Check that the infused oil is between 200 and 225°F (95 and 105°C), then place a strainer over the bowl with the chilis and pour the hot oil through the strainer into the bowl. It should bubble and instantly produce a nutty and toasty aroma. Stir the oil into the chili flakes, chili powder, and salt. Allow the oil to completely cool to room temperature before pouring into a glass jar. Cover and store at room temperature for up to 3 weeks, or longer if you're meticulous about never introducing any moisture into the jar or double dipping.

VARIATIONS

HONEY CHILI OIL: For a fun, easy twist, combine 3 tablespoons of chili oil with flakes and 3 tablespoons of honey to make a honey chili oil. Use this on a cheese board, or drizzle it over burrata, tomatoes, and stone fruit. Enjoy with crusty toasted bread and you'll be in heaven. Or for one of my favorite riffs, use as a spread for a fully loaded sandwich with turkey or ham.

DIPPING SAUCE: Add soy sauce, sugar, and black or rice wine vinegar to turn this into a dipping sauce for wontons and dumplings.

CHINATOWN CHILI BLACK BEAN SAUCE

辣豆豉
LÀ DÒU CHǏ

Makes a scant 2 cups (480 ml)

PETER: When Kathy and I sit down at a Chinese restaurant, the first thing we do is check out the chili sauce set out on the table. If the sauce is homemade, then we take it as a sign that the food might be quite good. If they are using some store-bought chili sauce, then we lower our expectations.

When I opened House of Nanking, I knew I had to make my own chili sauce. There are of course many different variations out there—some very spicy and heavy on the chilis, some salty, some a little sour—but the kind I enjoy most has milder spice and strong umami flavors from fermented black beans. That is exactly the style of chili sauce I created for Nanking, and our customers have enjoyed it for years.

- ¾ cup (90 g) fermented dried black beans
- 1 cup (240 ml) neutral oil
- 2 shallots, minced
- 3 cloves garlic, minced
- ¼ cup (30 g) chili flakes
- Red Thai bird chilis, minced (optional, for extra heat)
- 2 tablespoons soy sauce
- 1 tablespoon dark soy sauce
- 2 teaspoons sugar

Rinse the black beans, then drain and dry them with paper towels. Roughly chop the beans; your goal is smaller but not minced pieces.

In a medium saucepan, heat the neutral oil over medium heat, then add the shallots and garlic. Cook for 1 minute, or just until fragrant but not browned. Add the black beans, chili flakes, and Thai bird chili, if using, and continue to cook for 2 to 3 minutes to release the flavors of the beans and dry them out a bit. Season with the soy sauce, dark soy sauce, and sugar. Cook, stirring, for 1 minute, or until the flavors have melded. Remove from the heat and transfer to a glass jar. Let the sauce completely cool to room temp before closing the lid and storing. At room temperature, so long as you don't double dip, it can last for up to 2 weeks. In the fridge, it keeps for a month or longer.

SCALLION-OIL SOY SAUCE WITH GINGER

葱姜油
CŌNG JIĀNG YÓU

Makes a scant 2 cups (480 ml)

KATHY: This sauce right here is essentially soy sauce infused with ginger scallion oil. When I first had it with plain poached chicken as a kid, it blew me away. I started drizzling it over plain rice, congee, fried rice, and all sorts of eggs. Now when my kids need a little help finishing their rice or steamed protein and veggies, I'll drizzle "Mommy's sauce" and they will shovel that dinner down. Later, I will bake a simple piece of whitefish in the oven for my husband and drizzle some of the sauce on it, to change things up from his usual seasonings of salt, pepper, lemon, and butter (he has simpler tastes!).

- ¼ cup (60 ml) soy sauce
- 4 teaspoons sugar
- 1 teaspoon MSG
- ¼ cup (15 g) roughly chopped scallions
- 1 tablespoon finely grated ginger
- ¼ cup (60 ml) neutral oil

In a small bowl, whisk together the soy sauce, sugar, and MSG. Add the scallions and ginger. In a small saucepan, heat the oil until it smokes. Keeping your face above and away from the bowl (it will sizzle and splatter!), pour the hot oil over the scallions, ginger, and sauce. Whisk until fully incorporated. Cool, transfer to an airtight container, and store in the fridge for up to 1 week.

PLANNING A CHINESE FEAST AT HOME

KATHY: If you're new to cooking Chinese cuisine at home, you might be excited to host a dinner party for your friends and family, but unsure of how to organize the meal. Here's the good news: You have our permission to select whichever dishes from this book sound most appealing to you and just go for it! At both House of Nanking and Fang, we honor tradition but don't feel constrained by it. For that reason, we often design banquet meals that blend regional Chinese traditions with our own California-influenced way of eating.

Even in China, there isn't one set of rules for organizing a traditional Chinese meal; it varies greatly by region and by the type of cuisine. For example, in Shanghai in the old days, it wasn't uncommon to end with a light soup and dim sum. Today, heartier soups might be served at the start of the meal.

At Fang, our recipes encompass several regional Chinese cuisines, and many of our guests are American and used to eating a certain way. So we tend to divide meals into four courses: First cold apps, then hot apps (which include fried and steamed dumplings as well as soups). After a pause, the second course: mains plus stir-fried protein and veggie dishes. Another pause, then the third course, which is rice and/or noodle dishes. Finally, a sweet dessert.

Below we've included six sample menus, in case you'd like more specific guidance and inspiration. We can't wait to see how you cook for your loved ones from this book!

MENU 1:
Fang-Style Dinner at Home

COLD DISHES
(To be presented before guests sit down)

Heart Too Soft, aka Red Dates Stuffed with Sweet Glutinous Rice Balls 77

Marinated Chinese Celtuce Stem with Scallion Oil 59

HOT DISHES

Pork-Stuffed Gluten Puff 233

Grandpa Fang's Perfectly "Steamed" Whole Fish with Ginger and Soy Fish Sauce 256

Silk Squash with Dried Shrimp 175

STARCH

Classic Scallion and Egg Fried Rice 109

SOUP

Papaya, Fig, and Pork Bone Soup with Dried Chinese Almonds 128

MENU 2:
Simple, Classic Cantonese-Style Family Meal (Clean Eating!)

Watercress Pork Bone Soup with Figs and Dried Chinese Almonds 131

Steamed Chicken Wings in Black Bean–Garlic Sauce 210

Tomato Stir-Fried Egg with Egg Tofu 192

Garlic Yam Leaf Tips 172

Steamed white rice

MENU 3:
Simple, Classic Shanghainese-Style Family Meal

Five-Minute Soup with Tomato, Egg, and Seaweed 132

Grandpa Fang's Perfectly "Steamed" Whole Fish with Ginger and Soy Fish Sauce 256

Nanking's Dry-Fried Green Beans 167

Steamed white rice

MENU 4:
HoNK Dinner Party (the Modern Way)

COLD STARTER
Three-Tiered Baby Pea Shoot Salad 69

APPETIZERS
Nanking's Onion Cakes with Peanut Sauce 85

Wontons in Jalapeño-Soy Sauce 95

MAIN
Chicken in Tsingtao Beer Sauce 217

Honey Apple Shrimp 249

VEGETABLE SIDE
Sauteed Asparagus with Black Bean Sauce 184

Steamed white rice

MENU 5:
Vegan Dinner Party (HoNK Style)

Spicy Garlic Cucumbers 61

Nanking's Veggie Wontons paired with Nanking's Szechuan Eggplant 92 and 168

Crispy Tofu with Peanut Sauce 199

Nanking's Garlic Baby Pea Shoots 171

Steamed white rice

MENU 6:

Congee Party!
(A Modern Twist on the Classic)

BASE

Plain Congee, aka White Porridge 156

PAIRINGS AND TOPPINGS

Peanut butter sprinkled with sugar (trust us on this one!)

Spicy Garlic Cucumbers 61

Preserved Mustard Greens with Edamame 62

Spicy Pickled Long Beans with Ground Turkey 180

Chinese Chive and Egg Scramble 209

Soy-Marinated Jalapeños 265

Chili Oil 274

CLOCKWISE FROM BOTTOM CENTER: raw peanuts, dried barley, dried figs, dried anchovies, rock sugar, dried Chinese almonds, dried lily bulbs, lotus seed, dried tangerine peel (center)

Meat

Lap cheong (là cháng 腊肠 / laahp chéung): This red-hued, preserved pork sausage is often labeled "Chinese sausage" or "Cantonese sausage." It is made from pork and pork fat and has a sweet, savory, and slightly smoky flavor. When cooked, it has a chewy texture, and it's commonly used in stir-fries, clay-pot dishes, and fried rice. Look for lap cheong in the refrigerated or dried goods section of Asian markets by the checkout counter, typically vacuum-packed. Store lap cheong in the fridge after opening.

Lap yuk (Chinese cured bacon or pork belly, là ròu 腊肉 / laahp yuhk): Called là ròu in Mandarin, and sometimes Chinese-style cured bacon, Chinese-style cured pork strips, Chinese bacon (or, confusingly "Chinese brand uncured bacon"), this looks like a very thick slab of bacon that's been cured in salt and/or soy, sugar, and other spices, then air-dried. It is a savory, intensely flavored cured meat, used to add depth to stir-fries, rice dishes, and vegetables. It is usually found in shelf-stable sections of Asian markets, often near the checkout counter, vacuum-packed or hung unpackaged. When you unpackage it, it will be very hard in texture, but when you slice into it and cook it, the flavors and fat will get released into the food and it becomes tender, juicy, and translucent. As with lap cheong, when given the option, we prefer to buy the non-refrigerated ones. Store in the fridge after opening.

Salted duck leg (xián yā tuǐ 咸鸭腿 / hàahm aap béi): Also called dry-cured duck leg, this is duck leg that has been preserved through salting and drying. It's salty and rich, with tender meat and oily, soft skin when cooked. Look for it in refrigerated or frozen sections of Asian markets as well as shelf-stable sections next to là ròu/laahp yuhk. We prefer to buy non-refrigerated ones, and once opened, salted duck leg must be stored in the fridge.

Tofu

Egg tofu (yù zǐ dòu fu 玉子豆腐 / yuhk jí dauh fuh): A specialty tofu made with eggs and soy milk, resulting in a golden color and custard-like texture; slightly firmer than silken tofu with a rich, eggy flavor. It's often used in soups, stir-fries, or gently pan-fried; we use it in the dish on page 192. Look for egg tofu sold in cylindrical plastic tubes in the refrigerated section of Asian markets. To remove it from its packaging, slice the tube of egg tofu in half crosswise, cutting through the packaging. Gently squeeze from the ends and the egg tofu will pop out easily. If you can't find it, use regular medium or firm tofu cut into cubes.

Fermented tofu (fǔ rǔ 腐乳 / fuh yú): Also labeled "fermented bean curd," "preserved tofu/bean curd," or "soy cheese," thanks to the mouthfeel, which is similar to soft cheese. Tofu cubes are fermented in brine with rice wine, salt, and spices. This is a pungent, creamy condiment with a strong, salty flavor. We use it in small amounts in stir-fries, sauces, and braises, or as a spread. This is a very popular condiment to pair with white congee. Found in the jarred goods sections of Asian markets, typically in small glass jars, variations include red (with red yeast rice), stinky, and white. For the recipes in this book, use white fermented tofu.

Firm tofu (lǎo dòu fu 老豆腐 / louh dauh fuh): Firm tofu has a denser texture suitable for grilling or stir-frying, while medium-firm is more delicate.

Marinated tofu (dòu gān 豆干 / dauh gōn): Also labeled "marinated bean curd," or "braised bean curd/tofu." The direct translation from Chinese is "tofu dry," referring to the tofu being drier than regular block tofu. This firm, dense tofu has been pressed to remove excess moisture, then marinated and dried. It has a chewy texture with concentrated flavor, often smoky or spiced. Use it in stir-fries, cold in salads, minced as a filling for dumplings, sliced and then steamed, or as-is for a snack. Oakland-based Hodo makes a version that is distributed in many Western grocery stores, including Whole Foods. Chinese brands are available at Sayweee.com. Look for it vacuum-sealed in the refrigerated section along with other tofu.

Silken tofu (nèn dòu fu 嫩豆腐 / nyuhn dauh fuhu): A very soft, delicate variety of tofu with a smooth, silky texture. Its high water content gives it a custard-like consistency. We use it in soups, smoothies, desserts, or as-is for a refreshing cold dish.

Tofu puffs (dòu pào 豆泡 / dauh fuh paau): Also called "fried tofu blocks." These are deep-fried tofu cubes with a spongy, airy texture. The interior is light and white while the exterior has a yellowish hue. Due to its mild flavor and sponge-like texture, it absorbs seasonings and broths really well (there's nothing better than a juicy bite of tofu puff that has absorbed sauce or soup). As a result, tofu puffs are often used in soups, hotpots, or stir-fries, or stuffed with ground meat to create flavorful meatballs wrapped in tofu. Look for tofu puffs in refrigerated sections of Asian markets, typically in plastic bags; they come in different sizes.

Long beans (page 284)

Fruits and Vegetables

Bamboo shoot, winter (dōng sǔn 冬笋 / dūng seuhn): Winter bamboo plants are harvested and prepared for cooking, resulting in a crunchy vegetable with a mild, slightly sweet flavor. It's used in stir-fries, soups, and as a textural element in fillings for wontons, dumplings, and egg rolls. You can find fresh bamboo shoots vacuum-sealed in the produce section of Asian markets where the rest of the vegetables are sold. If you must use canned bamboo shoot, drain the liquid, then rinse three times under water to remove any lingering flavors from the can.

Bok choy, Shanghai (bái cài 白菜 / baahk choi): In the Shanghai wontons on page 150 and the cài fàn on page 113, we call for Shanghai bok choy, a smaller version of bok choy that is usually no more than six inches long. The smaller it is, the more tender, crisp, dense, and sweet. Slice it in half lengthwise through the core to expose the interior, then rinse it thoroughly to remove any dirt trapped in the core. Look for it in markets in the fall, winter, and spring.

Cabbage, baby napa (wá wa cài 娃娃菜 / wàah wàah choi), which is used in the recipe on page 176, are similar in size to endive and even sweeter and milder than large napa cabbage, with tighter leaves with more crisp firm stems. To prep them for cooking, slice them in half or quarters lengthwise and then rinse them. Try them grilled or roasted.

Cabbage, napa, aka Chinese cabbage (dà bái cài 大白菜 / daaih baahk choi): This mildly sweet, tender cabbage has crinkly, pale green leaves and more water content than other cabbage varieties. Look for firm cabbages with no wilted outer leaves, brown spots, or dots. The heads should have tightly packed leaves and their stems should not be split.

Cabbage, Taiwanese (gāo lì cài 高丽菜 / yèh choi): Similar to the green cabbage you see in Western markets, but flatter and more oblong, with a sweeter, more tender flavor. Used in stir-fries, soups, or raw in salads. Substitute green cabbage if unavailable.

Cauliflower, flowering (sōng huā cài 松花菜 / sàhn fā): Fun fact: sàhn fā is the most common cauliflower varietal eaten in China. But it didn't start popping up in American markets until fairly recently. Now, we find it at farmers' markets and even at Trader Joe's, which labels it as baby cauliflower. Flowering cauliflower is somewhat reminiscent of Broccolini, with skinny, crispy stems that are light and a little bit sweet. Look for it in the produce section of Asian markets, often sold in bundles; variations may include different stages of maturity, affecting tenderness and flavor intensity. Also known as "Chinese flowering cabbage" in some regions.

Celtuce (wō sŭn 莴笋 / wō sēun): Also known as stem lettuce, celtuce has a thick, crisp stem and small leaves. It is mild, with a slightly nutty celery-like flavor and crunchy texture. The tough exterior skin must be peeled off to reveal the edible interior flesh, which is used in stir-fries, salads, or as a filling for egg rolls. Look for celtuce in markets during its season in spring, summer, and fall. The more mature it is, the more fibrous the stem can get, which is less desirable. Celtuce is very suitable for people with diabetes (Peter and Lily's families have a history of it), as it regulates blood sugar and helps with metabolism.

Chive blossoms or garlic scapes (jiŭ cài huā 韭菜花 / gáu choi fā): Also called garlic chives, Chinese garlic scapes or Chinese chive blossoms. These are the flowering stems of Chinese chives, which feature small edible flower buds on top of slender round stalks that are thicker than the flat Chinese chives. Chive blossoms are juicer, sweeter, less pungent, and more crisp than Chinese chives. To use them, snip off and discard the ends by an inch, as they tend to be tough. Look for dark green, firm, and not flimsy chive blossoms with yellow flower tips that are tight and not bloomed out in spring and summer.

Chives, Chinese (jiŭ cài 韭菜 / gáu choi): Chinese flat-leaf chives, sometimes called Chinese leeks, are not to be confused with garlic chives (see above) or the skinny European chives you see in Western markets. Chinese chives are larger, with flat leaves that are at least two to three times longer than the Western counterpart. The flavor profile is also drastically different. European chives are much more delicate in flavor, whereas Chinese chives are pungent in smell and taste. Look for chives with firm stems and tips. The leaves should be bright dark green with no brown or yellow, and stand on their own without feeling flimsy and soft. Their season is spring, summer, and fall. Use them as a filling for dumplings, stir-fries, and even garnished over stews and soups to add crunch and bold pops of flavor, or in pasta dishes or added into quiche!

Eggplant, Chinese (qié zi 茄子 / kèh jí): Most recipes in this book call for Chinese eggplants, which are longer and thinner than globe eggplants, with purple skin ranging from violet to deep purple. They also have fewer seeds, which makes them sweeter and less bitter than Western varieties. When sourcing Chinese eggplants, make sure to choose ones that are deep dark purple and firm to touch.

Favas (cán dòu 蚕豆 / chàahm dauh): Often labeled "broad beans" in Chinese markets. These large, flat beans have a creamy texture and nutty flavor. They are often shelled before cooking and used in stir-fries, soups, cold dishes, salads, or dried and roasted into a crunchy snack. Look for fresh favas at the farmers' market or bags of frozen favas in Asian markets. For the recipe on page 187, buy shelled frozen favas so you don't have to shell them yourself!

Gai lan (jiè lán 芥兰 / gaai láahn): Also called "Chinese broccoli." Leafy green vegetable with thick stems and small florets; slightly bitter taste with a crunchy texture; commonly stir-fried, steamed, or blanched as a side dish. Variations may include younger, more tender shoots or more mature plants with larger stems.

Garlic: See page 47.

Ginger: See page 47.

Jujubes (hóng zăo 红枣 / hùhng jóu): Also called red dates, jujubes are a small, date-like fruit with a sweet, apple and honey flavor and chewy texture when dried. They are used in desserts, sweet and savory soups, teas, steamed or braised dishes, and traditional medicine. Look for jujubes in the dried goods sections of Asian markets, sold packaged or in bulk. Variations include fresh (less common) and dried forms, with different sizes affecting sweetness and texture.

Kalimeris indica (mă lán tóu 马兰头 / máah làahn tàuh): Sometimes labeled "aster indicus" or "Indian aster," this is the key ingredient in the mă lán tóu on page 65. Kalimeris indica is a wild vegetable harvested from young shoots. It's a tender, leafy green with a slightly bitter, very herbaceous, almost grasslike flavor, reminiscent of minced rapini or American parsley but with a kale-like chew. It's sold pretty much exclusively frozen in bags, so look for it in the frozen vegetable aisle of your Chinese market. If you can't find it, fresh chrysanthemum leaf is a great replacement. You would cook it the same way: blanch quickly in boiling water, remove immediately, run under cold water to bring the temperature down, then squeeze out all the water until dry. If you do find Kalimeris indica, try it on salads, mixed with ground meat as a filling for wontons, stir-fried with rice cakes and Chinese sausage, sauteed with orecchiette and red sauce in an Italian-style pasta, or over a white pizza with sausage.

Lily bulbs (băi hé 百合 / baahk hahp): Edible bulb scales of specific lily species. This starchy vegetable has a subtle, sweet flavor and crunchy yet tender texture. In recent years, fresh lily bulbs imported from China or

Japan have become easier to find in Chinese markets. Even so, it is unusual to find dishes featuring fresh lily bulbs on Chinese restaurant menus in the US. They are delicious in a stir-fry, like in the dish on page 183. Dried lily bulbs are not used for stir-frying—they are best in soups and traditional medicine. Look for fresh lily bulbs for stir-frying packaged in vacuum-sealed bags in the refrigerated section of your Asian market.

Long beans (cháng dòu jiǎo 长豆角 / chèuhng dauh gok): These elongated green beans can be 1 to 2 feet long. They have a slightly sweet, grassy flavor and extra crisp texture, similar to green beans but with a thicker skin and bite. We typically cut and use them in stir-fries or curries, but they can also be pickled, as in the recipe on page 180. Look for long beans in the produce section, often sold in bundles; variations include purple long beans, which have a similar taste. For info on pickled long beans, see page 284.

Lotus root (lián ǒu 莲藕 / lìhn ngáuh): Slice the rhizome of the lotus plant crosswise and you'll reveal a crunchy vegetable with a beautiful lacy interior. Lotus root is a very versatile ingredient used in many Chinese dishes. It can be enjoyed raw, boiled, stir-fried, or fried into chips. When eaten raw or lightly stir-fried, the texture is crunchy with a mild sweetness to it. When boiled in a soup, its texture becomes softer and starchier. To pick out the best lotus root, look for ones that have a white and smooth finish with no cracks, rather than those that are bruised with brown and dark spots. The lotus root should feel very firm when you push on it, and not soft. Buying fresh, unpackaged lotus root from the market is your best bet, as you can ensure freshness. When stored in packages, it can go rancid quickly as moisture collects.

Papaya (mù guā 木瓜 / muhk gwā): For the soup on page 128, use Maradol papaya, which is sold at many Chinatown markets and has orange flesh and greenish-yellow skin. If you can't find Maradol papaya, Hawaiian papaya will work, although it's sweeter.

Pea shoots (dòu miáo 豆苗 / dauh mìuh): At markets during their season in spring, you might find large (dà dòu miáo) or small (xiǎo dòu miáo) pea shoots. At Nanking, we call the latter "baby" pea shoots (sometimes called "baby pea sprouts"—but do not interchange with pea sprouts, which are larger), and use them in our Three-Tiered Baby Pea Shoot Salad (page 69) and garlic pea shoots. Pea shoots have a very crisp, grasslike flavor. Baby pea shoots are easy to prepare; just wash them and then they're ready to go. Look for bunches with no brown or yellow leaves that are not wilted and have firm, straight stems. Pea shoots are typically sold in bags or bundles, whereas baby pea shoots are usually packaged in boxes that are sold next to other sprouts like alfalfa.

Scallions: See page 47.

Silk squash (sī guā 丝瓜 / sī gwā): Also known as luffa, this is a long, slender squash with fuzzy skin that is bright to dark green and has a mild, slightly sweet flavor. Texturally, it is incredibly soft (even when raw) with a spongy and sometimes buttery mouthfeel. Because of its spongy nature, it's ideal for soups or stir-fries, where it can absorb a lot of flavor. When shopping for silk squash, do not be surprised if you cut into it and find that it's soft and spongy—the raw texture is often surprising to people who are used to cooking zucchini! The best way to tell if a silk squash is overripe is if it's slimy or has brown spots on the exterior skin, or if the exterior skin is soft enough for you to push your finger through easily.

Spinach, Taiwanese (Tái wān bō cài 台湾菠菜 / tòih wāan bō choi): We use this in our signature Nanking Noodles with Shredded Pork (page 117). It is similar to regular spinach, but with longer, crunchier stems and larger, stiffer leaves, plus an earthier flavor than common spinach. Taiwanese spinach is typically stir-fried, used in soups, or in fillings for wontons and dumplings. It is found in produce sections of Asian markets, often sold in bundles.

Yam leaf tips (fān shǔmiáo jiān 番薯苗尖 / fāan syú mìuh): Young, tender shoots and leaves from sweet potato vines with a slightly sweet, spinach-like flavor and silky texture. They are commonly stir-fried with garlic or added to soups and are found in Asian markets, sold in bunches with bright green stems and curled leaf tips. If you cannot find yam leaf tips, look for yam leaf, which is longer-stemmed and needs to be cut into smaller lengths before cooking.

Pickled Vegetables

Pickled long beans (suān dòu jiǎo 酸豆角 / syūn dauh gok): Long beans preserved in vinegar and salt brine are a tangy, crunchy vegetable condiment with a sour and salty flavor. They are a Hunan specialty and are typically sold in jars or vacuum-packed at well-stocked Chinese markets. To make your own, see page 180. The texture is very different from Western-style pickled green beans, which cannot be used as a replacement.

Pickled sour mustard greens (酸菜 suān cài / syūn choi): A fermented vegetable made from mustard greens that have been salted and allowed to naturally ferment, resulting in a sour, salty, and slightly funky flavor with a tender yet crisp texture. They are widely used across Chinese cuisine, particularly in Sichuan and Northern Chinese dishes, and can be found in vacuum-sealed packages or loose in brine at most Chinese grocery stores. Fresh sour mustard greens can also be found in the refrigerated section. Western sauerkraut, while also fermented cabbage, has a different flavor profile and texture and should not be used as a substitute.

Preserved mustard greens (xián cài 咸菜 / hàahm choi): Sometimes called "pickled cabbage leaf," "salted mustard green," "salted cabbage leaf," or "preserved vegetable," though the direct translation is "salted vegetables." This popular condiment is made from pickled thin mustard plant stem and leaves, typically from the species Brassica juncea. It has a crunchy texture, salty, slightly spicy flavor, and big umami notes. Use it in stir-fries, noodle dishes, or as a side. Look for xián cài in the pickled/preserved vegetable section of your Chinese market, where it might be sold in cans, jars, or vacuum-sealed packages. Different brands might have different spice levels, or the leaves might be cut or sliced differently. For the recipes in this book, buy xián cài that is pre-chopped and sold in vacuum-sealed bags. There are versions that are not chopped that are packaged in see-through plastic bags with a light yellow liquid—this is NOT what we are looking for, as these tend to be a lot saltier. (If it's your only option, rinse before use.) Chopped xián cài, by contrast, is perfectly seasoned and can be consumed right out of the package. Xián cài is not to be confused with zhà cài (see below), which is the salted stem of a mustard plant tuber. Zha cài is crunchy, whereas xián cài is not. When in doubt, show the Chinese characters to staff at your Chinese grocery store and they can help you! Once opened, store xián cài in the fridge (I like to transfer them to a glass jar with a lid).

CLOCKWISE FROM TOP: pickled sour mustard greens (suān cài), preserved mustard greens (xián cài), preserved mustard stem (zhà cài), pickled long beans (suān dòu jiāo), another form of preserved mustard greens (xián cài)

Preserved mustard stem / zhà cài (zhà cài 榨菜 / jaah choi): Packages of this are sometimes labeled "pickled radish," "Sichuan vegetable," "Chinese pickled vegetable," or "pressed vegetable." It is made from the fermented, bulbous stem of a specific species of mustard plant. Look for it in sealed packages at Chinese markets or online—the Yuquan brand, in bright green packaging, is fairly common. Different brands and packages might have varying spice levels and could be shredded, sliced, whole, or cut into chunks. For the recipes in this book, look for shredded zhà cài sold in vacuum-sealed bags, which are seasoned and ready to be enjoyed straight out of the bag. Whole zhà cài and zhà cài cut into larger chunks tend to be saltier and need to be rinsed before using. Look for zhà cài at the market or online at www.chinaglobalmall.com. Once opened, store zhà cài in the fridge (I like to transfer them to a glass jar with a lid).

Salted chopped chilis, aka chili chop (duò jiāo 剁椒 / dōk jīu): Duò jiāo, sometimes called pickled chilis, is a condiment with origins in the Hunan province. (Note that in

Chinese cuisine, "pickled" doesn't always equate to being sour—many salted things are referred to as "pickled.") Duò jiāo is made by dicing up red chilis then brining them in a salty solution that usually contains canola oil, garlic, and other ingredients that vary by brand. The result is a spicy condiment with a salty, fermented flavor and slightly crunchy texture. It's great for when you want to add spice to a dish in a visually and texturally appealing way—since the whole chilis are chopped, they tend not to disappear into dishes in the same way ground chili pastes can. Duò jiāo is sold jarred or in plastic containers. We like the brand Tan Tan Xiang. If you can't find it in your market, look for duò jiāo online. Store in the refrigerator after opening.

Noodles

Flour thread or fěn sī noodles (fěn sī 粉丝 / fán sī): Also called glass noodles. These are thin, translucent noodles made from mung bean starch, sweet potato starch, or pea starch. The noodles have a slippery, chewy texture and neutral flavor, which makes them well-suited for soups, stir-fries, steamed and braised dishes, or cold salads. Look for them sold dried in packages in the noodle section. Soak before using. They can be used interchangeably with mung bean noodles (see below).

Mung bean vermicelli noodles (lǜ dòu fěn sī 绿豆粉丝 / luhk dauh fán sī): Also called glass noodles. These typically need to be soaked before using, but they cook within minutes and absorb sauces and flavors very well. Pagoda brand is our go-to. They can be used interchangeably with flour thread noodles, aka fěn sī noodles (see above).

Rice stick noodles or mei fun (mǐ fěn 米粉 / máih fán): Mei fun are very thin noodles made from rice flour. They are sold dried (we like the brand Kong Moon) and are a great pantry item since they keep for a long time. Mei fun should be soaked in cool water for 30 minutes to soften before adding to stir-fries or noodle soups. Try substituting the wheat noodles in Yáng Chūn Noodle Soup (page 142) for mei fun. Because mei fun are rice-based and thinner than wheat noodles, in our family we often eat them when we're feeling under the weather. They're also great for older folks who need easier-to-digest meals, or toddlers who are still eating soft foods (just be sure to cut the noodles with scissors to make them all bite-sized).

Shanghai noodles (shàng hǎi cū miàn 上海粗面 / seuhng hói chōu mihn): Thick, chewy wheat noodles with a substantial, bouncy al dente texture. They are less smooth than udon noodles and thus pick up sauces beautifully when wok-tossed; typically used in stir-fries or with sauces; found fresh in refrigerated section or frozen noodle section in US markets. Some have egg added; some do not; some are thicker and some are thinner. Our preference is the more traditonal version, which does not have egg, and our feeling is, the thicker the better.

Shirataki noodles (mó yù sī 魔芋丝 / mō yuh sī): Shirataki "noodles" are translucent, gelatinous noodles made from a root vegetable called konjak. They are great if you're trying to cut back on calories or carbs. Look for them in water-packed bags in the refrigerated section of many grocery stores, including some Western-style groceries, near the tofu. They come in noodle-shaped strands or bundles, aka "knots." Rinse them well before using.

Thin dried wheat noodles (xì miàn 细面 / sai mihn): These are wheat flour noodles that are machine-extruded and sold fresh or dried. The result is thin, delicate strands with a smooth texture that become tender when cooked. For dishes like Yáng Chūn Noodle Soup (page 142), we prefer to use fresh noodles when possible. Dried noodles work if you can't find fresh. Wu Mu Dry Noodle is our preferred brand. You can sub spaghetti if needed.

Other Pantry Ingredients

Aji-mirin (wèi lín 味醂 / meih làhm): Mirin is sweet rice wine made by fermenting glutinous rice to create a golden, syrupy liquid with a mild alcoholic taste. Aji-mirin is actually sweeter than pure mirin and lower in alcohol content. Most American grocery stores that sell mirin will usually only carry Kikkoman Aji-Mirin (which translates to "tastes like mirin"). In this book, you can use hon-mirin (true mirin) or aji-mirin interchangeably. Store in a cool, dark place.

Anchovies, dried (jiāng yú zǎi 江鱼仔 / gōng yùh jái): Tiny, silvery anchovies are cleaned and sun-dried, resulting in a concentrated, salty flavor. They are used to make stock, add natural umami flavors to stir-fries or braises, or as a crispy topping when fried. Look for them in the dried seafood section, typically in plastic bags or containers. Store in a cool, dark place.

Chili crisp (lǎo gān mā 老干妈 / : "Chili crisp" has become synonymous with Lǎo Gān Mā, one of the most famous brands you'll find (though even Trader Joe's has its own version now). This Chinese condiment consists of crispy fried chili, soybean oil, garlic, shallots, various spices, and sometimes peanuts. It is essentially a hot oil with crispy bits that add texture and umami flavors.

Chili oil: See page 48.

Chili sauce (là jiāo jiàng 辣椒酱 / laaht jīu jeung): A condiment made from ground chili peppers, vinegar, and spices, resulting in a thick, bright red sauce with a spicy, tangy flavor. It's typically used as a dipping sauce or ingredient in marinades and stir-fries. Look for it in the condiment section, typically in glass or plastic jars. Variations include sweet chili sauce (for our homemade version, see page 271) and sambal oelek (see below).

Chili flakes (là jiāo suì 辣椒碎 or là jiāo fěn 辣椒粉 / laaht jīu seu): Look for Chinese chili flakes in the spice section of a Chinese grocery, usually in plastic bags or shaker bottles. Chinese chili flakes are different from the Korean and Italian versions; they are usually a darker, more vibrant red color and hotter. Korean chili flakes have slightly more complex flavors than Chinese chili flakes, which are more about heat. And Italian chili flakes are usually roasted longer than Chinese chili flakes before crushing, which means they can burn easily when you toast them in oil. If possible, find Chinese chili flakes for the best-tasting chili oils and sauces.

Chinese almonds, dried (xìng rén 杏仁/ hahng yàhn): Chinese almonds are actually apricot kernels (which is why you might find them labeled as "Chinese kernels") and have uses in traditional Chinese medicine and cooking. They come in two varieties: north (běi xìng 北杏 / bāk hahng) and south (nán xìng 南杏 / nàahm hahng) almonds. North almonds are slightly bitter, as they are mildly toxic and must be cooked thoroughly before consuming. When properly used, they are believed to help promote digestion, relieve constipation, and can act as a lubricant for your lungs to minimize chronic coughs. South almonds are slightly sweeter. Look for both north and south almonds packaged and sold in Chinese markets, or online (powingonline .com is a great resource).

Chinkiang vinegar: See page 48.

Cornstarch: See page 47.

Dark soy sauce: See page 48.

Dashi powder (yú tāng fěn 鱼汤粉 / yùh tōng fán): Granules made from dried bonito flakes, kelp, and sometimes other ingredients. This light, savory powder dissolves easily in water; it is used as a quick base for soups and sauces in Japanese cooking but also an umami-boosting flavoring agent for stir-fries. It's found in the soup or seasoning section, usually in small packets or jars.

Dumpling skins (jiǎo zi pí 饺子皮 / gáau jí pìh): Not to be confused with wonton skins, which are square and thinner. We use round dumpling skins for the veggie wontons on page 92, because wonton skins are too thin for the al dente texture I want for the dish.

Fermented dried black beans (dòu chǐ 豆豉 / dauh sìh): Soybeans fermented with salt and spices, then dried, resulting in small, black, wrinkled beans with a pungent, salty flavor. Used to add depth to sauces, steamed dishes, and stir-fries. Found in the preserved vegetable section, usually in plastic bags or cardboard containers—not to be confused with jarred black bean sauce (which is a sauce made from the actual beans). Store at room temp in a cool, dark place.

Fried gluten balls (miàn jīn qiú 面筋球 / mihn gān kàuh): A vegetarian protein made from wheat gluten that has been formed into small, puffy balls and deep-fried. They have a light, spongy texture with a slightly chewy interior that softens when cooked; often used in vegetarian dishes, stuffed with minced meat, soups, braises, and stir-fries and absorbs flavors very well. It is found in the shelf-stable section of Asian markets, typically sold in plastic packages. Use immediately or tightly seal to maintain freshness.

Hoisin sauce (hǎi xiān jiàng 海鲜酱 / hói sīn jeung): A thick sauce made from fermented soybeans, garlic, and spices, resulting in a dark brown, sweet and savory condiment with a slightly sticky and thick texture like BBQ sauce. It's used as a glaze, dipping sauce, marinade, or stir-fry ingredient and famously used as a sauce for Peking duck and dipping sauce in Vietnamese noodle shops. It is found in the condiment section, typically in glass jars or squeeze bottles. Store in the fridge after opening to extend shelf life.

La doubanjiang / chili broad bean sauce (là dòu bàn jiàng 辣豆瓣酱 / laaht dauh baahn jeung): A spicy, fermented paste made from broad beans and chili peppers. This chunky, deep red sauce with a complex, spicy-umami flavor is used as a base for Sichuan dishes to add heat and depth. Found in the condiment section, usually in glass jars or plastic pouches. Store in the fridge after opening to extend shelf life.

Maggi sauce (měi jí jiàng yóu 美极酱油 / méih gihk jeung yàuhu): A dark, hydrolyzed vegetable protein–based sauce with a strong, savory flavor reminiscent of beef bouillon. It's used as a seasoning in soups, stews, stir-fries, and marinades. Found in the condiment section, typically in glass bottles. Store in a cool, dark place.

MSG (wèi jīng 味精 / meih jīng): Monosodium glutamate, a flavor enhancer derived from glutamic acid; white crystalline powder

Thousand-year-old egg (pí dàn); see page 66

with a savory, umami taste. It's used to intensify flavors in various dishes. It is found in the seasoning section, usually in plastic bags or shaker containers; variations include different granule sizes and sometimes mixed with salt.

Neutral oil: See page 48.

Oyster sauce (háo yóu 蚝油 / hòh yàuh): A thick sauce made from oyster extracts, salt, and sugar. This dark brown, viscous liquid has a rich, savory-sweet flavor. Found in the condiment section, usually in glass bottles or plastic containers; variations include vegetarian versions made with mushrooms. Store in the fridge after opening to extend shelf life.

Peanuts (huā sheng 花生 / fā sāng): When we cook any dishes or soups with peanuts, they're always raw and not roasted.

Sambal oelek (cān bā là jiāo 參巴辣椒 / sāam bā laaht jīu): This raw chili paste has Indonesian and Malaysian origins. It is made from ground fresh red chilis, sometimes with salt and vinegar added. We love its bright, spicy flavor and coarse texture. Look for it in the sauce or international aisle of Asian and some well-stocked Western markets, typically in glass jars or plastic tubs. Store in the fridge after opening to extend shelf life. Note: The Mandarin and Cantonese pronunciations here are phonetic approximations. In Chinese markets, it's often labeled with characters that phonetically approximate the original name or describe it as a type of chili sauce.

Seasoned soy sauce for seafood (hǎi xiān jiàng yóu 海鮮醬油 / hói sīn jeung yàuh): This is less salty than regular soy sauce and is used as a dipping sauce or flavoring for seafood dishes, such as on page 256. Look for it in the sauce section of Asian markets, usually in glass or plastic bottles. Store in a cool, dark place.

Sesame paste (zhī ma jiàng 芝麻醬 / jī màh jeung): Chinese sesame paste is made from ground toasted sesame seeds. It has a rich, nutty flavor and slightly gritty texture. It is found in the sauce or condiment aisle of Asian markets, typically in glass jars, tins, or plastic tubs; variations include black or white sesame seeds. For the recipes in this book, use white sesame paste. Chinese sesame paste has a different flavor profile and consistency than tahini. Tahini uses untoasted sesame seeds, whereas Chinese sesame paste starts with toasted sesame seeds, resulting in a thicker, darker, more aromatic paste.

Shaoxing wine: See page 48.

Shrimp, dried baby (xiā mǐ 虾米 / hāh máih): Tiny shrimp that are salted and sun-dried, then used to add umami to stir-fries, fried rice, and soups, or as a garnish. Found in the dried seafood section, usually in plastic bags or containers; variations include different sizes and levels of saltiness. The larger the size, the harder the shrimp, so for first-time users, using the baby ones will be easier (see below). Baby shrimp might also be called "dried shrimp skin" (xiā pí 虾皮 / hāh pìh).

Sichuan pepper oil (huā jiāo yóu 花椒油 / fā jīu yàuh): Also called "prickly ash oil," this is oil infused with Sichuan peppercorns. It is fragrant with a numbing, tingling sensation and citrusy notes.

Soy sauce: See page 48.

Spring roll wrappers (chūn juǎn pí 春卷皮 / chèun gyún pìh): The recipes in this book call for square, 8-inch, wheat-based spring roll skins. This is not to be confused with the rice-based spring roll wrappers used for many Vietnamese and Southeast Asian dishes. They might also be called "wrappers," "pastry," "skins," or "shells," and are typically sold in the refrigerated or freezer section of Asian markets. Look for brands such as Spring Home.

Tangerine peel, dried (gān jú zi pí 干桔子皮 / gōn gāt jí pìh): Used in the soup on page 131. If you can't find sealed packages of dried tangerine peel in the dry goods section (alongside the dried grains and seeds) or dried fruit aisle of your Chinese market, look for it online.

Thousand-year-old egg (pí dàn 皮蛋 / pìh daahn): Also known as preserved egg, alkalized egg, century egg, or "peedan egg" in English, these eggs are preserved in clay, ash, alkaline salt, quicklime, and other ingredients. In our family we prefer duck eggs, but you can also find preserved chicken or quail eggs. During the preserving process, the egg yolk becomes dark green and creamy, and the egg whites become dark and translucent. Look for these online and in Chinese markets. They are typically sold in packs of 4 to 6. Since they are preserved, they are shelf-stable and might be sold on the shelf, or in the refrigerated section. You can store them for several months in the fridge or in a cool, dark place. (See photo opposite.)

Toasted sesame oil: See page 48.

White pepper: See page 47.

White rice: See page 48.

Wonton skins (hún tún pí 馄饨皮/ wàhn tàhn pìh): Some recipes call for wonton skins, which are square and thin, rather than dumpling skins, which are thicker and typically round. Twin Marquis is the brand we use at home. Look for them in the refrigerated section of Chinese markets near the fresh noodles.

Worcestershire sauce (wū sī tè jiàng 乌斯特酱 / wū sī daht jeung): Fermented liquid condiment with various ingredients; a tangy, savory sauce with complex umami flavors.

Yóu tiáo / Chinese donuts (yóu tiáo 油条 / yàuh tìuh): Deep-fried dough sticks with a crispy exterior and a light, airy, subtly savory interior. Typically eaten for breakfast with soy milk or as an accompaniment to congee; found in the bakery or frozen section of Asian markets, freshly made or frozen.

Zǐ cài (Chinese seaweed), also known as dried laver (zǐ cài 紫菜 / jí cho): When purchasing dried Chinese laver, make sure it comes as a round disc and is not the Japanese nori used for sushi. (Zǐ cài isn't suitable for wrapping around rice.) Chinese laver has a completely different texture and mouthfeel: It is incredibly thin, translucent layers of seaweed that are pressed into a cake and bloom into soft, ribbonlike strands when immersed in liquid. When it's saturated, nori results in a chewy bite that doesn't work in recipes like the soup on page 132 or soy milk on page 140. If you can't find laver, it's better to skip it than substitute nori. Look for zǐ cài on Sayweee.com.

Rice

Glutinous rice (nuò mǐ 糯米 / noh maih): Also known as sticky rice or sweet rice, this is used to fill lotus root in the recipe on page 162. It is a type of short-grain rice that becomes exceptionally sticky when cooked, and is prized for its chewy texture and ability to absorb flavors. Despite its English name, it doesn't contain gluten.

Common preparations include steaming in a bamboo steamer or rice cooker; using it to stuff dumplings, root vegetables, or bamboo leaves; and using it to make sticky rice dumplings, aka Chinese tamales (zòng zi 粽子) or lotus leaf wraps with minced meats. Always soak glutinous rice for at least an hour (or up to overnight) before you cook it.

Long-grain rice (cháng mǐ 长米 / chèuhng maih): This is most commonly used in Chinese stir-fries, fried rice, and as an accompanying side dish. We typically use fragrant jasmine rice as our everyday eating rice; its slender, elongated grains remain separate and fluffy when cooked. Basmati is another long-grained variety often used in South Asian cooking.

Medium-grain rice (zhōng mǐ 中米 / jūng lāp maih): We often use this to make Chinese rice porridge (congee) and some dim sum dishes. This rice has grains that are shorter and wider than long-grain, but not as short as short-grain, resulting in a slightly sticky texture when cooked, with a tender bite and subtle flavor. Look for specific cultivars like Calrose rice.

Short-grain rice (duǎn mǐ 短米 / faahn): Often called jān jyū maih, "pearl rice." These plump, almost round rice grains become sticky and clump together when cooked. They have a chewy texture with a slightly sweet flavor. Short-grain rice is most commonly used in sushi, rice balls, and sweet rice desserts.

RESOURCES

We hope that in reading this book, you've developed an even greater appreciation for Chinese produce and ingredients, and the people who grow and sell them. Whenever possible, we urge you to seek out local, independent farmers and Chinese grocers! You can find small Chinese markets almost everywhere in the United States.

Produce & Pantry Ingredients

CITY SUPER:
1108 Stockton Street, San Francisco, CA

Peter is basically the unofficial mayor of this classic Chinatown spot. Maybe you'll run into him there!

D&T MARKET:
1118 Stockton Street, San Francisco, CA

This is where Kathy and Peter most often find themselves if they're not at City Super.

MANILA ORIENTAL MARKET:
950 King Drive, Suite 112, Daly City, CA

Offers a wide variety of Asian produce.

NEW MAY WAH SUPERMARKET:
707 Clement Street, San Francisco, CA

Located in the Richmond District of San Francisco; known for its extensive selection of Asian produce.

SUNSET SUPER:
2425 Irving Street, San Francisco, CA

A Chinese supermarket in the Sunset District with a good selection of produce and other Chinese ingredients.

SAN FRANCISCO FERRY PLAZA FARMERS' MARKET:
1 Ferry Building, San Francisco, CA

Located at the end of Market Street on the Embarcadero, this market is known for its diverse selection of local produce. It does not specifically focus on Chinese vegetables, but some vendors do carry Asian produce that can be used in Chinese cooking; for example, Chue's Farm, Heirloom Organic Gardens, Star Route Farms, Dirty Girl Produce, and K&J Orchards. (Keep in mind that the availability of specific Chinese produce can vary greatly depending on the season and the individual vendor's crops.) Visit ferrybuildingmarketplace.com for hours and info.

H MART:
Hmart.com

This Korean supermarket chain has locations nationwide, carries many Chinese ingredients and produce, and is expanding rapidly! Check to see if you have an H Mart in your city.

99 RANCH MARKET:
99ranch.com

With many locations across the US, this Asian supermarket chain carries a vast array of Chinese produce and ingredients. Check to see if you have one your area.

WEEE!:
Saywee.com

Our favorite online retailer for fresh produce, pickles, and other jarred goods. Weee! offers quick delivery in many regions across the country; check the website to see if delivery is available in your area.

Equipment

If you have the time, we highly recommend going to a local shop to find your wok. Not only are you supporting local businesses, but you'll also get the chance to hold and feel various woks to pick one that works best for you. And, you can learn from knowledgeable staff members about wok essentials and how to care for your specific wok. Below are three San Francisco shops you can visit:

WOK SHOP:
718 Grant Avenue, San Francisco, CA 94108

This Chinatown shop is known for its wide variety of woks and Chinese cooking utensils. The shop offers wok seasoning classes and carries both traditional and modern wok styles. Better still, owner Tane Chan is knowledgeable about wok selection and use, and happy to chat with customers.

KAMEI RESTAURANT SUPPLY:
525 Clement Street, San Francisco, CA 94118

Also in the Richmond district, this store has a large selection of restaurant-grade kitchen supplies, including woks. This is a good spot for finding professional-grade woks.

If you don't have a local retailer, we recommend the following brands, which are available on Amazon:

- Craft Wok
- Joyce Chen
- Lodge

ACKNOWLEDGMENTS

KATHY: Six months into writing this book, what had at first been a joy—filling my journal with recipes, stories, and memories—became a struggle. Both my parents started suffering from health issues. Although they are now through the worst of it and back to working every day, they are clearly slowing down. Here I was, reminiscing and writing about all my joyful memories of them doing everything they possibly could to take care of me, well beyond just putting food on the table. Suddenly, I saw an arc I didn't want to see and didn't feel prepared for. Our roles have reversed, and now I am managing doctor visits, medications, and the difficulties that arise when your age catches up to you. I lay awake many nights overwhelmed with unexpected emotion.

I'm not an emotional person. In fact, I'm the opposite. Being raised first-generation Chinese American, I never learned to be in touch with my emotions. We are incredibly stoic; we never say "I love you," or "I'm proud of you." We don't say "thank you." We don't say "I appreciate you." We always say we show it through our actions, our sacrifices, our tough love, our criticism, our never-ending desire to feed and cook for you, to keep you layered so you don't catch a cold. I guess what I'm trying to say here is, while I can't find the courage to say it in person, this book has become an opportunity for me to say what I can't vocalize. Sometimes it's easier to write it down for another to read; I suspect that's how some of the greatest songs are created.

I love my parents more than my heart can hold. I thank them for giving me the life I have, and for teaching me all the best values to be a good person first and foremost, and to work as hard as possible to be successful. House of Nanking has many meanings for those who love it. But to me, House of Nanking is the home my parents built for our family, and I can't think of a better way to keep the legacy, the story, the dedication, the commitment they have than to share it on these pages, which can live forever.

My parents' generation is special, and I know that I am not the only child of immigrants who feels the way I do. While I'm obviously dedicating this book to my parents, I feel compelled to dedicate this to all the immigrant parents out there who have sacrificed for their families. Our stories may be different, but the love is not. And when words can't do the talking, food can.

I truly hope this book speaks to you. I hope you hear the words of love in these pages, through the recipes, and the stories. Because it's everywhere in this book. Every single dish was created because of love, whether it was for family, the business, the customers, or the city of San Francisco. And, last, for our love for Chinatown. It's the first home my parents stepped foot into that welcomed them, and to this day, they have not left. I hope our fellow Chinatown pó pos and gōng gongs can be proud to see a small, immigrant-founded mom-and-pop shop represented on these pages, highlighting how far we've all come since we landed here.

Things are changing. Exciting Asian chefs, some first and some second gen, are doing cool things in the Chinese food space. But don't forget about the OGs, the ones who didn't do it for write-ups, Michelin stars, or accolades. The ones who didn't land in any food and wine magazines for their wok hei. The ones who would never have a cookbook . . . until now.

致谢

凯西：写这本书六个月后，最初的快乐（在日记本里记录食谱、故事、和回忆）都变成了一种挣扎。我的父母都开始出现健康问题，虽然他们现在已经度过了最糟糕的时期并且重返工作岗位，但他们显然是在放慢脚步。在这里，我回忆并书写着所有关于他们尽其所能照顾我的快乐记忆，远不仅仅是把食物摆上餐桌。突然间，我看到了一个我不愿看到也没有准备好的转折 - 我们的角色已经转换。现在是我在管理医生访问、药物以及当年龄追上你时出现的种种困难。很多个夜晚，我因意想不到的情绪而辗转难眠。

我不是一个感性的人。事实上，我恰恰相反，作为在美国长大的第一代华裔美国人，我从未学会如何与自己的情感建立联系。我们非常坚忍，我们从不说"我爱你"或"我为你骄傲;" 我们不说"谢谢"。我们不说"我感激你。"我们总是说我们通过行动来表达，通过我们的牺牲，我们的严厉之爱，我们的批评，我们永无止境地想要给你做饭和给你添衣以免着凉。我想说的是，虽然我找不到勇气当面说出这些话，但这本书给予了我无需通过语言表达的机会。有时候把想说的话写下来让别人读更容易，我猜想，一些最伟大的音乐作品就是这样创作出来的。

我对父母的爱超出了我的心所能承载的范围 - 我感谢他们给了我现在的生活，教会我首先要做一个好人，树立正确的价值观并尽可能努力地追求成功。南京小馆对那些喜爱它的人来说有许多含义，但对我而言，南京小馆是我父母为我们家庭建立的家园。我想不出有比在这些永远流传的书页上分享他们的传承、故事、奉献和承诺更好的方式了。

我父母那一代人很不一样，我知道我不是唯一一个对移民父母有这种感受的移民子女。显然，我是把这本书献给我的父母，但我觉得有必要把它献给所有为家庭做出牺牲的移民父母。我们的故事可能不同，但爱是相同的。当言语无法表达时，食物可以。

我真心希望这本书能引起你的共鸣。我希望你能在这些页面中，通过这些食谱和故事听到爱的话语，因为它在这本书的每个角落，每一道菜都是因为爱而创造的。无论是对家人的爱、对事业的爱、对顾客的爱和对旧金山的爱。最后，是对唐人街的爱。这是我父母踏入的第一个欢迎他们的家，直到今天他们都没有离开。我希望我们的唐人街婆婆公公们能为看到一个小型的，由移民创办的夫妻店在这些页面上得到展示而感到自豪，突显出自从我们来到这里以来我们所取得的进步。

时代在变迁，令人兴奋的亚裔厨师们 - 有些是第一代，有些是第二代，正在中餐领域做着很酷的事情。但别忘了那些元老们 - 他们不是为了报道、米其林星级或荣誉而做事的人。那些不会因为锅气而登上任何美食杂志的人和那些永远不会有烹饪书的人......直到现在。

MORE THANKS

KATHY: When I think about the journey that led to this cookbook, my heart swells with gratitude. This book wouldn't exist without the incredible souls who've touched my life, believed in me, and helped shape not only these pages but also the person I've become.

Mom and Dad, you're my everything. The courage it took to open House of Nanking, the endless hours you poured into making it succeed, the sacrifices you made so I could have a better life—I see it all now with such clarity and profound appreciation. To my extended family who became my second parents while Mom and Dad were at the restaurant: Your love nourished me in more ways than just the delicious food you shared. Every recipe in this book carries a piece of the warmth and joy you brought to my childhood.

Caleb, my wonderful husband, you taught me that having big dreams wasn't enough—it was about finding smarter ways to achieve them. Remember when you first encouraged me to hire a PR firm? I used to say, "I'm not good at selling myself, I can only be myself," and you showed me I didn't have to do it alone. Your practical wisdom—that I could hire people to advocate for me while I focused on what I do best—changed everything. You researched the top firms and pushed me to invest in myself, and your aggressive, practical approach opened doors I'd been knocking on for years. That single piece of advice set off a chain of events that transformed my career. Thank you for always championing me and being the pillar of our family—your unwavering support means everything.

James Gutierrez, executive producer of *Chef Dynasty*, you found us during the darkest days of the pandemic and saw something special in our father-daughter story. Without ever meeting us in person, you crafted a vision that would become our show—and that sparked something magical in my dad's heart, finally convincing him that our legacy deserved to be preserved in this cookbook.

Gregory McKnight, my mentor and friend, you taught me that it's okay to step into the spotlight, to voice my dreams out loud. You helped me balance my cultural roots with the confidence to reach for what I want. When I shared my cookbook dream, you didn't just open a door—you helped me find the courage to walk through it.

To my book dream team: Brandi Bowles, my incredible literary agent, you got it from the very first moment. To everyone at Abrams Books, thank you for believing in this project and pouring your hearts and expertise into making it exceptional. Holly Dolce, my editor at Abrams, your enthusiasm and clear vision for our story has been nothing short of extraordinary—this book wouldn't be what it is without your guidance and unwavering support.

And Emily Timberlake—where do I even begin? You weren't just our ghostwriter; you became the guardian of our family's legacy. These past two years have given me not just a beautiful book, but a friendship I'll treasure forever. Your dedication went so far beyond the role of a writer—you fought for our vision at every turn, ensuring each recipe, each story, each photo captured the true essence of House of Nanking. Those late-night texts about the perfect word choice, the way you coordinated with every member of our team to maintain excellence throughout the process, your tireless attention to even the smallest details—you poured your heart into this project as if it were your own family's story. The warmth and authenticity in these pages? That's your gift. You didn't just write our story; you understood it, protected it, and helped it shine. You've become family, Emily, and this book is as much your triumph as it is ours.

Our visual storytellers brought such magic: Quentin Bacon, our phenomenal photographer, you made our food look the way it feels to eat it—full of love and life, even during those scorching San Francisco days! Diane Shaw, our brilliant art director, your few days with us left such an imprint on these pages. Natalie Popova and Natalie Drobny, our talented prop and food stylists, your styling touched everything with beauty.

Kevyn Allard, our dedicated recipe tester, your meticulous work has ensured that every home cook can bring our flavors to life, and I smile every time I see your creations online. Teacher Jenny, our Chinese translator, thank you for helping bridge the language gap—you've helped preserve not just recipes but the heart of our heritage.

This book is more than paper and ink—it's a love letter to everyone who's been part of our House of Nanking family. It's the taste of my childhood, the echo of my parents' dreams, and the result of so many helping hands and loving hearts. To everyone who's walked this path with me: You've helped create something that will outlive all of us, something that will tell our story long after we're gone.

And finally, to our beloved customers—from those who've stood in line since we opened our doors in 1988 to the new faces we see each day: You are the heart and soul of House of Nanking. Your loyalty and enthusiasm, and the stories you've shared with us over the years, have transformed our restaurant from a small family business into a San Francisco institution. Through three generations, you've embraced our family's vision of Chinese cuisine, trusted us to feed you "chef's choice," and made our restaurant a part of your own family traditions. This cookbook is also for you—a chance to bring a piece of House of Nanking into your own homes and create new memories with your loved ones.

From the bottom of my heart, thank you all for making this dream come true.

EMILY: Kathy's is an impossible act to follow, so I'll keep this short. Thank you to the brilliant, talented, and always kind Kathy Fang for inviting me into her world, and trusting me to help share this beautiful story. Working with you has been a joy from beginning to end . . . I'm not sure I can say that about anything else in my life, hah! Thank you for being a dream collaborator and true inspiration. Thank you to Peter and Lily Fang for building a Bay Area institution that has nourished our community for generations. I'll never forget my little daughter taking her first bite of fried sweet potato—and the delighted grin that followed! Thank you to my agent, Rica Allannic, for being the best in the biz. Thank you to our passionate and talented team at Abrams: Holly Dolce, Diane Shaw, and Hannah Braden, you are perfect and we are so grateful to you all. To Ethan and Ramona: I love you bigger than the sky.

$13.95

大排滷蛋湯麵
酸菜魚片湯麵
加喱牛肉湯麵
雪菜扣肉湯麵
香酥雞滷蛋湯麵
雪菜肉絲湯麵
雪菜肉絲拌麵
蒜味大蝦湯麵
蒜蓉大蝦拌麵
开洋葱油湯麵
葱油开洋拌麵
雪菜肉絲湯年糕
雪菜肉絲炒年糕
麻醬干拌麵
麻醬拌撈雲吞

大排滷蛋飯
南京辣牛肉飯
香酥雞滷蛋飯
雪菜扣肉飯
椒鹽魚柳飯
酸菜魚片飯
麻婆豆腐飯
馬來加喱牛肉飯
南京雞球燴飯
麻辣雞丁飯
麻辣魚片飯
蝦醬肉末茄瓜飯
加喱素菜豆腐飯
宮保大蝦飯
四季豆肉末飯

INDEX

D

E

I

J

K

L

M

N

O

P

Editor: Holly Dolce
Designer: Diane Shaw
Managing Editor: Lisa Silverman
Production Manager: Denise LaCongo

Library of Congress Control Number: 2025931669

ISBN: 978-1-4197-7787-5
eISBN: 979-8-88707-456-6

Printed and bound in China
10 9 8 7 6 5 4 3 2 1

Abrams books are available at special discounts when purchased in quantity for premiums and promotions as well as fundraising or educational use. Special editions can also be created to specification. For details, contact specialsales@abramsbooks.com or the address below.

ABRAMS is represented in the UK and Europe by Abrams & Chronicle Books, 1 West Smithfield, London EC1A 9JU and Média-Participations, 57 rue Gaston Tessier, 75166 Paris, France.
abramsandchronicle.co.uk and media-participations.com
info@abramsandchronicle.co.uk

ABRAMS The Art of Books
195 Broadway, New York, NY 10007
abramsbooks.com

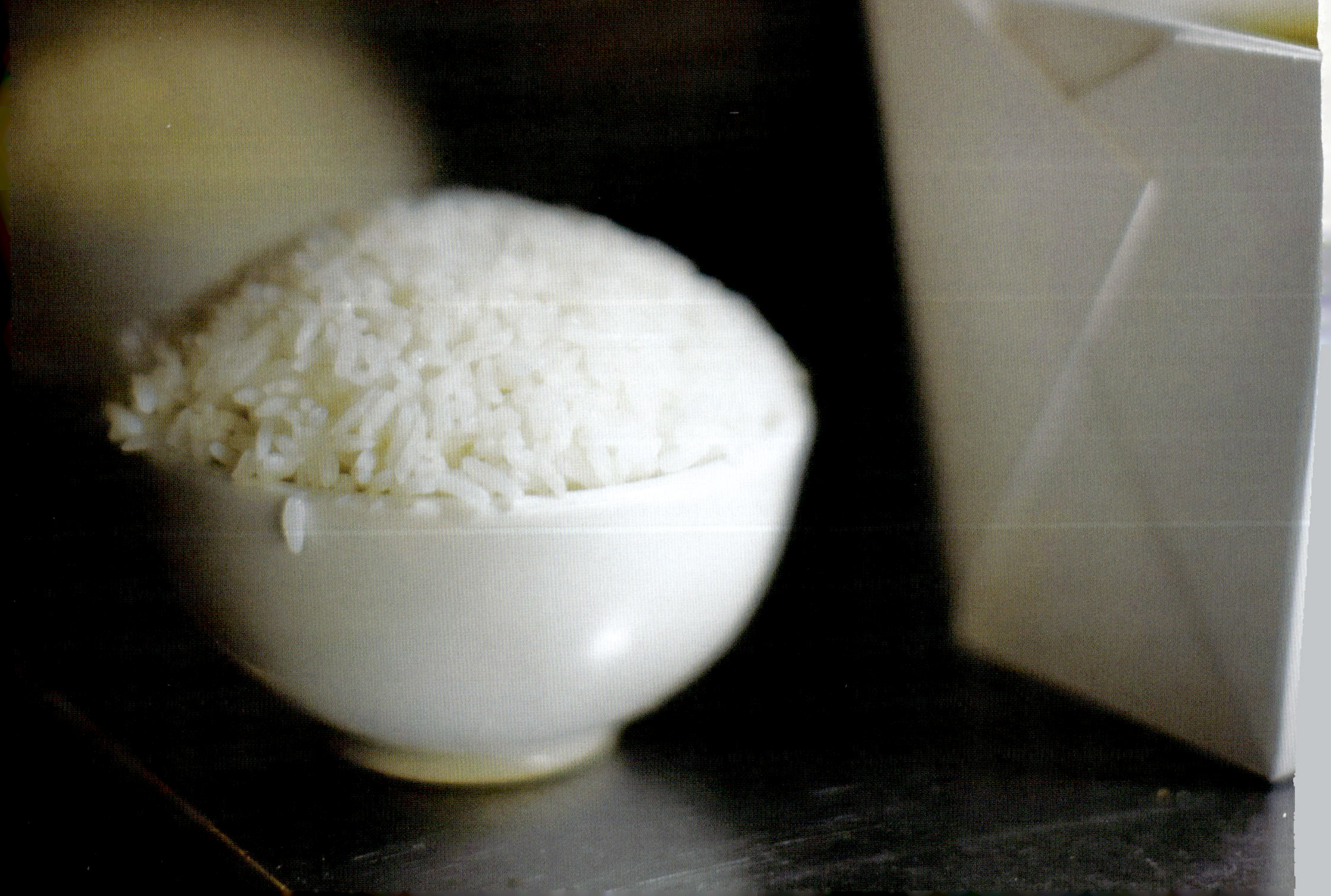

"House of Nanking isn't just a restaurant—it is a San Francisco icon, bursting with bold, authentic Chinese flavors and a rich family legacy. In this cookbook, Peter and Kathy Fang share the magic that's inspired me, blending their unforgettable father-daughter journey with a trove of cherished recipes. I'm beyond excited that I can cook these celebrated Chinese classics at home!"

MICHELLE TAM, *NEW YORK TIMES* BESTSELLING COOKBOOK AUTHOR AND CREATOR OF NOM NOM PALEO

"As with the best startups, the Fang family blended tradition with innovation to create something extraordinary. This book captures their remarkable journey and mouthwatering cuisine."

BEN HOROWITZ, INVESTOR, ENTREPRENEUR, AND BESTSELLING AUTHOR

"There are few restaurant dynasties in America that compare to the Fang family's. From their origins in Shanghai to their beloved House of Nanking, Peter, Lily, and Kathy Fang pour their hearts into the most delicious and innovative Chinese food in San Francisco. I'm proud to share the city with them, and I will be cooking out of this beautiful book for years to come—it's a love letter to Chinatown."

TYLER FLORENCE, CHEF, TV HOST, AND AUTHOR OF *AMERICAN GRILL*

"House of Nanking and Fang are more than restaurants—they are San Francisco institutions. Eating there always feels like coming home, with unforgettable flavors of food, family, and tradition. This beautiful cookbook opens those doors to everyone."

MARC BENIOFF, CHAIR, CEO, AND COFOUNDER OF SALESFORCE